THE POLITICS OF BANKING

THE POLITICS OF BANKING

The Strange Case of Competition and Credit Control

Michael Moran

St. Martin's Press   New York

© Michael Moran 1984

All rights reserved. For information, write:
St. Martin's Press, Inc., 175 Fifth Avenue, New York, NY 10010
Printed in Hong Kong
Published in the United Kingdom by The Macmillan Press Ltd.
First published in the United States of America in 1984

ISBN 0-312-62635-5

Library of Congress Cataloging in Publication Data

Moran, Michael.
   The politics of banking.

   Includes bibliographical references and index.
   1. Banks and banking—Great Britain. 2. Banks and banking—Government policy—Great Britain. 3. Credit control—Great Britain. I. Title.
HG2988.M67   1983   332.1'0941   83-16068
ISBN 0-312-62635-5

For Winifred

Contents

Preface   ix

1   **The Politics of Complexity**   1
    1   The subject of the book   1
    2   Why write the book?   3
    3   The politics of complexity   5

2   **The Politics of Lombard Street**   9
    1   Custom, policy and politics   9
    2   The stage and the actors   10
    3   Bankers and the economy   12
    4   Bankers and the Bank of England   16
    5   The Bank of England and the government   22
    6   Esoteric politics and monetary policy   27

3   **The Politics of Policy Change**   29
    1   Breaking the policy code   29
    2   Competition and Credit Control: a summary   30
    3   Fashion and policy change   33
    4   Academic enquiry and policy change   35
    5   Adversary politics and policy change   39
    6   Economic interests and policy change   41
    7   Bureaucratic politics and policy change   47
    8   The decline of esoteric politics   53

4   **The Politics of the Money Supply**   55
    1   Control, complexity and the money supply   55
    2   The quintessence of complexity: money and politics, 1971–3   58
    3   Complexity triumphant: politics and money since 1974   73

5	Crisis, Crash, Rescue	76
	1 Trust, crisis and banking	76
	2 Banking, prudence and property	79
	3 Law, trust and supervision	84
	4 Rescuing an industry	97
6	Rules, Risks and the Law	113
	1 Markets, regulation and formality	113
	2 Crisis, change and regulation	114
	3 Legislating for complexity	118
	4 Complexity magnified: supervising supranational markets	133
7	Complexity, Trust and Policy Making	140
	1 The problem of opportunism	140
	2 Complexity and capitalism	144
	3 Living with complexity	150

Notes and References   163
Index   182

Preface

Those who helped me most with this book can only be thanked anonymously. While writing it I was able to talk to over twenty individuals – bankers, politicians and civil servants – who were closely concerned with the politics of money in the 1970s. These conversations – they were too informal to be called interviews – rarely provided new information, nor were they designed for that purpose. I approached people after writing a first draft of the book from published sources, and used the conversations to present my impressions and tentative conclusions. The responses were always stimulating and often chastening. To all who gave their time I express warm thanks. I owe a special debt to three individuals who both talked to me and subsequently made very valuable comments on a second draft of the manuscript. Comparing my impressions formed as an outsider with the views of those inside the policy machine reinforced a conviction which I have long held: that British government is much less secret than is commonly believed. Much supposedly secret information awaits the researcher, scattered in numerous, obscure but still public sources.

It is a pleasure to thank by name some others who have helped me. Anthony King commissioned the book and commented on a draft in his usual meticulous and perceptive way. My colleague Martin Burch also made valuable comments on the manuscript; even more important, he shared with me his views about policy making in the graduate course in Policy Analysis which we have taught together for some years. Richard Harrington generously allowed me to pick his brains about monetary economics. Mrs. Marjorie Gray and Miss Catherine Knowles turned virtually illegible manuscripts into a succession of immaculately typed drafts. The University of Manchester kindly paid some of my travelling expenses.

My family helped me survive the whole experience by constantly reminding me that hardly anything is less important in life than a book about public policy.

Victoria University of Manchester   MICHAEL MORAN
2 September 1982

1 The Politics of Complexity

A notion prevails that the money market is something so impalpable that it can only be spoken of in very abstract words. ... But I maintain that the Money Market is as concrete and real as anything else; that it can be described in as plain words; that it is the writer's fault if what he says is not clear.*

1 THE SUBJECT OF THE BOOK

This book is about money, power and policy. Money is examined in various forms. Part of the study concerns that mystical quantity the money supply which, apparently invisible to mortal man, can only be imperfectly apprehended through a variety of indirect signs.[1] Some plainer senses of money are also examined: money used (up to £3,000 million) to support collapsing banks and property companies in the middle of the 1970s; money lost (in excess of £300 million) by public institutions in that crisis; more money lost (£50 million and still rising) by the commercial clearing banks in the same affair.[2]

'Power' hints at a way of examining banking usually neglected in the orthodox economic literature. The succeeding pages describe how public institutions – notably the Treasury and the Bank of England – try to shape the behaviour of banks and other credit-giving agencies. It is conventional to picture these shaping influences as working to two different ends: ensuring that financial institutions are managed prudently; and ensuring that they create credit in the amounts, and for the purposes, desired by the authorities.[3] These matters have been exhaustively examined by economists, yet the problems raised in the control of money and banking go far beyond technical difficulties of economic intervention: they concern the connections between government and

* The quotations at the heads of Chapters 1–6 are from Walter Bagehot, *Lombard Street: a description of the money market* (first published 1873).

powerful private interests, the capacity of government to engage in extensive economic management and the degree to which complicated social institutions can be subjected to close public regulation.

Viewed thus, the control of money and banking acquires a strongly political character. This is emphasised by a peculiarity of British monetary policy. Until very recently public efforts to control money and banking in Britain rested on another more private system of power, encompassing an enclosed elite at the top of government, the Bank of England and a small number of commercial banks. To anticipate: one of the chief themes of this study concerns the way problems of control and supervision levered open and partly destroyed this enclosed system.

Money and power are the meat of the book; policy is the organising skeleton. In September 1971 the Bank of England, in the name of the Conservative Government, introduced changes in the way banks were to compete for business and were to be regulated by the authorities. 'Competition and Credit Control' (CCC), as the new arrangements were called after the consultative document that preceded them, was the product of negotiations within the enclosed elite that had traditionally shaped decisions.[4] In the more public world of Parliament the reforms were announced merely as 'changes in method without changes in basic policy'.[5]

These comparatively obscure reforms were actually as ambitious as anything attempted domestically by Mr Heath's Government. They were designed to reverse a century-long trend to cartels and other restrictive practices between the banks; to change a system of monetary control in which credit was largely rationed by administrative decision into one in which price was the decisive influence; and greatly to increase the part played in the banking system by competition and the free market. By contrast with the early partisan reforms of the Heath Government – such as industrial 'disengagement' and the Industrial Relations Act – Competition and Credit Control was esoteric and uncontentious. Yet the ambitions behind the scheme, and the results it produced, were as significant as anything connected with those more controversial measures.

This book is a study of these ambitions and consequences. It begins by examining the connections that have grown up between bankers, politics and policy in Britain. This background material sketches the growth of the enclosed system of power that linked Whitehall, the Bank of England, and the world of commercial banking. Chapter 3 describes how this enclosed system was challenged, and how it produced Competition and Credit Control in response to that challenge.

The two succeeding chapters are concerned with what happened after 1971 to the two conventional objectives of policy: control of credit creation and allocation (Chapter 4); and prudential regulation of banks (Chapter 5). 'Rules, Risks and the Law' (Chapter 6) concludes the case-study by describing the changes that came over the system of prudential control after the great banking crisis of the mid-1970s. The chapter presses an argument which recurs throughout, and which is aptly summarised in Lowi's aphorism that 'policies determine politics': the policies introduced in money and banking in the 1970s altered the power of established institutions, and introduced new participants into decision making.[6] The result was considerably to reduce the autonomy and the cohesion of that enclosed elite which had dominated policy at the beginning of the decade.

The book is about economic events, but it is not an economic analysis of those events; nor could it be, since my technical competence is slight. The technical details of monetary policy are examined lightly, and only in so far as they are essential to the narrative. There are dangers in this, but good economic analyses of Competition and Credit Control already exist.[7] The chief aim is rather to examine, with particular reference to monetary policy, some general problems of policy making and execution. This gives the concluding chapter a special purpose. In all case-studies there is a tension between the substance of the particular study and the wider analytical questions prompted by that individual case. For most of this book (Chapters 2–6) the tension is resolved in favour of the first of these: the pages are dominated by narrative, and by the politics of money and banking. By contrast, the final chapter neglects banking to examine wider problems of policy making and execution. This shift was forced on me by the experience of writing the case-study, for it became clear that the difficulties revealed by the history of Competition and Credit Control, though in part peculiar to money and banking, also exemplified problems common whenever policy is made and executed.

The tension in a case-study between the particular and the general is often fruitful, but it is always uneasy. This sense of unease prompts an obvious question: why spend so much time on a narrow range of events and institutions? In short, why write the book?

2 WHY WRITE THE BOOK?

Academic case-studies of public policy are in disrepute.[8] Their faults are obvious: they lack the immediacy of journalism, the authority of history or the analytical scope of conventional social science. The best answer to criticism remains the power of example. If a general justification exists for adding another study to a large literature it must lie in any merit the succeeding chapters might have; but the particular reasons for choosing Competition and Credit Control do require explanation. They are part historical, part analytical. Competition and Credit Control is an important episode in the history of both British banking and British politics. Banking markets were transformed by the new policy: the years since 1971 saw dazzling innovation, fierce competition and rapid changes in official means of monetary control. The immediate effects were even more spectacular. In the two years following the introduction of CCC the authorities at first did not understand what was happening, and when they did they were hindered from taking corrective action by a combination of reluctance and incapacity. The consequences were painfully significant. There was a great expansion, neither anticipated nor desired, in the volume of credit in the economy. This newly created credit flowed disproportionately into property investment, inducing a mania of speculation. The sudden exhaustion of that mania at the end of 1973 left behind what the Governor of the Bank of England has called 'the worst financial crisis since the 1930s'.[9] The direct costs to the public purse and to the commercial banks are still being counted; the costs in lost confidence and wasted resources are incalculable. Even in these difficult times an episode that shakes the foundations of the financial system is unusual enough to justify special attention.

Yet the significance of Competition and Credit Control goes beyond these immediate events. Just over two years after introducing CCC the authorities greatly modified its most distinctive feature, the use of free market mechanisms to control credit creation and allocation. The experiment with Competition and Credit Control, spanning the period from September 1971 to November 1973, thus coincides with a better known experiment: the attempt by Mr Heath's Government to solve the problems of the British economy by inducing a rapid spurt of economic growth. This commonly misnamed 'Barber boom', so abruptly stifled in 1973, was a turning point in the history of British economic policy. It was the last attempt by a British government to practise demand management in the Keynesian fashion. After the failures of that episode – which were also the failures of Competition and Credit Control – the power exercised over policy by financial markets rose greatly. The most important sign of this alteration was the increasing attention paid to controlling the money supply: from 1974 there existed internal targets for monetary growth; in 1976 the targets became public commitments; after 1979 the effort to meet targets threatened to dominate all other objectives.[10]

These changes within government were connected to alterations in the more open world of party debate. The individuals who remade Conservative Party policy after Mr Heath's removal in 1975 concluded that his Government failed because neither the money supply nor the level of public borrowing were effectively controlled. The economic history of Mrs Thatcher's Government after 1979 was dominated by the fear of repeating these errors. The economic policies pursued after her election were thus in part a consequence of certain obscure changes in the means of monetary control introduced in the early 1970s. Nor were the effects of Competition and Credit Control confined to the high politics of money and economic management. 'The worst financial crisis since the 1930s' also penetrated the more mundane world of banking regulation. For the first time banks were subjected to a comprehensive legal code, the structure of the industry greatly altered and a transformation effected in the kind of power exercised over commercial banks by the authorities.

The high politics of money and the more obscure politics of regulation provide the historical substance for the book. This substance produced in turn two themes of a more analytical character. The first asserts that in monetary policy, as in other parts of political life, we have in recent years seen a shift from *esoteric politics* (private, informal and technical) to *exoteric politics* (open, formal and partisan). This argument arises naturally in the narrative, and is best left there; but a second theme requires a preliminary sketch.

3   THE POLITICS OF COMPLEXITY

The fate of Competition and Credit Control emphasises the complexities involved in designing and executing public policy. The seasoned observer of the British economy will retort that it is hardly necessary to read a book, let alone write one, to realise that economic management is a complex business; the evidence is all about us, in the deserted factories and in the miseries of the unemployed. Yet the argument is not as trite as first appearances might suggest, for 'complexity' is itself an appropriately complicated notion. In everyday language 'complex' is merely a synonym for 'very difficult', as in 'complex problems'. In the literature on public policy it has acquired more specialised meanings which have been used to explain why decisions are made in particular ways and why they so often fail to achieve desired ends.

Three different senses are commonly stressed: intellectual, social and administrative complexity. The recognition over two decades ago of the first of these helped destroy models of decision which presumed that rational men operated with clear objectives in a predictable world. In the contemporary study of public policy the assumption that *intellectual complexity* is ever present has been the foundation of influential 'incrementalist' theories, which argue that since decision makers cannot gather or understand all relevant information they typically proceed by 'muddling through' piecemeal, and are wise to do so.

Intellectual complexity is in part due to problems of observation: policy makers, faced with a stream of information, are never sure whether it is correct, appropriate to the problem or up to date. These complexities of observation are compounded by complexities of understanding. Policies as different as those designed to cure inflation, crime or poverty are all shaped by notions about the springs of human behaviour. Put pompously, policy rests on theory; but theoretical understanding of how the world works, and of how it might be made to work differently, is very limited.[11]

Policy makers are thus social theorists of a kind. Were it the case that successful policy demanded only an act of understanding, intellectual complexity would be a lone obstacle. Since success also depends on human cooperation and control, *social complexity* presents an additional set of difficulties. Policy is generally made and executed in a world peopled by recalcitrants. The fact that the policy maker typically tries to compel or cajole individuals into behaviour which they would not otherwise adopt makes his work a constant battle with human inventiveness. Whatever the object – to restrain bank lending, to levy taxes or to forbid drunken driving – those responsible for policy have to cope constantly with the human capacity to find new ways of evading or avoiding control.

Social complexity is ubiquitous, but the problems it creates are especially serious in advanced industrial societies. With industrial advance complexity is organised into formal institutions, intensified by a refined division of labour and spread by growing relations of dependence. La Porte and his colleagues have begun the task of exploring these matters.[12] It is already clear that to accomplish even comparatively mundane objects of policy – getting commuters to work or building a single hospital – involves creating a complicated chain of obedience and agreement.

Since social complexity creates great problems of control it commonly calls forth an increase in the resources of controllers. This is one reason why those who execute policy in modern governments typically do so by setting in motion a large administrative machine. This solution itself intensifies the problems of *administrative complexity*. Policy execution in the modern state is almost never in the hands of one individual.[13] Tasks as great as waging war, or as small as taxing a single citizen, are accomplished by putting together the separate, specialised activities of many public servants. Whether the tasks are carried out well or badly depends critically on how far the separate activities are coordinated. Problems of coordination grow with increases in the size of government, in its internal complexity, in the range and difficulty of its tasks, and in the degree to which it subjects those tasks to a refined division of labour. The consequence is that in modern government great resources have to be devoted simply to assembling a machine which will work reasonably coherently. This is why 'the quest for coordination', to use Harold Seidman's words, has become 'the twentieth-century equivalent of the medieval search for the philosopher's stone'.[14] The search for the stone was among the historic concerns of administrative science; it has been renewed in the last decade in the literature on implementation.

To stress complexity in the manner emphasised here is to risk a charge of excessive pessimism about the capaicty of government to carry out ambitious tasks. Much of the literature certainly is pessimistic. Recognising intellectual complexity led advocates of incrementalism to recommend slow change and piecemeal solutions as the best way of making policy. Recognising the significance of organised social complexity has led others to conclude that the tasks now required of government are beyond its present capacities.[15] Students of implementation began examining administrative complexities in surprise that things often went wrong in government, and ended in amazement that anything ever went right.[16]

Recognising complexity need not lead to this pessimism. The puzzles and problems facing the policy maker can be, and often are, overcome by exercising the common human capacities to learn and adapt. Pessimism or optimism about the ability of government to cope with complexity rests on a judgement about its ability to use these common capacities in recognising problems and in devising appropriate solutions. It is plain that in come cases adaptation is swift; in others, painful and slow, or completely absent. These difficult matters are taken up in the concluding chapter.

The politics of money and banking exemplify complexity. Complexities of observation and understanding are intertwined: making sense of financial indicators is intimately connected with the theoretical problem of appreciating the significance of monetary policy and monetary institutions for the economy at large. The problems of social complexity are acute. The actors in the field are mainly sophisticated financial institutions whose profits are greatly affected by public policy. These institutions have an extraordinary capacity to innovate and adapt, notably as a way of lawfully avoiding the effects of public controls. This in turn has intensified administrative complexity. New financial practices have created novel problems of regulation. As a result both the rules, and the ways in which they are administered, have become progressively more complicated. All of these features make the politics of money and banking a politics of complexity.

2 The Politics of Lombard Street

The briefest and truest way of describing Lombard Street is to say that it is by far the greatest combination of economical power and economical delicacy that the world has ever seen.

1 CUSTOM, POLICY AND POLITICS

The silent assumptions in policy making are usually more important than any open arguments; most of what government does results from the unthinking use of customary rules and customary solutions. Understanding policy thus demands not only a description of the visible arguments which bring it about but also an examination of the submerged mass of customary assumptions on which it rests.

These truisms apply with special force to money and banking in Britain. Customary assumptions long excluded most of what we conventionally understand by 'politics' from Lombard Street (itself a conventional image for the banking community). To identify them as customary is to establish that their roots lie in the past. Understanding the politics of banking thus requires a sketch of the way historical experience produced a unique pattern of politics. In the succeeding pages this is accomplished by sketching three key features: the economic setting of banking; the connections between bankers and the Bank of England; and the links between the Bank of England and the rest of the government. The argument of the chapter is that these features show a history unique by comparison both with banking abroad and with other great interests at home; that this history in turn produced a distinctive set of assumptions about how policy should be made; and that these assumptions intimately affected how Competition and Credit Control was shaped and executed.

The historical sketch shows bankers in Britain to have formed a small enclosed community. One legacy of this tradition has been to make banking and finance unfamiliar to most outsiders. My historical sketch is therefore preceded by an elementary introduction to the financial community. Readers with any superficial acquaintance with the City may skip this next section.

2   THE STAGE AND THE ACTORS

The stage is Lombard Street; the actors are bankers. Lombard Street was the original home of London's banks and money markets. It is now a gloomy, anonymous place distinguished only by Hawksmoor's exquisite church of Saint Mary Woolnoth. To T. S. Eliot – who endured a brief time in banking – the bankers who flowed into Lombard Street each morning seemed like the lost souls in Dante:

> Sighs, short and infrequent, were exhaled,
> And each man fixed his eyes before his feet.
> Flowed up the hill and down King William Street,
> To where Saint Mary Woolnoth kept the hours
> With a dead sound on the final stroke of nine.

The observer today sees something less impressive, and less terrifying. Lombard Street is now part of a small area where most banks of any significance have their head offices. This compactness is remarkable: in a ten-minute stroll a walker can pass almost every British financial institution of importance. This is why 'Lombard Street' refers not only to a place, but is also a conventional image describing in shorthand a geographically compact banking community.

Lombard Street is itself part of the wider stage of 'the City'. The City of London is, to be precise, an anachronistic local government unit covering about a square mile of the East End. More commonly, it is an image used to describe the many markets trading in and out of this area. Within living memory (at least of the very old) the City was important in manufacturing and in trading goods; now, City markets deal almost exclusively in financial claims and instruments. Of these markets the best known are run by regulating institutions: for instance the Stock Exchange, which organises markets in company securities and in public ('gilt-edged') borrowing; and Lloyds, which organises the world's greatest insurance and reinsurance market.

Banking, too, is divided into distinct institutions. The *London Clearing Banks* ('the clearers') are, exactly, the six banks with a seat in the Bankers' Clearing House which 'clears' customers' cheques. More commonly and loosely 'the clearers' refers to five banks (Barclays, Lloyds, Midland, National Westminister and Williams and Glyn's) whose branches dominate retail banking in England and Wales. (There exists a separate group of Scottish clearing banks, all of which are owned in whole or in part by the London clearers.) The clearing banks are best known by their retail services – taking deposits, making loans, providing a national money transmission system – but their entry during the 1970s into *wholesale money markets* has reduced this dependence on retail banking. Wholesale markets trade large sums of money (typically from £50,000 upwards) for any period ranging from a night to several years. The markets are, broadly, divided into those trading in *sterling* and those dealing in *eurocurrencies*. Nomenclature is rarely exact in financial life: a eurocurrency is actually any currency traded outside its country of origin.

The clearing banks are joined in the wholesale markets by other important banking institutions. The *Discount Houses* dominated money market trading until the 1960s. In the *Discount Market* the banks lend and borrow funds at short term. The Discount Houses also make a market in *Treasury Bills*, three-month bills issued by the Bank of England to cover the government's own need for short-term borrowing. The Discount Houses and the Discount Market are closely controlled by the Bank of England, the Houses in particular being virtually its agents.

During the 1960s the Discount Market was first challenged, and then eclipsed, by a set of *parallel* or *secondary* wholesale money markets. These markets – they include those in local authority debt, in loans made directly between banks, and in loans made directly between companies without a banking intermediary – were subject to little official surveillance or control.

The rise of the new money markets accentuated the divide between *primary* and *secondary* banks. Primary banks (they include the clearing banks and the Discount Houses) made regular returns to the Bank of England, and were supervised by it. The secondary (or 'fringe') banks were a heterogeneous group: they ranged from long-established finance houses providing credit in the mass market for hire purchase, to institutions set up to provide virtual black market credit during the period of very tight official controls on bank lending in the 1960s. The language of primary and secondary banking became obsolete with the passage of the Banking Act 1979, which introduced Britain's first comprehensive legal framework for banking regulation.

Everything about British banking is subtle and complicated and nowhere more so than its connections with the state. The Bank of England (conventional shorthand 'the Bank' with a capital 'B') emerged as the first modern central bank while still nominally under private ownership; the formality of nationalisation occurred in 1946. The Bank's many – and often conflicting – duties include acting as the Treasury's agent in financial markets, advising Whitehall on economic policy, regulating the conduct of banks and many other financial institutions, and acting as the voice of City interests in government.

The last of these duties has in the 1970s been increasingly taken on by organised interest groups. The *Committee of London Clearing Bankers* – which actually does have offices in Lombard Street – has in recent years been transformed from a trade association operating restrictive practices into a highly efficient lobbyist in Whitehall. The *British Bankers' Association* was roused from a dormant state in 1972 to lobby for the wider interests of all bankers, especially in Brussels.

3 BANKERS AND THE ECONOMY

The economic history of banking in Britain can be summarised in three words: separation, concentration, cartels. The first of these marked an important divide between banking and manufacturing industry. When in the later part of the nineteenth century Germany and the United States challenged Britain's economic supremacy they did so through an industrial revolution in part sponsored and controlled by banks; the consequence was that in their cases banking and industrial capital became entwined. By contrast, Britain's industrial revolution was accomplished before a national banking system developed, so the resources for investment consequently came largely from outside the banking community.[1] Banks were left to provide short-term trade credit, and were happy to do so: generations of bankers were taught to view sceptically any loans which locked money up in long-term projects. Though periodic crises in British industry have modified these attitudes, it was not until the mid-1970s that bankers shed their dislike of long-term loans and of being entangled in the affairs of their industrial customers.[2]

This historic separation was widened by another peculiarity: the country's financial capital was already a great international commercial and banking centre before Britain's industrial supremacy was established. 'London's financial organisation', as the Macmillan Committee put it, 'adapted itself to the needs of... world-wide commerce and it was there that the great private merchant banking houses settled and flourished'.³ By the end of the nineteenth century British banking was a key influence in international trade and in the international monetary system; by contrast, it was marginal to domestic manufacturing investment. One sign of this ascendancy of the cosmopolitan over the domestic was the City's domination by internationally minded merchant banks which were often – as in the case of Rothschild – part of financial dynasties spanning several countries.⁴

The economic consequences of this separation have been long disputed; the political results are less commonly noticed. In Germany and in the United States the fusion of banking and industrial capital stimulated a fear of 'money power' which made banks the object of fierce political argument; in Britain, as Sir Oswald Mosley and the radical Left both discovered, attacks on bankers aroused little popular response.⁵ The most important political argument involving the banks in the inter-war years was, for instance, an esoteric dispute about the degree to which they were sensitive to industry's demand for credit.⁶

This separation from political controversy was reflected in a distinct kind of interest representation. During and after the First World War the business community increasingly organised itself into pressure groups designed to lobby and bargain in Whitehall. The banks largely stood aside from these efforts, preferring to work informally through the City and the Bank of England.⁷ In this way the economic divide between banking and industry was mirrored in the relations of the two to government.

This distinctive kind of representation, stimulated by separation from industrial interests, was further encouraged by the history of ownership in banking. The banks were able to neglect formally organised pressure group politics because the concentration of ownership and control in a few hands made commercial bankers a cohesive political force, able to act in unity without the need of much formal organisation. The case of the clearing banks illustrates the point. The amalgamations which were brought to a climax by mergers during the First World War left branch banking dominated by only five London clearing banks. The mergers of 1917–18 increased the share of total deposits lodged with the 'Big Five' from approximately 50 per cent to 80 per cent; less than forty years before the comparable figure had only been 25 per cent.⁸ The mergers established a pattern of ownership which was not seriously disturbed for fifty years, and the cohesion implied by this economic concentration was further supported by powerful social influences. Thus, the amalgamations had been accompanied by a convergence on London: by 1918 almost every English bank of significance had its head office in the City, and was hence part of that intimate social network remarked on time and again by observers of the financial community.[9]

The unity which this proximity supported also rested on a much more important source of social cohesion. The mergers brought together not just banks, but their controlling families. As Lisle-Williams has shown, the most senior posts in the clearing banks were (and to a lesser degree still are) occupied disproportionately by members of the original founding families. These families were assimilated into English aristocratic society, by kinship and by education at elite institutions; and through kinship and interlocking directorships were part of great financial empires which connected clearing banks, insurance companies, merchant banks and associated trading enterprises such as shipping. Not until the years after the Second World War did the clearers' connections with industrial enterprises begin to rival their links with finance.[10]

This pattern of concentration, social exclusiveness and continued proprietorial influence was even more marked in other parts of the banking community. Long after the joint stock revolution had transformed ownership and control in industry, many of the great merchant banks continued under the private control of families whose names were by-words for social exclusiveness. But even more pertinent to Competition and Credit Control were conditions in the Discount Market. Until the 1960s the Market was the only wholesale money market of significance in London. It was a key mechanism both for the clearing banks and for the authorities. The banks used it to even out their flow of funds by trading their short-term surpluses. The authorities used it as a market for Treasury Bills, the principal instrument used to fund short-term public debt. By trading in the market, and by lending to the Discount Houses who dominated it, the authorities also influenced the working of the whole banking system, and thus the flow of credit in the economy at large. At the insistence of the Bank of England, ownership and control had originally been sharply concentrated during the inter-war Depression: in the decade after 1933 the number of Discount Houses fell from twenty-two to eleven, remaining stable thereafter.[11] The Houses displayed in extreme form the social characteristics of the banking community: even in 1980, after two decades of great change in the City, a third of their directors were from families with large shareholdings in a House; two-thirds of directors were from families with an entry in *Burke's Peerage*; every owner-director of a House had been educated at a Clarendon School; and – extraordinary proportion – three-quarters of these were old Etonians.[12]

This social exclusiveness was a marked feature of the whole financial community, distinguishing it from the comparatively more open industrial elite. The economic implications of these differences in social status have long been discussed; the political consequences are as important. The sense of identity between banking and the rest of the City was strengthened at the expense of the banks' connections with industry. The fact that the people who mattered were few in number and were drawn from a narrow social stratum strengthened the predisposition to coordinate action informally. Bankers, like the rest of the City, thus had little need for the cumbersome apparatus of pressure group politics. 'If I want to talk to the representatives of the British Banks, or indeed of the whole financial community', said the Governor of the Bank of England in 1957, 'we can usually get together in one room in about half-an-hour.'[13] From these features a distinct political style developed. Banks and other financiers did not bargain in Whitehall. Matters affecting the City were decided in the City, in a community where doing business, deciding policy and keeping up friendly social contacts were all intermingled. Against the increasingly formal and bureaucratic character of government and industry, bankers and financiers put personal qualities above formal qualifications, the spoken word above the written agreement and the power of trust above the force of law.

This outlook was in part a natural product of the social unity of the financial community, but it was also supported by more brutal economic forces: the effects of separation and concentration were reinforced by cartels and restrictive practices. There is an unsurprising coincidence between the rise of concentration and the decline of competition. In the mid-nineteenth century branch banking was highly competitive: new entrants to the industry were common, banks competed over the rates offered to depositors and borrowers, and there was rivalry over such services as hours of opening. The amalgamations before the First World War produced a loose and unstable cartel fixing interest rates for depositors. The emergence of the Big Five in 1918 made this cartel totally effective, and over the next two decades killed almost every kind of visible competition in retail banking.[14]

There were similar developments in the money market. In the early 1920s the clearing banks and the Discount Houses agreed a minimum rate of interest for the clearers' funds in the Discount Market. In the decade after 1925 the Bank of England used its influence to extend this informal arrangement into a comprehensive set of restrictive practices. The clearing banks agreed not to compete with the Discount Houses in tendering for Treasury Bills. The Houses in turn agreed to bid a common price at the weekly tender, allotting the Bills between each other according to a fixed formula. In this way the Bank protected the Discount Houses from the consequences of the Depression, and ensured a stable market for short-term government debt.[15]

At this time also began a practice which still persists: the Governor or his Deputy met representatives of the Houses weekly. In this informal setting many things could be discussed. The representatives heard the Bank's view of the immediate economic prospects, and fixed their offer price at the tender accordingly. The Bank in return was able to keep close contact with institutions who were virtually its agents, to communicate views via the Discount Houses, and to gather from them information about the financial community.[16] Thus was created one of the more complex features that Competition and Credit Control tried to unravel: the connections existing between debt management, credit control and the restrictive practices which were an inseparable part of the socially cohesive banking community. The links between restrictive practices and social cohesion were common throughout the financial system. Informality and trust could be relied upon in regulating financial life because entry into markets was tightly controlled, and competition between existing members severely curtailed. The penalties of exclusion and the rewards for inclusion were powerful incentives to acceptable behaviour.[17]

Separation, concentration and cartels thus gave the banking industry in Britain a special economic history. This history in turn drew banking away from the normal channels of interest group politics into the enclosed politics of the City. Privacy and informality were sustained because powerful controls held disruptive competition in check. But curbing competition in a market economy is hazardous because individuals and institutions are constantly inventing new ways of bidding for business. That restrictions in banking held for so long owed much to the part played by the Bank of England.

4 BANKERS AND THE BANK OF ENGLAND

In English public life, laws often seal existing arrangements rather than make new ones. The case of the Bank of England epitomises this. When it was nationalised in 1946 the law merely recognised what Lord

North had noted over one hundred and fifty years before: that the Bank was 'from long habit and usage of many years... part of the constitution'.[18] The fact that its public responsibilities were developed outside the statute book deeply affected the Bank's relations with the banking community, and intensified those political peculiarities which grew from the special economic history of banking. The Bank's influence was decisive in three areas: prudential regulation, interest representation and monetary management.

The system of prudential control in Britain still bears some of the imprints of its nineteenth-century origins; indeed before the secondary banking crisis and the 1979 Banking Act it was almost entirely shaped by those origins. Evolving a stable banking system in the first industrial society posed problems of great intellectual and social complexity: rules for the prudent allocation of a bank's resources had to be devised, and a mechanism had to be invented which would prevent the difficulties of any particular institution from destroying confidence in all banks.[19] The intellectual problem of devising prudent banking rules was met by agreeing conventional (as distinct from statutory) ratios prescribing the proportion of a bank's resources to be held in cash or in assets easily convertible into cash. The social problem of maintaining confidence in the whole system even when some institutions were failing was solved by the device of a lender of last resort who, in Kindelberger's words, 'stands ready to halt a run out of real and illiquid financial assets into money, by making more money available'.[20]

To act effectively as lender of last resort an institution had to have, or be believed to have, limitless cash. The only bank which could expect to fulfil that condition in the nineteenth century was the Bank of England: as the manager of government debt it was closely identified with the power of the state, and under the Bank Charter Act of 1844 it had a virtual monopoly in the issue of banknotes. Solving the problems of intellectual and social complexity was nevertheless slow and painful, as is clear from recurrent banking crises, notably in 1825, 1847, 1857 and 1866. The pressure of these crises eventually forced the Bank to act as the guardian of stability, but it was not until the publication of Bagehot's *Lombard Street* in 1873 that its role as lender of last resort was fully acknowledged; and only after the 1870s was the Bank's narrow function of providing support in a crisis broadened into a general responsibility for the security of banking institutions. Only when it rescued the House of Baring from collapse in 1890 was its duty to safeguard the health of individual banks fully established.[21]

This obscure history is vital to understanding the events of the

1970s, for it emphasises how far banking regulation in Britain originated as the concern of a private institution controlled by the City elite. Such laws as did affect regulation largely appeared after the Second World War, and their content only emphasised the marginal relevance of the statute book: they either exempted banks from statutory requirements (such as the disclosure obligations imposed on the rest of business by company law) or gave to the Bank of England extensive administrative discretion in licensing institutions as banks for a variety of particular purposes.[22]

This history drew regulation away from the politics of Parliament and Whitehall, and into the City. The style of supervision and control practised by the Bank was in turn influenced by the City's hostility to formality and bureaucracy. Regulation was pictured as an exchange between partners, not as an exercise in authority. The Bank extended its jurisdiction only when it offered some privilege in return. The Discount Houses, for instance, put themselves under supervision in return for access to the Bank as a lender of last resort. The Bank's judgements in regulation were also partly 'market-determined', to use its own phrase: it relied less on detailed scrutiny of an institution, and more on the signals about that institution which it received from the market. This method was perfectly expressed in the notion of a ladder of status. Institutions were first acknowledged by the Bank to have banking status for certain limited purposes. Using this recognition they could improve their standing in the financial markets, which in turn brought wider recognition from the Bank. An institution might in this way try to climb to the position occupied by a leading merchant or clearing bank.[23]

This self-conscious cultivation of an anti-bureaucratic style was emphasised by the fact that, from the late nineteenth century until the secondary banking crisis, supervision was the responsibility of the Bank's Discount Office. The Office's primary function was to manage business with the money market. Supervision and control were in large degree by-products of this task, since the Office's extensive dealings were an important source of information about how banks were conducting their affairs. The City's informality was also exploited by encouraging bankers and financiers to treat the Office as open to a host of informal calls and conversations. In this way the Bank believed it could acquire information and exercise influence in a more subtle way than more formal legal controls would have allowed.[24] Informality was also encouraged by keeping small the number of people concerned with regulation and, in true City fashion, by taking on trust the information supplied by bankers.

Prudential regulation is an instructive example of how the Bank's connections with bankers were shaped by the informality and social cohesion of the City. It also shows how different were the politics of Lombard Street from the politics of economic policy in general. Take the case of public responsibility for firms who got themselves into difficulties. In the last two decades the role of the state in industrial rescues has been the subject of fierce partisan political argument. By contrast, in the 1960s the Bank supported about a dozen institutions without any publicity or controversy, and in the 1970s organised the much larger secondary banking rescue with only a little public argument. The contrast strikingly illustrates the widely held assumption that what needed to be fiercely debated in the case of industry was a private technical matter when banks were involved.[25] The difference is both a particular clue to understanding the secondary banking crisis, and a general clue to the politics of the banking community.

The persistence into the 1970s of a style of regulation based on informal understandings between a small number of people was due partly to the social characteristics of the banking community; but it also arose from the way the Bank had intertwined prudential regulation, interest representation and control over the wider economic impact of the banking system.

Since the First World War interest representation in banking, as in the City generally, has been increasingly accomplished through representative associations. In this, financiers followed the pattern established throughout the economy; but whereas other great interests established direct connections with central departments, and were thus drawn into the bargaining which goes on inside government, bankers relied until the beginning of the 1970s almost totally on the Bank of England to express their views in Whitehall.[26] The Bank in turn increasingly used the representative associations to control financial markets, both for prudential stability and to accomplish other obligations which had been laid on it by government.

To gain the compliance of the associations, and to give them the means of controlling their members, it favoured them in various ways. The most visible of these favours went to institutions who had historically been close to the Bank. Members of the London Discount Market Association had access to the Bank as lender of last resort, while the seventeen leading merchant banks in the Accepting Houses Committee could have their bills re-discounted at the Bank.[27] Less visibly, the Bank acquiesced in – and to some degree encouraged – the restrictive practices administered by the Committee of London Clearing Bankers.

The advantages of these arrangements were particularly clear during and after the Second World War. As public control of the economy extended, the Bank had to carry out a growing range of highly complex tasks. After 1940, for instance, it was responsible for detailed exchange controls, and domestically had to give guidance to the banks as to how much, and to whom, they could lend. By relying on representative associations to control their own members the Bank was able to carry out the tasks required of it by government without replacing informality by more legal and bureaucratic arrangements. In this way the banking system remained insulated from the politics of economic management in Whitehall and in Parliament. The Act which nationalised the Bank in 1946, true, gave it the power 'if so authorised by the Treasury' to 'issue directions to any banker', but this power of compulsion was never used, despite the fact that for most of the post-war years banks were under instructions to restrain lending and to direct their loans in directions favoured by government.[28] These 'quantitative' and 'qualitative' guidelines (as they were commonly called) were always issued as 'requests' by the Bank. This language was in part a mere politeness, since the clearing banks treated the requests as instructions. Yet the language was not just politeness, for it signified the Bank's determination to carry out an increasingly wide range of public duties without resort to the statute book, and to the range of political forces which the statute book involved. The Bank could only do this by creating a system of control outside the law, and its chosen instruments were the representative bodies and trade associations. Thus its 'requests' generally went to the associations rather than to individual banks.[29]

This is how, in the years after the Second World War, prudential regulation, interest representation and credit control became entwined. The system of control through representative associations was the Bank's attempt to cope with great problems of social complexity without opening the City up to Whitehall or Parliament. Those who controlled the Bank believed, in common with most people in the City, that the law was too inflexible to control effectively a highly sophisticated financial system, and that its use would open banking to the influence of those unqualified to make expert judgements. To keep out such undesirables as lawyers and politicians 'moral suasion' – seeking compliance by appealing to voluntary restraint – was elevated to the status of a philosophy of regulation.[30]

The reader will hear an odd echo in all this: during the 1960s right-wing bankers rejected legal controls on much the same grounds as those put forward by left-wing trade unionists concerned to keep the statute book out of industrial relations.[31] But the price of 'moral suasion' was a banking system riddled with restrictive practices. To regulate markets independently of the statute book it was necessary to hand over extensive powers to trade associations. The associations in turn needed restrictive practices as instruments of control. From the early 1960s, however, these limits on competition became decreasingly effective. The financial system grew in size and complexity. New institutions, markets and financial instruments developed rapidly. The revival of London as an international financial centre attracted large numbers of branches and subsidiaries of aggressively competitive foreign banks.[32]

The Bank of England struggled vainly to maintain the established system of control in the face of these changes. When the system of 'requests' to restrain lending first began in the Second World War it was sufficient to have the agreement of the clearing banks, indeed of the Big Five alone, to exercise effective control; by the end of the 1960s the Bank had been forced to extend the 'requests' to cover more than 260 institutions.[33] The extension was accomplished by trying to recreate in the new markets the traditional system of control through trade associations. The case of the finance houses illustrates the Bank's response, and the difficulties which it faced in making the response effective. The rapid expansion of the post-war market in consumer credit had helped the finance houses to challenge the clearing banks in the mass market for loans. In the 1950s the Bank attempted to strengthen the Finance Houses Association, and in 1961 extended the system of 'requests' to the finance houses via the FHA.[34] It also encouraged the houses and the clearing banks to agree to restrictions on competition. This sufficed for the immediate purpose of controlling the volume of lending, since at the end of the 1960s the Association's members took 90 per cent of all instalment credit business. The remaining 10 per cent was, however, accounted for by numerous small companies – the Radcliffe Committee put their number at about 1,200 a decade before – who were 'sufficiently insecure to resent well-meaning interference and requests for moderation in an environment of fierce competition'.[35] The consequence was that big companies who voluntarily exercised restraint found their business nibbled away. The Bank met similar problems whenever it organised a market to limit competition: those who were 'responsible' suffered at the expense of the aggressive parvenus produced by a highly adaptable financial system.

It would be wrong to conclude from this that the Bank's influence was wholly directed to stifling competition. Its actions were ambiguous. The informal, consciously anti-bureaucratic style of regulation which was practised in London was actually a great attraction to banks from more tightly controlled countries, notably the United States. The influx of foreign banks in the 1960s was a competitive shock to domestic institutions. The ladder of banking status was likewise designed to encourage new entrants into the industry, by allowing enterprises to operate first on a modest scale before gradually building up their resources. The very success of this approach, by stimulating growth and innovation, weakened the social and economic fabric of the Bank's traditional ties with the banking system. The continued resistance to more bureaucratic means of control in the face of these difficulties had much to do with the Bank's place in the machinery of government.

5 THE BANK OF ENGLAND AND THE GOVERNMENT

Informality, privacy, freedom from partisan political argument: these features have marked the policies of the banking community. Their persistence owes a great deal to the connections existing between the Bank of England and its chief point of contact with government, the Treasury. These connections in turn were above all shaped by the effort to solve one problem: how to reconcile the rise of elected governments intent on ambitious programmes of economic management with the Bank's desire to keep control of money and banking in its own hands. The search for a solution to this problem affected the way responsibility for policy was allocated between the Bank and government, the institutional connections existing between the two, and the way the Bank was organised internally. Examining each of these in turn illustrates the Bank's changing role.

Before the First World War the problem of who should control money and banking was settled largely in the Bank's favour by a set of customary assumptions rarely challenged in political argument. These assumptions defined prudential regulations as something which was a private concern of the Bank and the City, not the public concern of Parliament and government. In monetary policy the rules of the Gold Standard pictured control as a purely technical banking matter, thus placing it firmly in the Bank's hands.[36] Only in its traditional role as the manager of government debt was the Bank the acknowledged servant of government.

This customary allocation of responsibilities was reflected in institutional arrangements. The Bank largely worked in isolation from Whitehall. Only the Governor kept up personal contact with the Treasury, and his communications were infrequent. The Bank was organised on a small enough scale to be dominated by the Court, a group of directors drawn from the City elite who generally treated their duties as part-time. The Governorship itself was rotated between the members of the Court at two-yearly intervals according to a seniority rule modified occasionally to exclude the incompetent.[37]

The great political and economic changes which occurred in the half century after the First World War inevitably altered these hermitic arrangements. The destruction of the Gold Standard destroyed the notion that monetary policy could be treated as a technical banking matter isolated from the wider conduct of economic management. The visible sign of this change was the fate of Bank Rate, the key monetary instrument under the Gold Standard. After a long struggle by the Bank to retain control over the Rate it was finally fully established by the 1950s that no alteration could be made without Treasury agreement.[38]

Against this significant loss of control must be set the Bank's success in preserving some areas of autonomy and in creating others. The Bank of course retained responsibility for prudential regulation. It also controlled the structure of the industry having emerged with the dominant voice on bank mergers after the report of the Colwyn Committee in 1918.[39] The way the Bank dominated and organised interest representation also gave it considerable independence, for the customary assumption that bankers would not directly approach central government also involved the converse notion that government would not deal directly with the banks. Even Mr Dalton, of all post-war Chancellors the one most hostile to the Bank of England's power, nevertheless told the Radcliffe Committee in 1958 that he would not have thought any Treasury officer should have official contacts with the clearing banks.[40]

The Bank was able to establish a right to stand between the Treasury and the City in part because the economic consequences of two wars forced government to rely on its expertise to manage the financial community. The expense of war sharply increased the volume of long-term and short-term public debt.[41] This debt was largely funded through the capital and money markets. The Bank, because it was the traditional debt manager and because of its closeness to the financial community, was vital to successful funding. Although formally only the agent of the Treasury, the complexities of managing the markets meant that it developed considerable freedom of action. As Lord Bridges (a former permanent secretary to the Treasury and Head of the Civil Service) put it at the end of the 1950s: 'The high officials of the Bank of England ... have long and intense training and experience in their particular field ... officers of the Treasury are laymen'. Consequently, 'policy springs to a very sharp extent out of the practical experience of the Bank'.[42] Although the Bank's freedom to manage financial markets in its own way was challenged within the Treasury in the late 1960s, the customary assumption that the Bank was the expert in dealing with the markets was important to the development of Competition and Credit Control.[43]

The independence which the Bank retained gave it in some radical circles a reputation of immense power. When Labour was in office after 1964 the Governor's complaints about such matters as public spending and taxation aroused widespread suspicion in the labour movement that the Bank was stifling the Government's radical intentions.[44] The indignation aroused by these interventions showed a misunderstanding of the Bank's position. Its influence did not rest on the ability to shape fiscal policy but came from those customary assumptions spiriting important subjects – prudential regulation, control over interest representation, management of financial markets – away from Whitehall into the City. Complaints by the Governor were indeed a sign of where the Bank was weak, for they indicated areas where it was a more marginal participant in the machinery of policy making.[45]

This marginality itself arose in part from the way the Bank insisted on organising its institutional links with government. After 1914 it was never again possible for the Bank to remain isolated from Whitehall, but it nevertheless persistently tried to minimise communication. It particularly resisted formal involvement with the committees into which economic policy making was increasingly organised. In Whitehall itself the reforms implemented after the First World War during Warren Fisher's time as Head of the Civil Service transformed a disparate grouping of departments into a close community, particularly in the Administrative class of the Service.[46] From the very beginning the Bank self-consciously stood aside from all this. Montagu Norman, its greatest Governor (1920-44), emphatically believed that central banking should be carried on independently of politicians, and of their civil servants.[47] In Norman's time the Bank's contacts with Whitehall were made almost entirely through the Treasury, and these contacts in turn were channelled largely through the Governor.[48] This reflected in part his temperamental preference for informal personal dealing, but it had the effect of keeping the Bank clear of the Whitehall machine.

That this emphasis on informality was not just due to Norman's personal whim is shown by the persistence of the style after his departure. When the Radcliffe Committee gathered evidence at the end of the 1950s it found that the volume of contacts with Whitehall had increased over the years, but that the emphasis was still on informality. At the highest levels, according to the Governor, hardly anything was recorded in writing.[49] In the 1960s, partly as a result of the Radcliffe Committee's criticisms of this state of affairs, the Bank became increasingly involved in the Whitehall committee network, and broadened its range of contacts beyond the Treasury. Yet almost on the eve of Competition and Credit Control a well-informed observer could still write of the most important contacts between the Bank and central government that 'more of the real business is done in conversation and less is put down on paper here than anywhere else in Whitehall'.[50]

This separation from the Whitehall machine was prompted by the Bank's determination to retain tight control over its own affairs. It had long tried to preserve its independence by claiming that it conducted two kinds of activities: those where it was legally the agent of the Treasury, and those 'affairs of the Bank' where it was its own mistress.[51] Even in the late 1960s the Bank was insisting that in managing its own affairs it was entitled to much greater independence from central government than was enjoyed by other publicly owned bodies. The Select Committee on Nationalised Industries found in 1969 that it published no conventional accounts, was subject to none of the usual limits put on bodies disposing of public money, and did not even reveal to the Treasury what its senior officials were paid.[52] This state of affairs could be defended on two grounds. The Bank could point to the letter of the law, for the Charter under which it operated did indeed leave it mistress of its own affairs. But this merely begged the question, why a publicly owned institution should have been given such unusual independence? Sir Leslie O'Brien therefore offered a second, more substantive defence: the Bank needed autonomy the better to perform its 'independent advice function' in government. The advice it offered, he suggested, was probably more independent than that given by civil servants who 'living in the same departments as the Ministers who lead them become impregnated with the Ministers' enthusiasms and aspirations'. This special independence, he went on,

> rests on our ability to run the Bank as an independent institution, to recruit such people as we see fit . . ., to pay them what we regard it is necessary to pay them in order to get them and generally to conduct our affairs as an independent institution.[53]

This control over its own affairs allowed the Bank to develop very differently from other bodies concerned with economic policy. It paid salaries competitive with those offered in the City, and drew leading officers from there: every Governor from Cunliffe to Cromer had family connections with the financial elite. It is thus not surprising that the Bank acquired an outlook more attuned to the City than to Whitehall. It shared in particular the City's scepticism of abstract theory and systematic evidence in making decisions. 'I do not attach importance to great elaboration of statistical information', said Montagu Norman to the Macmillan Committee, explaining that statistics were 'more valuable for the purpose of testing conclusions arrived at independently than for providing the foundation on which to base conclusions'.[54] Almost thirty years later one of his successors, in responding sceptically to demands that the Bank acquire more academic expertise, remarked in a similar spirit that it 'must be a Bank and not a study-group'.[55]

This scepticism about the relevance of intellectual argument has attracted predictable hostility from academic economists. Reviewing the evidence of how the decision to change Bank Rate was arrived at in 1957, for instance, Thomas Balogh was scathing: the affair, he remarked, showed 'casualness and absence of expert knowledge'; in all the discussions it was 'difficult to find a relevant and intellectually coherent observation'.[56] Yet stressing practical experience over academic theory and statistical evidence, whatever it did to the substantive worth of policy, decisively strengthened the Bank's influence at the expense of Whitehall. The Treasury could acquire formal expertise; only the Bank had the practical experience of actually managing markets. By accepting the customary notion that experience mattered above all, senior civil servants were induced into the state of deference well illustrated by Lord Bridges' views. 'Monetary policy', he remarked to the Radcliffe Committee, 'resides in practical wisdom and experience, and not in very clearly thought out theory.' Consequently, 'something of the independence of the Governor's position does spring from the fact that he is a man who in his own person embodies the practical experience and wisdom which resides partly in the Bank and partly in the financial institutions of the City'.[57]

By the end of the 1960s the supremacy of 'practical experience and wisdom' was being challenged. In the Treasury, the Bank and even the City academically trained economists were becoming more numerous and influential. Since the beginning of the decade the Bank had been systematically gathering economic intelligence; by its close, economists were being hired to carry out theoretical work. The declining prestige of practical experience, and the rising influence of technical economic analysis, were to decisively shape Competition and Credit Control.

6 ESOTERIC POLITICS AND MONETARY POLICY

Nearly two decades ago W. J. M. Mackenzie argued that theory and practice in English politics are deeply influenced by competing models of our political life. These models provide both representations of the past and images of the present. Mackenzie emphasised in particular the contrast between *esoteric* and *exoteric* models of English politics. The first of these pictures politics as shaped by the social cohesion of an elite; the second represents politics as a matter of open political argument located in popular assemblies such as Parliament.[58]

Until the early 1970s money and banking in Britain were run almost totally according to the esoteric model. Banking was dominated by an elite selected by birth and united by kinship, common education and economic interests. These features connected banking more closely to the City than to manufacturing industry. In the City both business and policy were carried out informally. With little written down, and even less revealed, it was very difficult for outsiders – even such well-informed outsiders as senior Treasury officials – to understand how things were done. Managing the banking system was pictured as a task for experts of a special kind. The skills needed could not be acquired by formal training, nor could they be reduced to academic principles; they grew from long practical experience in managing markets which, as a senior Bank officer put it, took 'a life-time to understand'.[59] Outsiders could contribute little, whether as voters, academics, backbench MPs, ministers or even senior civil servants.

Elements of esoteric politics can be found in many parts of our political life but the model was especially influential in money and banking because of the unusual social cohesion of the banking elite, and because the Bank of England exploited that cohesion to protect the system from exoteric influences. To sustain esoteric politics for so long was an extraordinary achievement in a society where elites of birth and kinship were under attack, where bureaucratic organisation was spreading rapidly and where partisan political argument was engaging an increasingly wide range of issues. By the end of the 1960s the esoteric system was finally showing signs of stress. Competition and Credit Control was a response to that stress. The problems caused by implementing Competition and Credit Control further weakened esoteric politics and made the politics of money and banking even more exoteric in character.

3 The Politics of Policy Change

The best thing undeniably that a Government can do with the Money Market is to let it take care of itself.

1 BREAKING THE POLICY CODE

The origins of public policy are mysterious, for the choices made or neglected by government derive from a subtle compound of influences. These influences are inadequately conveyed by simple historical narration since apparently plain narratives are inevitably constructed from hidden assumptions about why policies alter. To account for the introduction of Competition and Credit Control these assumptions must be made visible. This is done in the succeeding pages by discarding the conventions of historical narration. The discussion begins at the end, with a summary of Competition and Credit Control. Attempts are then made to explain the existence of the new arrangements using five different accounts of how policies are formed. These accounts have the merit of making clear their assumptions about the influences which shape policy. In using them we can illuminate both the forces which produced Competition and Credit Control and the utility of different accounts of change.

The five accounts in question variously suggest that policy is the product of: (a) the rise and fall of fashions among those who make decisions; (b) enquiry carried out by professional academics; (c) party competition in a system of adversary politics; (d) the demands of powerful economic interests; (e) the workings of what Allison and Halperin call 'bureaucratic politics'.[1]

The choice of these five is a little arbitrary. They are nevertheless very common ways of explaining policy, and they contain very different assumptions about how it is made. Though sometimes described as models or theories they might be more illuminatingly spoken of in the language of code-breaking. All policy making is full of puzzles. New policies are preceded by a jumble of events, and each new policy is made up of a jumble of actions and aspirations. Each of the five accounts gives a key which makes sense of some of the jumble. Some keys convey more sense than others; none breaks the policy code entirely. Fashion, academic influence and adversary politics all have something to offer; but the accounts which stress economic interests and bureaucratic politics, as will appear, tell us much more.

2 COMPETITION AND CREDIT CONTROL: A SUMMARY

Competition and Credit Control takes its name from a consultative document issued by the Bank of England in May 1971 'for discussion with banks and finance houses'.[2] The document was the considered product of long thought and discussion, and while the ensuing consultations were perfectly genuine the scheme which was implemented in September 1971 differed only in minor details from what had been proposed four months before.

The aim of these changes was, as the Governor of the Bank put it, 'to permit the price mechanism to function efficiently in the allocation of credit, and to free the banks from rigidities and restraints which have for too long inhibited them'.[3] Competition and Credit Control thus tried to alter practices which had developed in banking over a century, and to reform methods of credit control which had existed for a generation. Since the Second World War governments had generally preferred to ration credit by administrative guidance rather than through the price mechanism. Banks had worked almost continuously under official 'requests' to restrain the volume of loans, and to give priority to particular groups of borrowers. In the 1960s 'quantitative' guidance – to use official language – was extended to a wide range of institutions. It also became more precise, for after 1965 the level of all bank advances was put under common arithmetic ceilings.[4] 'Qualitative' guidance about the direction of lending also became increasingly elaborate, its content reflecting in part the political influence of different interests. The 1970 Budget, for instance, urged the banks to discriminate against importers and personal borrowers, and suggested priority for farmers, exporters and those needing money for manufacturing investment and as bridging loans for house purchase.[5]

CCC abolished most of these efforts to ration credit by administrative decree, and also abolished many restrictive practices in banking. The ceilings on lending – as they were commonly called – were dismantled. The Bank also ceased to give formal guidance as to which borrowers were to be favoured: the flow of credit was in future to be 'primarily determined by its cost'.[6] As a consequent change – though it was not formally part of CCC – all restrictions on credit for hire purchase were abolished in July 1971, in accordance with the arguments of Lord Crowther's *Committee on Consumer Credit* which had reported in December of the previous year.[7] CCC also ended the agreement between the clearing banks offering uniform rates to borrowers and lenders; abolished the cartel under which the Discount Houses submitted a common bid at the Treasury Bill tender; and ended the agreement by which the clearing banks declined to compete with the Houses in bidding for Treasury Bills. Encouraging competition between banks implied that such administrative controls as did exist should be applied uniformly to all institutions. The special cash and liquidity ratios observed by the clearing banks were therefore abolished, and were replaced by a common reserve ratio which applied to all banks.

Since it was a guiding principle of Competition and Credit Control that credit should be allocated by its price – measured by the rate of interest – it followed that official financial transactions would have to be modified accordingly. The tactics guiding official dealings in both Treasury Bills and gilt-edged stocks were thus changed so as 'to leave more freedom for prices to be affected by market conditions'.[8] In abolishing the ceilings on lending, all hire purchase controls and most qualitative guidance, the authorities gave up three powerful instruments of credit control. The principles which inspired CCC rejected these administrative restraints in favour of control through the price mechanism: in plain language, if credit grew excessively interest rates would be pushed up to choke off demand.

This obvious change in the means of control was accompanied by a more subtle shift in the quantity to be controlled. The system of 'requests' had been designed to control credit by restricting bank advances. This rested on the increasingly dubious proposition that a group of institutions conventionally labelled banks monopolised credit creation and allocation.[9] CCC recognised, in the Governor's words, 'that financial systems are infinitely adaptable and the channels whereby money and credit end up as spending are many and various.'[10] The new arrangements thus shifted attention away from bank lending to 'the money supply under one or more of its many definitions'.[11] In view of what happened during the first two years of its life it is worth emphasising, however, that CCC was never designed to allow direct official control of the money supply. The authorities' intention was to influence the level of interest rates and, by thus varying its price, to affect the demand for credit.

The Bank of England had two main instruments to help it achieve these objectives: Bank Rate and Special Deposits. The first of these was technically the rate of interest normally charged by the Bank when it lent to the Discount Houses in its role as lender of last resort to the banking system. By varying the Rate the Bank could thus influence the price of funds in the system. More important, Bank Rate signalled official views of what the trend of interest rates should be. For the first thirteen months of CCC it was set by administrative means, the Bank announcing the Rate after consultation (which sometimes meant hard private argument) with the Treasury. In October 1972 a formula more sensitive to market pressures was introduced: the Rate was linked to the level set at the weekly Treasury Bill tender, and was renamed 'Minimum Lending Rate'. Even MLR was still under strong official influence, however, since the Bank continued to indicate its view about what the appropriate level of interest rates should be by the price at which it dealt daily in Treasury Bills and by numerous informal communications.[12]

The effect of Bank Rate/MLR on interest rates was reinforced by the power to call Special Deposits from the banks. A call for Special Deposits required them to place a prescribed percentage of their own liabilities in cash at the Bank of England. The intended effects were simple though the mechanism involved complicated adjustments between institutions: to drain reserves from the banking system, push up the rate of interest on selected financial instruments and thus influence interest rates generally.[13] Special Deposits hence worked in part by their effects on the reserve ratios observed by banks. The reserve asset ratio was one of the most complex features of CCC. In some theoretical accounts of banking, reserve ratios are pictured as levers which give the authorities precise control over banking behaviour. By controlling the supply of assets which count as reserves, the authorities can put exact arithmetic limits to credit creation. The ratio devised under CCC was never of this kind: it was, in one economist's phrase, 'a rag-bag' of financial instruments, some of which were beyond official control.[14] Its composition reflected the complex array of forces which shaped policy. Some financial instruments were defined as reserves to encourage prudent banking; some were assigned to the reserve category to support the market in government debt; others were classified as reserves to support the Bank's agents, the Discount Houses, by encouraging the commercial banks to place funds with the Houses. These complexities were to be part of the undoing of CCC, for the inventiveness of the banks in manufacturing reserves was one of the influences facilitating the extraordinary growth in credit after 1971.

In all the technical details of CCC lay a change familiar to any observer of the politics of the British economy. As has happened periodically with collective bargaining and also with industrial policy, the power of the state was partly displaced by the influence of the market. Rationing by price replaced rationing by administrative decree. These fluctuations have attracted various explanations. It is time to see how far our five accounts of policy change make sense of Competition and Credit Control.

3 FASHION AND POLICY CHANGE

To those who take part in government, decision making often seems the result of fashions which sweep the policy making community. Similar new ideas inexplicably appear in different places at the same time, so that everybody concerned with an issue seems to arrive independently at a new set of common conclusions.

The ideas behind Competition and Credit Control certainly have these marks of fashion. The new scheme was made up of two connected elements: reform of the system of credit control, and changes in the competitive character of the banking industry. The first of these involved a shift of attention from bank advances to the supply of money as a whole. According to one well-informed outside observer the view that 'money mattered' became 'fashionable overnight in the policy-making world' in the late 1960s.[15] An even stronger case can be made for the notion that opposition to restrictive practices in banking was a sudden fashion. For almost a century restrictions on competition developed with no official criticism and much official encouragement; then within less than a year from the spring of 1967 two official broadsides were fired at the banks. In May 1967 the National Board for Prices and Incomes, in a report on the level of bank charges, argued that restrictive practices caused serious misallocation of resources, both in banking and in the whole system of credit allocation. The report anticipated Competition and Credit Control in many ways: it recognised that restrictive practices were bound up with the means of credit control, so that both would have to be reformed together; it suggested that the interest rate cartel be abolished; and it argued that all banks should be subject to common reserve ratios.[16]

Eight months later the Monopolies Commission was even more critical. Using a report on proposed mergers between four clearing banks as the occasion, it argued that restrictive practices 'have such a soporific effect on the banks that, so long as they exist, no foreseeable change in the structure of the clearing bank system could greatly increase the degree of competition'.[17] Like the PIB, the Commission recognised that reform in the industry could not come without change in the system of credit control. The Commission's report was followed soon after by the appointment of the Crowther Committee on Consumer Credit, whose *Report* in turn was a sustained argument in favour of a free market in credit allocation.[18] These officially sponsored arguments were matched in circles on the fringe of the official world: in the late 1960s and early 1970s numerous articles discussing the virtues of free competition suddenly began appearing in the specialist banking press.[19]

Academics dislike accounts of change which are phrased in terms of fashion, for such language seems to locate policy, in Dunleavy's words, 'outside the area of political analysis altogether'.[20] This need not be so. We can reconcile fashion and policy change by reflecting for a moment on the circumstances when fashion is most likely to influence human conduct. Two conditions must exist: the choices facing individuals must involve matters of taste which cannot sensibly be guided by rational argument; and individuals must choose in social circumstances which favour imitation, and the diffusion of ideas and habits. Thus fashion strongly guides choice in clothes, drink and food; and it spreads quickly in enclosed communities, like universities and lunatic asylums, where personal contact and rapid communication encourage imitation of fashion leaders.[21]

Both these conditions are present in some degree in public policy making. Though the choices facing decision makers are rarely trivial matters of taste, it is also rare for any particular option to be indicated by intellectually coercive arguments. The cases for and against competition in banking (or incomes policy or capital punishment) can never be resolved in an intellectually conclusive way. What Keynes said of economics is true of most debates about public policy: 'you cannot *convict* your opponent of error – you can only *convince* him of it'.[22] This intellectual uncertainty leaves a crucial area of freedom which can be subjected to the influence of fashion. This influence is strengthened when, as with the case of money and banking, policy making is esoteric. When a small number of like-minded people constantly communicate privately and informally, and read the same reports and journals, they reproduce exactly the social conditions which make the spread of fashion likely. Indeed some of the most significant policy changes in recent years are explicable precisely in such terms. The commitment to monetary targets embraced quite suddenly by a wide range of industrial economies in the mid-1970s, for instance, plainly reflected a fashion which central bankers communicated to each other in their small, enclosed world.[23]

When those concerned with monetary policy sometimes privately link CCC to the rise of certain newly fashionable ideas their account is thus not to be dismissed. The influence of fashion was connected to both the kind of choices facing policy makers and to the esoteric system of politics in which choices were made. The reports of the PIB and the Monopolies Commission dropped powerful challenges and arguments into the enclosed world of money and banking; the ensuing discussions, said Sir Leslie O'Brien, Governor of the Bank 1966–73, 'served much the same purpose as a full-dress public enquiry, and perhaps the better so for being less formal'.[24]

'Fashion', then, is not a way of rendering the origins of CCC inexplicable; it is a key to some of the jumble of events which preceded the 1971 changes. Yet it plainly leaves unanswered the most important question in the whole affair: why were particular ideas fashionable at a particular time? Part of the answer might lie in the influence of academics.

4 ACADEMIC ENQUIRY AND POLICY CHANGE

That academics influence policy makers is well documented. Sometimes particular individuals establish themselves as experts in the eyes of powerful men. More commonly, academic knowledge is organised as a professional orthodoxy used to train decision makers, as Dunleavy found in architecture and planning. More common still, intellectuals with a shared outlook work as an informal lobby, pressing their arguments on policy makers: the history of such lobbies stretches from the Benthamites to the modern activities of the 'Nuffield School' of industrial relations research.[25]

The influence of economists generally works through the second and third of these routes. As government, banks and industry hire more professional economists, so academic orthodoxies penetrate institutions. But since economics is a deeply divided discipline only a few fundamental ideas are unquestioningly accepted as constituting orthodoxy. Like-minded economists who want to influence policy therefore typically work as an informal lobby. In Britain these activities are assisted by various institutions: thus the Institute of Economic Affairs and the National Institute of Economic and Social Research have been important in sponsoring (respectively) liberal-market and Keynesian arguments.

To show that an intellectual lobby helped change monetary policy three conditions must be established: the lobby must have pressed new ideas; the ideas must have been communicated to policy makers; and policy makers must have been convinced by them. The first condition is amply fulfilled. In the 1960s economists began analysing both monetary policy and the banking industry in novel ways. From Chicago Friedman and his colleagues pressed the increasingly influential argument that control of the money supply was the key to successful economic management. By the end of the decade economists in Britain were replicating both Friedman's research and his arguments.[26] Some of the same individuals were also changing the way economists analysed the banking industry. Until the 1960s the dominant academic tradition in Britain – exemplified by the work of R. S. Sayers – emphasised the history and institutions of banking.[27] It also inclined to the belief that banking was an activity where intense competition would endanger prudent judgement. By the end of the 1960s an alternative view was becoming popular. Banking was treated as an industry which like any other could be examined with the highly abstract tools of micro-economic analysis. Viewed thus, cartels and restrictive practices were not an aid to prudence; they obstructed efficiency and harmed consumers.[28]

Two of the most important elements in Competition and Credit Control – greater concern with the money supply and with stimulating competition – thus reflected changes which had come over economists in the preceding decade. There is ample evidence that these views were widely communicated to politicians, officials and bankers. Some lines of communication were indirect. The International Monetary Fund team which scrutinised the British economy after devaluation was deeply influenced by Friedman's ideas. In October 1968, at Sir William Armstrong's instigation, a conference was held between IMF and British officials to discuss the relevance of the money supply to economic management, and in the following year the Government had to commit itself to a target for monetary growth as a condition of IMF assistance.²⁹ The new economic analysis of banking was also indirectly communicated. The style and substance of the PIB Report, for instance, was influenced by the writings of Professor Harry Johnson, a powerful critic of the bank cartel.

These indirect communications were reinforced in more direct ways. Walters' application of Friedman's work to Britain was published in a popular version by the Institute of Economic Affairs in 1969, was widely noticed in the banking press and was discussed at conferences and meetings where academics and officials were present.³⁰ Griffiths' *Competition in Banking*, also published by the IEA, drew similar wide attention in the banking press. The reforms it advocated resembled, but went further than, Competition and Credit Control.³¹ The most effective of all communicators was the late Harry Johnson, who simultaneously held chairs at the London School of Economics and the University of Chicago. Johnson's outstanding intellect and energy are shown not only in his specialist academic work, but also in a stream of less technical articles and conference papers which addressed the case for greater competition to officials and to bankers.³² In the late 1960s Johnson had an even more direct line of communication, for he ran an informal seminar which was regularly attended by Treasury officials interested in the new ideas. (The higher journalism he practised also illuminates the important part played by the specialist banking press in communicating academic ideas: *The Banker* and *The Bankers' Magazine* became in the 1960s – and remain – important in transmitting the policy implications of technical research.)

All these activities are a good example of an informal academic lobby at work. The effort to communicate with policy makers was undoubtedly further helped by the growing contacts in the 1960s between professional economists and the world of policy. The signs of this change are numerous: the increasing number of economists employed as specialists in Whitehall and the City; the existence of conferences and study groups (such as the Money Study Group founded in 1970) where academics and policy makers gathered; and the increasing use of academic advice at all levels in the Bank of England.³³ These developments exposed bankers and policy makers to a professional orthodoxy which instinctively suspected cartels and restrictive practices. It is remarkable, for instance, how the arguments of the socialist economist Roger Opie – a member of the Monopolies Commission when it reported on the banks – resemble the criticisms voiced by Brian Griffiths, an economist of an otherwise very different intellectual persuasion.³⁴

It is therefore clear that economists were thinking about money and banking in new ways, and that these novel ideas were widely communicated. It is much less certain that the ideas convinced policy makers of the need to reform. The impact of arguments about the significance of the money supply was discernible, but slight. Competition and Credit Control certainly did signify growing interest in measures of the money supply, and disenchantment with the practice of controlling credit by limiting bank advances; it emphatically did not indicate any intellectual conversion to monetarism. The views of Robert Armstrong (Head of the Home Finance Group) and of Leslie Dicks-Mireaux (a senior adviser at the Bank) well represent official orthodoxy at the end of the 1960s. At a conference held in October 1969, where most of the leading economists in the field gave papers, they were both sceptical of monetarist theories, and Armstrong was politely critical of what he described as the inability of monetarists to translate elegant theory into a form useful to policy makers.[35] One of those who helped draft Armstrong's remarks says that it was intended to be less chilly than the bare text suggests, and was designed to prompt the monetarists into more practically useful research. Armstrong was nevertheless voicing a common scepticism whose survival, we shall see, was an important clue to what happened after 1971.

The influence of academic arguments favouring more competition in banking cannot be so easily dismissed. Intellectual influence can be exercised in various ways: policy makers may be conscious of the force of an argument or – as in the case of Keynes's famous defunct economists – ideas may just seep into the store of conventional wisdom held by practical men. Both sorts of influence were observable in the late 1960s. According to the Governor of the Bank of England the arguments in the PIB Report, which reflected the views of economists, were taken seriously within the Bank.[36] At a less conscious level, the language used by policy makers in the period leading up to CCC echoed the critical terms – rigidity, misallocation of resources – common in the academic literature.

The activities of academic economists do, therefore, give a further inkling of where CCC came from. Policy makers were prone to the influence of fashion; academics were well placed to shape fashion. The new monetarism had a small but discernible influence in making those responsible for policy marginally more sensitive to the importance of the money supply. More significantly, academic arguments favouring greater competition were transmitted by such leaders of policy fashion as the Prices and Incomes Board.

Any attempt to estimate the influence of ideas on action faces a perennial problem: do particular ideas become popular because of the power and clarity with which they are presented, or because they coincide with the demands of particular political forces or economic interests? It is sensible to suspend judgement about the influence of academic enquiry until these other forces and interests are examined. The account of policy change which stresses adversary politics gives an important place to politicians and to their parties.

5 ADVERSARY POLITICS AND POLICY CHANGE

'Adversary politics' is both a description and a criticism of how important policies are made in Britain. The adversary tradition, so the argument runs, encourages the main opposition party to exaggerate its differences with government, and to adopt policies which reflect 'ideology' rather than the practical pressures of office. New governments are thus elected with damagingly unrealistic commitments. Since power alternates between two big parties, this lack of realism is compounded by instability, each administration reversing its predecessor's policies.[37]

The notion that the adversary system produced Competition and Credit Control is supported by a striking coincidence. The Conservatives were elected to office in June 1970 committed to disengage government from the economy; nine months later the Chancellor, in his first full Budget, announced that plans were to be drawn up to disengage government from the banking industry.[38] The idea that CCC can be traced to the Conservative Party, and notably to that curiously insubstantial figure, 'Selsdon Man', is oddly attractive to bankers and economists, both in private and in print.[39]

The conclusion prompted by coincidence is wrong. 'Competition and Credit Control was seventy per cent the Bank, twenty-five per cent the Treasury, five per cent the politicians', says someone who was a senior Treasury official at the time. Even this may overstate the politicians' influence. CCC had little to do with adversary politics, for reasons which illuminate both the adversary system and the politics of money and banking. Adversary politics is a theory of the exoteric politics of partisan argument in Parliament and in the country; it cannot make sense of those important policy changes which result from private negotiations between small elites removed from partisan politics. In the late 1960s, when the Conservatives were settling their plans for disengagement, customary assumptions pictured money and banking as abstrusely technical. Few politicians were interested in the issues, and those who were rarely gave them a partisan expression. The focus of party argument was elsewhere: on industrial policy, reform of collective bargaining, taxation. These subjects absorbed the energies of those who remade policy before the 1970 election. The few comments from the Conservative front bench on the revival of interest in monetary policy at the end of the 1960s confirm that the Conservatives saw little of partisan importance in such matters.[40]

The Conservatives thus came to office with no plans for monetary reform. The desire to move to a more competitive system was indeed already present in Whitehall and in the Bank before the election. In his last Budget, for instance, Mr Roy Jenkins committed himself to removing the ceilings on clearing bank lending, announced that more use would be made of Special Deposits, and anticipated that the appearance of the Crowther Report would prompt reforms in the way lending by finance houses was controlled.[41] It was already plain that Crowther's proposals would favour strengthening free competition at the expense of administrative control. Since the markets in different kinds of credit were linked it was unthinkable that consumer credit could be reformed independently of changes elsewhere in the banking system.

There still remains the possibility that the election of a government committed to disengagement accelerated the speed with which reform took place. It is certainly true that the Chancellor had to agree to (and could thus have vetoed) the proposals; and it is also true that the Bank presented CCC to the Chancellor as a reform which was in sympathy with the Conservatives' economic philosophy. The return of the Conservatives, however, changed ministerial attitudes to competition less dramatically than public appearances might suggest. Mr Roy Jenkins had gathered round him ministers whose social democratic outlook made them sympathetic to arguments for greater competition. On the choice of timing the Governor has suggested convincingly that immediate economic circumstances were the key consideration: 'low international interest rates, relatively slack demand for loans and a strong balance of payments' gave the authorities the freedom to risk the delicate experiment of removing ceilings and steering the monetary system through interest rates.[42]

Politicians were insignificant in working out CCC. Customary assumptions pictured the exercise as technical, though involving important technicalities. Ministerial assent was a gate through which the scheme had to pass; it was allowed through because it appeared in the guise of a technical reform with which ministers could sympathise. Esoteric politics organised the politicians out of decision making; by contrast, it organised great economic interests, notably the clearing banks, into an important place.

6 ECONOMIC INTERESTS AND POLICY CHANGE

That economic interests shape public policy is widely believed, though that belief takes many different forms. Various Marxist accounts see policy as a response to forces lying deep in the capitalist economy. Less strikingly, orthodox pressure group theory simply expects that in a country like Britain, where consultation with groups is common, well organised interests will play a significant part in policy making.[43] Both Marxist and non-Marxist accounts would expect the big banks to be a powerful influence on CCC; just how much power they are assigned depends on the nuances of different theoretical approaches.

This expectation is amply fulfilled. To understand why, it is necessary to sketch the extraordinary changes which have come over banking in the last two decades; changes which, it has been said, altered banking more than in the preceding two centuries. In the 1960s both retail and wholesale banking began changing in ways which attacked the restrictive practices operated for so long by the clearing banks. The severity of the attack was indicated by the fall in market shares experienced by the clearers: in 1951 they held nearly 80 per cent of all domestic bank deposits; by 1967 the figure was down to just over half, and the clearers only had 30 per cent of deposits with all financial institutions.[44]

Part of the challenge to clearing bank supremacy came in retail banking, especially from the building societies: between 1964 and 1970 the building societies' share of all sterling deposits rose from 18.4 per cent to 28.9 per cent; in the same period the clearing banks' share actually fell, by just short of three per cent, to 32.2 per cent.[45] The banks responded to this challenge by competing more aggressively in areas not covered by restrictive practices. This is why the 1960s saw great innovations in retail banking services: the introduction of credit cards, of personal loans as an alternative to overdrafts, and the rapid spread of the network of local branches. It was the intensity of this non-price competition which prompted the PIB to argue that the interest rate cartel diverted competition into wasteful investment on unnecessary branches.[46] The period also saw a new emphasis on advertising and marketing: in 1968 Barclays appointed one of their most talented assistant general managers to head a new Marketing Division. This first marketing department in a clearing bank indicated both the growing acceptance of modern management techniques and the declining influence of the traditional English banker's passive attitude of merely standing ready to accept deposits.

These changes were important in altering relations between the clearers and the mass of their customers, but they were trivial compared to what was happening in the wholesale money markets. When ceilings and qualitative guidance first began the Discount Market was the only wholesale money market in London, and its operations were tightly controlled through restrictive practices agreed between the clearers, the Discount Houses and the Bank of England. By the end of the 1960s these sedate arrangements were being transformed by the growth of new markets and new institutions. To the Discount Market was added a connected set of 'parallel' or 'secondary' markets, dealing in a variety of funds: local authority debt, loans between banks and loans between companies. The markets in turn stimulated the development of a system of 'secondary' banks, distinguished by this label from the primary banks which the Bank of England traditionally supervised.[47]

These changes were the early stages of a banking revolution which was consummated in the 1970s. Branches first emerged as the dominant feature of domestic banking in the generation before the First World War because a large retail network was the most efficient and prudent means of accumulating vast deposits. The rapid growth in the 1960s of wholesale deposits raised in the new money markets marked the rise of an even more effective, if less prudent, way of attracting funds. In the decade after 1962 the amounts traded in the new markets rose almost threefold; by the end of the 1970s they had more than doubled yet again, far outstripping the volume of funds in the branches. In some areas the growth was even more rapid: deposits in the inter-bank market rose by nearly one thousand per cent between 1962 and 1972, and doubled again in the next five years.[48] Even this growth was exceeded by the rate of expansion in the international money markets. Partly as a result of the Bank of England's encouragement London became the leading centre for eurocurrency dealings, a supremacy it retains. Before CCC the special liquidity requirements imposed on the clearing banks prevented them from dealing in the international markets, except through subsidiaries. The common reserve ratios for all banks introduced under CCC freed the clearers from these restrictions, and five years after the new scheme was introduced almost a third of London clearing bank deposits were in foreign currencies.[49]

The wholesale markets which flourished in the 1960s and which dominated banking in the next decade were very different from those in which UK banks traditionally operated. Unlike the Discount Market they had no lender of last resort, and until the great crisis of the mid-1970s were subject to little public supervision. This lack of supervision also signified the absence of those social and economic controls over entry, and over the terms on which business was done, which restrained competition in traditional markets. Entry (especially into the sterling markets) was comparatively easy in the 1960s, and competition for business fierce. The participants were often innovators in new banking techniques and practices, and in new means of organisation. The numerous American banks which came to London in the 1960s, for instance, imported both new financial instruments (such as Certificates of Deposit) and novel management techniques derived from the most advanced parts of American business.

The competitive challenge of the new markets and the new institutions helps explain the great changes which came over the clearing banks at the end of the 1960s. There developed a new interest in marketing and in applying advanced business techniques such as Management by Objectives.[50] In 1968 two big clearing banks merged to form the National Westminster Bank, Barclays swallowed up one of the few remaining small independent clearers, while Barclays and Lloyds were only prevented from merging by the opposition of the Monopolies Commission. This spate of amalgamations, the first significant alteration in the structure of the banking industry since 1918, was prompted by the growing scale of financial markets.[51] Yet another sign of change came in 1969 when the clearing banks renounced their right to keep their inner reserves secret, in favour of publishing figures of true profits. The change, though partly the result of government pressure, also reflected a new competitiveness. By the end of the decade every big clearing bank was breaking the rules of the cartel on interest rates, by operating through subsidiaries in the new money markets; when CCC was introduced the proportion of clearing bank profits derived from their subsidiaries' money market operations was rising sharply.[52]

These competitive responses were seriously obstructed by an obstacle which can be described in one word: ceilings. The uniform quantitative limits on bank lending kept the growth of advances well below the rate at which the new money markets were expanding; in some periods the clearers were even being 'requested' to cut back the total volume of lending. The subsidiaries allowed the clearers to break the cartel, but were not a way of avoiding ceilings because subsidiaries were also covered by the Bank of England's 'requests' to limit advances.[53] The clearers' problems were illuminated in 1969 when they exceeded the targets for lending set by the authorities. At the Treasury's instigation the banks were penalised by a 'fine' which reduced the rate of interest paid on their deposits at the Bank of England.

This fine intensified the clearers' dislike of ceilings, and turned their private complaints into an unprecedented series of public protests. Their views were summarised by the Chairman of the Committee of London Clearing Bankers in April 1970. He expressed concern about the clearers' declining market share; attacked the ceilings as arbitrary; and anticipated a key element of CCC by arguing that credit control should include the principle that a bank successful in attracting deposits would be able to expand lending accordingly.[54]

Policies bearing the same name can signify very different things to different people. To some, Competition and Credit Control meant a welcome if limited assertion of free market principles. To others it (incorrectly) signified the influence of 'Selsdon Man'. To the clearing banks it meant something simpler: the end of ceilings, objections to which had increasingly dominated their private and public communications with the authorities. The new arrangements were, in the words of a senior executive of Barclays, 'a management boon'.[55] Another banker privately puts it more brutally: after CCC was introduced the clearers, he says, were able to play freely in the 'casino' of the money markets. They also played enthusiastically, reorganising their money market operations and bringing subsidiaries back into the parent company. By 1973 over 45 per cent of London clearing bank sterling deposits were raised in the wholesale markets.[56]

Competition and Credit Control thus considerably assisted forces which were already destroying the traditional organisation of English banking. It accelerated the decline of the branches as a source of funds and encouraged the expansion of the highly competitive wholesale markets. In freeing the clearers from restrictions it provided the conditions for their transformation from domestic institutions largely concerned with traditional retail banking into multinational corporations marketing a wide variety of financial instruments and services in a range of domestic and international markets.

Viewing CCC as a response to the changing character of banking, and to the clearers' problems in adapting to change, decodes the new policy more satisfactorily than any of the accounts previously offered. The rapid rise of fiercely competitive wholesale markets immediately makes sense, for instance, of the fashion for competition and modern management practices which developed in the late 1960s. The role of academics also now seems less important: the popularity (though not the existence) of the new economic analysis of banking, with its novel stress on competition, is explicable as a result of the changed competitive climate in financial markets. When CCC is pictured as a response to the interests of the clearing banks some puzzles are also immediately solved. If the new scheme was the result of an intellectual fashion favouring competition, for instance, it was inexplicable why the clearing banks were able to retain the common practice of not paying interest on current account deposits. Professor Harry Johnson had argued with great cogency that this restrictive practice was unfair to customers and an obstacle to the efficient allocation of resources.[57] Its retention is immediately understandable when we know that current accounts provide an important source of cheap funds for the clearers; in the last decade of high interest rates this cheap money has helped make them very profitable. The failure to pay interest on current accounts was, true, not a restrictive agreement in the explicit manner of the cartel in, for instance, the Treasury Bill market. But it was plainly the result of collusion by the clearing bank oligopoly, and the authorities plainly had the power to exact a change in return for the other reforms which the clearers earnestly wanted.

Implementing the full schemes for competition favoured by academic economists would have damaged a powerful banking interest. Picturing CCC as a solution to the clearers' problems thus makes sense of much that was in the scheme, and of some things which were omitted. Yet many puzzles are unsolved. If the new policy was a response to clearing bank demands why were ceilings not simply removed, without involving other major competitive reforms? An answer with which a Marxist might sympathise is that the more powerful and commercially aggressive wing of banking favoured competition because it was attuned to the demands of the new financial markets. Thus Barclays and National Westminster, the two banks which benefited most from the mergers of the late 1960s, were also the most innovative and most eager to grasp the opportunities offered by the end of ceilings. By contrast Sir Cuthbert Clegg, the Chairman of a smaller clearing bank which Barclays took over, was left to voice traditional bankers' fears about the prudential dangers of competition.[58]

Yet there remains an important puzzle which cannot be solved by picturing CCC as a response to the interests of the clearing banks. All accounts which represent public policy as due to the pressures of private economic interests have to explain how private desires are turned into public actions. The need for explanation is especially pressing in the case of banking, for in Britain the industry has long been closely regulated. Even actions normally controlled by the banks require official approval: thus the original entry of clearing bank subsidiaries into the new wholesale money markets had to await Bank of England permission for several years. The key changes in CCC – the end of ceilings and the introduction of common reserve ratios – could only be carried out by the Bank and the Treasury.

The readiness with which the authorities responded to clearing bank interests will not surprise anyone who holds the view, common among radicals, that the Treasury and the Bank are especially sympathetic to banking capital. More generally, a large literature documents the fact that regulatory bodies are commonly 'captured' by the interests they are supposed to control.[59] These arguments provide a ready explanation for official willingness to introduce CCC: the measures were demanded because of the changed character of the banking industry, and were granted because public institutions were responsive to private banking interests.

In assessing this explanation it is important to distinguish between the Treasury and the Bank. The notion that the former was 'captured' by the clearing banks is implausible. At the end of the 1960s there were few direct contacts between the Treasury and the clearers, and the policies advocated by the Treasury – ceilings, 'fining' the clearers when they broke through the ceilings – were harmful to banking interests. The position of the Bank of England was more complicated. Its senior officials candidly sympathised with the clearers' arguments, and certainly thought of CCC as a way of helping them to compete more effectively. But to picture the Bank as the captive of clearing bank interests makes no sense. The modern history of the British monetary system rather demonstrates the reverse: it is the Bank which dominated and shaped institutions and markets. Nor has the modern Bank ever had any of the institutional marks of a regulatory body liable to capture. It is powerful and prestigious, with an ample independent income. Of course the Bank, as has often been said, is a Janus-like institution, with one face sympathetically turned towards the City. Its

The Politics of Policy Change 47

other face is, however, turned towards government. The Bank consequently responds to the internal politics of Whitehall and to the demands created by its role as a central banker. The influence of these entanglements is recognised by the account of policy change which emphasises the importance of 'bureaucratic politics'.

7 BUREAUCRATIC POLITICS AND POLICY CHANGE

'Where you stand depends on where you sit.'[60] Don Price's cryptic aphorism captures the essence of bureaucratic politics. A verbose translation would run as follows. The policies defended by particular individuals in government reflect the positions which they occupy in public institutions, and the responsibilities and interests of those institutions. Because policies are made in bureaucracies – that is, in rule-governed institutions – arguments over policy are conducted as games with prescribed rules. These games, in Graham Allison's words, 'determine decisions and actions'.[61]

Decoding Competition and Credit Control in these terms involves beginning with the institutions which put together the proposals. This means the Bank of England, and to a smaller degree the Treasury. If the bureaucratic politics account makes sense the policies pressed by these institutions should reflect the public duties with which they were charged. Policy change should mark either a change in these duties, or an alteration in official capacity to carry them out. New policy should be traceable to how the games of decision were played.

It is natural to begin with the Bank, for the customary assumptions formed by historical experience gave it a dominant role, especially in controlling credit and in prudential regulation. This experience also shaped the assumption that politics would be esoteric in character, while the social and economic history of banking provided the conditions needed for this esoteric style. Customary assumptions thus gave the Bank wide responsibilities, and dictated that those responsibilities be carried out by the informal and private exercise of restraint over the competitive appetite of bankers.

Developments in public policy and in financial markets combined to threaten these esoteric arrangements in the 1960s. The drift of public policy had long been a danger to esoteric politics, for the increasing scope of economic intervention practised by Whitehall was a constant challenge to the autonomy of the banking sector; hence the Bank of England's gradual loss of independent control over Bank Rate, and thus over interest rates as a whole. As intervention increased so the challenge could be expected to grow. This is exactly what happened after the level of government intervention began to rise steeply in the early 1960s. In 1965 the Treasury turned the Bank's general requests to restrain lending into precise arithmetic ceilings on the level of bank advances. The object – a familiar one – was to restrain credit growth without raising interest rates. The precision of these figures put great strains on relations within the small elite which influenced monetary policy. The clearing banks had constant difficulties in keeping within the targets, in part because the overdraft system made it very difficult to control exactly the amount which customers could borrow. These problems were viewed impatiently at the higher political and official levels of the Treasury. Whitehall's irritation partly explains why the banks had to bear the unprecedented embarrassment of investigations by the PIB and the Monopolies Commission. Irritation culminated in the 'fine' on the clearers in 1969 for failing to stay within the ceilings.

Private recollections of the late 1960s confirm what the public sources already strongly suggest: the Bank disliked all these developments. It disliked opening up questions about monetary policy to the PIB, and to the public arguments which were usually prompted by PIB investigations. It disliked introducing the Monopolies Commission into questions usually settled privately between itself, the banks and the Treasury. Above all, it disliked the ceilings because their command-like quality was a danger to esoteric politics. The Governor's speeches and other official comments in the late 1960s endlessly repeat the same themes: ceilings put an excessive strain on relations between the authorities and the banks, and distorted the workings of the banking system.[62] It is thus no surprise that the most senior officials of the Bank were impressed by some of the arguments of the PIB Report and that they gave it very serious consideration.[63] The imposition of ceilings endangered the esoteric politics through which the Bank accomplished its public duties.

These dangers were compounded by developments in the financial markets. The new, fiercely competitive wholesale money markets, and the secondary banking system, were partly stimulated by the tight controls on the primary banks: like all systems of administrative rationing, the 'requests' prompted the appearance of unofficial markets to meet unsatisfied demand. The Bank's established response to new markets and institutions was – as we saw earlier in the case of the finance houses – to organise the market under the control of a trade association. This association then operated restrictive practices, and negotiated with the Bank. This way of preserving esoteric politics depended on limiting entry to markets and suppressing 'excessive' competition. These conditions became increasingly difficult to enforce in a banking system which was invaded by highly competitive foreigners, and which was responding to the invasion by rapid growth and adaptation. In the later 1960s policy makers began to meet increasing problems of social and intellectual complexity. Within both the Bank and the Treasury there developed agreement that existing credit controls were being avoided on a large scale, and that the diversion of credit outside officially controlled and monitored institutions made official indicators unreliable.[64]

The threat to esoteric politics came also from the growing scale of the banking community: we have already seen that by 1969 'requests' covered over 260 institutions. The informality and personal knowledge so central to esoteric politics were plainly endangered. This increase in scale went with a decline in the social cohesion which had allowed the Bank to exercise delicate control by private, personal communications. Parvenus were often insensitive to the broadest hints about their behaviour: the chairman of one fringe bank, called to be rebuked by the Governor for some transgression, emerged from the meeting with the remark that he had enjoyed his visit and hoped he would be invited again.[65] (Similar problems of control afflict other City markets, such as Lloyds and the Stock Exchange.)

These problems could have been solved in a number of ways. The authorities might have armed themselves – as they were forced to do in the late 1970s – with legal powers and created a formal apparatus of control. In the Bank and in the City this solution was unthinkable, in the exact sense of that word: it was excluded from consideration by the customary assumption that regulation should, if at all possible, be kept away from the political forces connected with Parliament and with the statute book. In extremity the Bank was certainly willing to use the law; indeed in the 1950s it had gone so far as to draft a Bill – which was aborted in Whitehall – giving it statutory powers over the finance houses for the purpose of credit control. But this kind of extremity was far off at the end of the 1960s: the Bank made it clear to the Crowther Committee that it wanted nothing to do with a formally organised system of large-scale controls.[66]

A more attractive alternative was to strengthen those banks which would respond to control by traditional means. Of these, the clearers were the most important. From the appearance of the PIB Report, therefore, the Bank of England's aim was to reform the monetary system to the advantage of the clearing banks, especially at the expense of the fringe. As the Governor said in commenting on the PIB Report:

> I entirely accept the dictum that the technical implementation of monetary policy must accommodate itself to the commercial banking system as it evolves. If it were to evolve so as to bring more of the many diverse banking and credit facilities now available into the clearing bank system, the task of the monetary authorities might perhaps be made easier. There would, so to speak, be fewer taps for us to turn off and on.[67]

We have it on the authority of Sir Leslie O'Brien's successor as Governor, and of the Bank's written evidence to the Wilson Committee, that it was the conscious purpose of Competition and Credit Control to allow the clearers to compete aggressively and in this way to 'contract' the fringe.[68] (For similar reasons the Bank in 1968 favoured mergers between the clearing banks: the Governor pointed out to the Monopolies Commission that 'there would be advantages for the Bank in having only three large banks to deal with'.)[69]

This account makes sense of many important parts of CCC. It explains why dismantling ceilings was accompanied by so much stress on competition, for it was important that the clearers should compete aggressively against the fringe. It also explains why a common reserve asset ratio for all banks was introduced: the special ratios traditionally observed by the clearing banks were agreed to hinder their ability to compete in some of the wholesale markets.[70] This concern to strengthen the clearers also explains of course why the Bank's emphasis on equality in competition did not extend to tampering with the advantages the clearers derived from the cheap funds raised in non-interest-bearing current accounts.

That Competition and Credit Control was a 'management boon' for the clearers was thus no accident, but neither was it the result of some conscious grand design inside the Bank. Like all policy, CCC was shaped by instinctive preferences which were rarely articulated: a reluctance to transform the way the Bank carried out its (bureaucratic) public responsibilities by adopting more formal powers; a desire nevertheless to reassert control over the banking industry; and a sense that these varying preferences and desires could be reconciled by strengthening those institutions with whom the Bank felt most comfortable in dealing in the traditional ways, of which the clearing banks were the most significant.

The Politics of Policy Change 51

The Bank could not, however, accomplish change alone. The customary division of responsibility meant that the assent of Treasury officials was needed. This necessity was strengthened by the comparative indifference of ministers to the techniques of monetary management. It was plain that the political masters would be influenced by the way the scheme was presented by official advisers. In the Treasury's changing attitude lies the final important clue to the origins of Competition and Credit Control.

Throughout the 1960s the Treasury had consistently favoured policies designed to produce cheap credit. In doing so it was responding to forces influentially represented in the Whitehall community: industrial investors who wanted low interest rates and, more visibly, electorally influential mortgagees in the housing market. The Treasury's preference for administrative controls on the level and direction of bank lending was due to the belief that these were an effective alternative to rationing by price. Treasury officials had likewise been an obstacle in dismantling the clearing bank's interest rate cartel because they believed that competition would simply push up the cost of borrowing. Thus when in 1963 the clearing banks produced a modest proposal to relax the cartel it was vetoed by the Treasury, fearful that a rise in interest rates would hinder Mr Maudling's programme of rapid expansion. Five years later Treasury officials repeated similar objections against competition to the Monopolies Commission team investigating the bank mergers.[71]

To fully understand why these views were apparently abandoned in 1971 would demand a close description of the bureaucratic politics of monetary policy in the late 1960s. But here the trails are confusing and indistinct. This is partly because the outsider cannot see the official papers, but it is also in part a result of esoteric politics: so much depended on informal understandings that the story can never be adequately reconstructed. There exist in private recollections two accounts of what happened, corresponding broadly to the City's and Whitehall's view of events. Everyone recalls the same basic facts. From late 1969 until the end of the following year there existed a committee (more like a seminar, one participant recalls) which discussed the relevance to economic management of monetary policy and monetary instruments. The committee had been set up as a result of the new interest in monetary policy stimulated by the attentions of the IMF. It was composed of both Bank and Treasury officials and its high status was evident from the fact that the chairman was Sir Douglas Allen, the Treasury Permanent Secretary.

The Bank undoubtedly seized this opportunity to make its case for reform. Some of the key documents which destroyed the intellectual arguments for retaining the ceilings were originally prepared for the committee's meetings. They included a paper which stressed how far ceilings had merely driven credit out of officially measured channels; and a paper prepared within the Bank which used econometric analysis to show that interest rates could be more effective than administered ceilings on bank lending in influencing credit conditions.

On one view the politics of this committee were 'bureaucratic' in an exactly Weberian sense: there took place a rational argument, the Bank won the argument, and was thus able to replace the ceilings with Competition and Credit Control. By the autumn of 1970, on this view, the Bank was receiving informal but obvious signs from Whitehall that proposals for reform would be welcome.

Recollections from Whitehall picture what happened as less intellectually rational. On this view, the Bank bounced the Treasury: produced its own scheme in the autumn of 1970 while the Allen committee was still pondering various options in a leisurely way, and used the Governor's special access to sell the package to an inexperienced new Chancellor.

My own guess – it is nothing more – is that both these accounts exaggerate: the first overestimates the influence of rational argument, the second overstates the Bank's cunning. Esoteric politics worked informally, depending heavily on allusions and unspoken understandings. It was very easy for the Bank – which wanted something like CCC – to interpret any allusion as indicating that proposals would be welcome. Within the Treasury it was difficult to find a defender of the view that ceilings should continue. To this extent the Bank had indeed won an intellectual argument. But as the failure of the Allen committee to produce proposals showed, there was no clear agreement on what exactly should replace existing administrative controls. When the Bank produced its proposals Whitehall had thus lost faith in ceilings, but was uncertain about where to go next. Officials were reduced to reminding ministers that the Bank's proposals could mean putting up interest rates in the future. Ministers happily accepted this: they were flush with electoral victory, interest rates were then low, and not even the gloomiest Treasury official thought they would be well into double figures within three years.

The introduction of CCC was a sign that the cheap credit lobby in Whitehall had been eclipsed. The eclipse was brief. The first serious efforts to allow interest rates to rise after 1971 produced a powerful reassertion of influence by those sensitive to the demands of industrial investors and mortgagees in the housing market; this is part of the story in the next chapter.

8 THE DECLINE OF ESOTERIC POLITICS

Those who make and execute policy in the modern state do so in conditions of great intellectual, social and administrative complexity. By the end of the 1960s these three factors were reinforcing one another in the markets for credit. The extraordinary inventiveness of financial operators was constantly creating new financial instruments, new markets and new institutions, in part as a way of avoiding administrative controls on credit creation and allocation. Avoidance (and in some cases evasion) meant that official indicators of credit growth were increasingly unreliable. The growing scale of financial markets made regulation a task beyond the informal administrative style practised by the Bank.

These developments endangered the privacy, informality and freedom from partisan political argument which are the essentials of esoteric politics. In doing so they threatened powerful institutions and interests: the Bank of England, which was the key actor in the esoteric system, and the banks which were freed from the close attentions of politicians, civil servants and lawyers. Competition and Credit Control was an effort to restore the dominant position of institutions which could practise esoteric politics in the established manner.

The destructive forces described here are not confined to the banking community. In the rest of the City, private, informal ways of taking and enforcing decisions have been severely challenged in the 1970s.[72] In other policy spheres, too, esoteric arrangements have been disrupted by exoteric forces: the 'Whitehall village' which settled policy when Heclo and Wildavsky examined public spending has since the mid-1970s been opened to a variety of more public influences; the 'private politics' of energy policy has in the same period been similarly disrupted, notably by publicly organised campaigns against nuclear power; in defence policy 'technical' issues of strategy and weapons choice have been converted into open political controversy by the activities of pressure groups and party politicians.[73]

The argument that esoteric politics is in retreat will be unfamiliar, because British politics is commonly supposed to be marked by extraordinary and growing secrecy. Doubtless there exist powerful interests favouring privacy and informality as a way of excluding other interests from influence. Esoteric politics is nevertheless a fragile social form. It can only be practised by small, socially cohesive elites so united that internal differences show themselves merely as limited technical arguments. The complexities of modern policy making destroy cohesion, privacy and informality. Regulation and control increasingly require the support of the statute book and with the law enter new, more public forces. This is not only a matter of securing parliamentary approval, though that is more irksome than some critics of Parliament allow. It is also a question of what accompanies parliamentary intervention: the lobbying and partisan argument which goes with the parliamentary process, and the legal arguments and the apparatus of formality which grow up as a statute is clarified and adapted in the courts.

These forces are abetted by other developments. The spread of pressure group activity – itself partly due to imitation of existing successful groups – further widens the range of interests which enter policy debates. The 'positive mania for information' – as a banker once unkindly described the desire for more publicity about monetary policy – represented in the activities of journalists, MPs and even academics further challenges the privacy of elites.[74]

The problems of esoteric politics in banking were thus not unique. The vigorous effort at reassertion contained in Competition and Credit Control was due to the fact that the social and economic foundations of the esoteric system were still fairly strong in banking. It is notoriously the case, however, that the political forces needed to make a policy are often different from those necessary for its successful execution. In this simple observation lies a clue to some of the problems experienced after 1971.

4 The Politics of the Money Supply

Banking is a watchful, but not a laborious trade

1 CONTROL, COMPLEXITY AND THE MONEY SUPPLY

The important events in the life of a government are not always those which excite most attention or argument; quiet omissions can also have resounding consequences. The point is aptly illustrated by the case of the money supply when Mr Barber was Chancellor, especially after the introduction of Competition and Credit Control. The great political arguments of the early 1970s were focused away from money and banking, on to the problems of EEC entry, trade union reform and the role of the state in managing industry. Yet what was happening to the monetary system, largely unnoticed except by those with specialist interests, had profound economic and political results. Competition and Credit Control unleashed powerful competitive forces in banking; these forces were for a time so far beyond official control as to make it impossible for the authorities to fulfil their traditional duties of controlling the volume of credit in the economy and preserving the prudential soundness of banks.

This chapter is about the first of these failures, whose nature can be simply illustrated. In the two years following the introduction of CCC, the most commonly used measure of the money supply (conventionally called M3) rose at an annual average rate of 26 per cent. This increase was startling compared both with the past and with the record for other economic indicators. In no year since records began had the growth of the money supply reached double figures. In the two years in question industrial output expanded at only a quarter of the rate at which the money stock was growing, prices rose by only a third, and even wages by less than a half. The recorded increases were also remarkably consistent: in the first three months when CCC was operating M3 rose at a rate, expressed in annual terms, of 23 per cent while the increase for the first year was the same.[1]

Just as remarkable as these figures was the authorities' reaction to them. Such extraordinary increases might have been expected to prompt determined efforts at credit control. The record shows, to the contrary, that the measures taken were hesitant, limited and late. CCC provided two instruments for restraining the growth of credit, Bank/Minimum Lending Rate and Special Deposits. The appropriate response to a rapid rise in the money supply, according to the logic of CCC, was to induce a sharp increase in interest rates; the mechanism involved raising Bank Rate and calling for Special Deposits. The introduction of the scheme was actually accompanied by a cut in Bank Rate from 6 per cent to 5 per cent. (In April 1971 it had already been reduced from 7 per cent.) During the first nine months of CCC, when M3 was rising at over 20 per cent, the Rate remained unchanged. The currency crisis which caused the pound to be floated in June 1972 led to a rise to 6 per cent. In the following October a new formula was introduced for fixing Minimum Lending Rate, as it was now renamed. MLR was tied to a level set at the weekly Treasury Bill tender. All the qualified observers nevertheless agree that it was still under close official control. The new formula produced only a modest rise in the Rate (to just over 7 per cent), and for the next nine months MLR drifted in a range between just over 7 per cent and just under 9 per cent. When a sharp increase came in July 1973 it was prompted by external pressures on sterling, not primarily by the desire to control credit expansion at home. In the following November the formula linking MLR to a money market rate was abolished, and the Rate was raised by administrative decision to the unprecedented level of 13 per cent.[2]

The history of Special Deposits reveals a similar story of delayed and limited response. Only in November 1972 did the Bank make its first call for Deposits of 1 per cent. Subsequent calls took the figure to 4 per cent by the beginning of 1973, but despite the fact that credit expansion continued unabated there were no further calls until the crisis measures of the following November. These measures also signalled the end of the first part of the life of CCC. Its most distinctive feature – controlling the volume of credit by price – was abolished in favour of official controls over the rate at which banks could contract new liabilities. After just over two years experience with the market the authorities thus returned to administrative rationing.[3]

The Politics of the Money Supply 57

This brief, painful experiment had great economic and political results. It is now generally agreed that the credit expansion of the early 1970s stimulated wild speculation in the market for houses and offices, encouraged imprudent lending by banks, and thus contributed to the financial crisis of 1974. Some monetarists go further, tracing the great inflation of 1975 and 1976 to the expansion of credit under Mr Barber.[4] In the realm of policy the rise of what we conventionally call 'monetarism' owes much to the lessons drawn from experience of the first two years of CCC. Monetary targets were first set privately in the Bank in 1974. Within a few years these private targets had become public obsessions. Mrs Thatcher's Government committed itself to hitting monetary targets set several years in advance because of the common Conservative belief that Mr Heath's policies failed in large part through poor control of the money supply.[5]

This practical political conclusion echoed an influential theoretical argument, to the effect that failure to control the money supply was one of the economic consequences of democracy. This view was widely asserted in the gloomy days after Mr Heath's loss of office. The argument helped revive the old central bankers' dream of taking control of monetary policy from the hands of elected politicians. This clear attack on democratic control over a key part of economic management has been resisted, but in Britain since the mid-1970s there has nevertheless been a constant tension between two ways of running monetary policy: on the one hand, allowing policy makers discretion in the choice of objectives and instruments; on the other, relying on non-discretionary objectives and mechanisms, such as monetary targets and monetary base control.[6]

It is thus beyond question that influential policy conclusions were drawn from the experience of the early 1970s; how far the prevailing images of that period faithfully picture reality is more doubtful. Representations of the past are commonly influential, not in proportion to their accuracy, but in the degree to which they portray the past in a series of vivid and simple images. In political arguments about the economic policies pursued by the Heath Government such simple images abound: they include pictures of a 'U-turn' in 1972, a weak Chancellor, and a strong Prime Minister insistent on growth at all costs. Less polemically, a recurrent image pictures a government desperately trying to cope with the electoral pressures of democracy. These images convey some of the truth, but the succeeding pages suggest that the problems of monetary control transcended particular individuals, or even particular institutional arrangements. They were rooted in complexity, in its intellectual, social and administrative forms.

This recondite argument has an important practical implication. The attractions of monetarism undoubtedly owe much to the fact that it offers to policy makers the possibility of practising economic management without entangling them in the appalling complexities of controlling wages or prices. Monetarism disengages government by offering a few fixed, automatic rules to guide policy. This mechanical image of policy making is aptly conveyed by Friedman's argument that economic management should rest on control of the money supply, and that monetary control in turn should be accomplished through physical control of a single asset which would satisfy the reserve requirement of banks. The device is as simple, he has suggested, as controlling the supply of cars by rationing the availability of steel to the motor vehicle industry.[7] The argument in these pages is that no such fixed, non-discretionary rules allow us to escape complexity. Controlling credit is the same kind of activity as controlling prices, wages or a multitude of other parts of social life: they are all efforts to influence tricky and inventive individuals and institutions who will use their resources and ingenuity to evade or avoid restrictions which threaten their interests. It should thus be no surprise to discover that the politics of the money supply since 1971 are the politics of complexity.

2 THE QUINTESSENCE OF COMPLEXITY: MONEY AND POLITICS, 1971-3

Understanding the behaviour of those concerned with monetary policy after 1971 can best begin (though it cannot end) by examining their contemporary view of the circumstances in which they found themselves. In plain language, when the figures suggested that there was occurring an extraordinary growth in credit, what did they think was happening? For about the first year of CCC the answer is simple: they did not understand what was going on. This observation is not at all shocking; indeed, were policy makers normally in possession of an accurate picture of the world they would be surprisingly and alarmingly omniscient. Managing the economy is commonly compared with steering a vessel; more accurately, it is like guiding a ship whose instruments tell the pilot, not where he is now, but where he probably was some months ago, and where he might expect to be some months hence. The statistics available to policy makers are typically only available after considerable delay, are incomplete, are of doubtful accuracy, and are difficult to interpret because of the intrusion of a variety of short-term influences. British monetary statistics were until quite recently even poorer than the usual run of economic statistics: only after the Radcliffe Committee's criticisms (1959) did the Bank of England begin extensive monitoring of financial institutions, and only from 1963 were figures for the money stock gathered systematically.[8]

These special imperfections were not the result of accident, nor of any unusual technical difficulties in gathering monetary statistics; they were the product of esoteric politics. The notion that financial markets should be managed privately and informally by those with long practical experience in the markets meant that there was hostility to collecting and publishing statistical data. Even after the Bank was persuaded to gather information systematically it remained reluctant to compel institutions to provide data. As the Governor explained in 1969, when defending the slow rate at which statistics were being improved, the Bank could only gather information which the financial institutions were ready to supply: 'It is an expense to them ... we are strongly questioned as to our need ... we are probably going ahead as fast as tolerable to those who have to provide the statistics'.[9]

That imperfections in the figures loomed large in the minds of policy makers is clear from the comments of the joint Bank–Treasury team which reported on monetary policy in 1969: they stressed that many key statistics were historically incomplete, were consequently difficult to adjust accurately for seasonal variations, and contained large residual errors.[10] These elementary complexities of observation were compounded by one of the results of social complexity. Competition and Credit Control had been introduced in part because the ceilings on bank advances caused credit to be created and allocated outside officially controlled institutions. The authorities knew that this avoidance had occurred on a large scale, but they had no accurate measure of its size. (The parallel is obvious with arguments about the size of the 'black economy' created by tax evasion.) By abolishing the ceilings on lending they hoped to draw credit back into officially monitored and controlled institutions; indeed, that was one reason for encouraging the clearing banks to bid aggressively for business. Faced with a sharp rise in the measured money supply the authorities thus could not know in the early months of CCC how much was due to 'reintermediation' (banking jargon for the return of existing credit to the officially monitored banking system) and how much to credit created to meet new demand stimulated by the end of restrictions. To the extent that it was the former, it was to be welcomed; to the extent that it resulted from the excessive creation of new credit it suggested the use of the instruments of control available under CCC.[11]

The entwined problems created by social complexity and the complexities of observation were deepened by complexities of understanding. Policy makers, whether their responsibilities lie in money and banking or elsewhere, receive a constant stream of information, much of it statistical. Some sense is extracted from this raw material by assimilating it to a picture of how the world works. In this way an effort is made to cope with complexities of understanding by adopting a theory, though the theory may amount to no more than a set of half-conscious assumptions. The understanding suggested by this theory dictates which information is acted upon, and which neglected. A trivial example makes the point: the authorities have long had a measure of the volume of banknotes in circulation, but variations in the size of the note issue are ignored for the purposes of economic management because it is assumed that the quantity in circulation has no significant effect on the economy.

To make a judgement about the money supply after 1971 involved just such a decision about which information to act upon and which to neglect. Those responsible for policy had available four measures of the size of the money stock. This variety itself reflected intellectual complexity, for it arose from lack of agreement about a fundamental theoretical question: how can money be defined and measured? This uncertainty in turn results in part from the inventiveness of financiers, who have continually created new instruments which function as money, often in response to official efforts to control existing forms of credit. In the United States, which has the most inventive of all financial systems, the result has been to create a wide range of instruments, and thus a multiplicity of measures of money. The experience has been expressed by a senior economic adviser at the Bank of England in a form now lightheartedly called 'Goodhart's Law': any financial indicator ceases to be a reliable measure when it is subject to official control. Thus does social complexity magnify intellectual complexity.[12]

Of the four measures of the money stock possessed by policy makers at the beginning of the 1970s the two usually labelled M1 and M3 received most attention. The first was chiefly a measure of those assets which function as a medium of exchange. It thus matched roughly our everyday conception of money. M3 was a wider and more abstruse measure; in the Bank's words 'more institutional in character, depending not so much on the nature of the asset as on the fact that the financial intermediary with which the deposit has been made is a member of the banking sector'.[13]

These technical differences had great implications for interpreting the money supply figures under Competition and Credit Control. It was an important purpose of the scheme to draw credit back into the monitored banking sector. M3 was a measure of the level of activity in that sector. It was thus to be expected that if the purpose of CCC was accomplished the indicator would rise sharply, while the less institutionally defined M1 would show no comparable increase. This is exactly what happened. The two years after September 1971 saw a wide, persistent and unprecedented gap between the two measures. In the first year of the scheme M1 rose at just over half the rate of M3; for the two years after 1971 its annual rate of increase was less than half (10 per cent against 26 per cent). In some periods there was even a difference in the direction of change: in the first quarter of 1973 M1 fell slightly, while M3 rose by over 5 per cent.

It is not difficult to show that both the Bank of England and the Treasury were aware of all these considerations; indeed the picture of complexity presented here is in part derived from official reactions to the figures. When senior policy makers responded in a considered way on important public occasions to worries about the money supply they also expressed themselves in the language of complexity. Speaking to an audience of bankers in October 1972, for instance, the Governor argued that CCC was producing important structural changes in the banking system. These changes inflated M3 without expanding credit in the economy as a whole: 'If you encourage the banks to become more competitive, you must expect them to take a larger slice of the available business, and this kind of expansion carries no connotation of excessive monetary ease.' He noted the gap in growth between M1 and M3, and argued that the former was free of the distortions created by the introduction of CCC, and was therefore a better guide to the rate of monetary expansion than was M3.[14] In April of the following year the Deputy Governor, in a speech to the Lombard Association, laid even more stress on the significance of complexity. He repeated the argument that changes in banking behaviour had made M3 an unreliable indicator; confessed to being unsure how to allow for the distortions caused by such changes; and expressed the 'hope' that the distortions were only transitional. To emphasise the difficulties he stressed the highly speculative quality of what he called existing 'estimates' of the money stock and emphasised the great scope which existed for measurement error.[15] That these views were communicated to other policy makers is clear from private recollections, from the fact that they were echoed in official Treasury commentaries, and from the public remarks of ministers.[16]

This public emphasis on the problem of making sense of the figures was often the subject of sardonic scepticism from critics of the Government, who believed that the authorities were only publicly rationalising their unwillingness to curb excessive monetary growth.[17] According to this view, from the middle of 1971 the Government was intent on economic expansion and was not going to allow higher interest rates to stand in its way. Since a curb on the money supply would have meant increasing rates sharply, the Bank was unable to take corrective measures, and so was forced to make the best of a bad job by stressing unreliability in the figures.

There is a small, important, nugget of truth in this view, but it has to be expressed with great care. It is certainly the case that public comments on sensitive economic indicators offered by senior policy makers are phrased according to the kind of audience which will be listening. Policy makers will in particular speak defensively in commenting on economic trends which appear in any way alarming, since they know that financial markets pay close attention to official announcements, and often act upon them. This commonsense observation is, however, a long way from the assertion that there was a wide gap in 1971 between what was felt privately in government and what was said publicly. All the private recollections of the period which I have gathered emphatically deny that such a gap existed; indeed the spontaneous emphasis on the problems of making sense of the figures is a common feature of such recollections.

The public official comments on the figures, far from concealing some special private anxiety, in one important case actually mislead by suggesting greater concern than was felt in reality. From the columns of *Hansard* between 1971 and 1973 can be culled an anthology of remarks about the money supply by Treasury ministers. These remarks stressed the familiar problems of observation and understanding and emphasised the Government's determination to keep the money supply under control. Taken out of its parliamentary setting the anthology suggests that great thought had been given to pondering the implications of the figures. The truth is otherwise. A small number of backbench Conservatives of a monetarist outlook persistently asked questions about the money supply, compelling some considered official reply. These MPs were viewed as monetary cranks both within the

Treasury and within the 1922 Committee. In the Treasury comparatively little attention was paid to the money supply figures, because the customary division of responsibility in government pictured the management of money as the Bank's responsibility. (One – perhaps atypical – economist who worked as an adviser in the Treasury in the early 1970s told me that at the time he had only the faintest notion that there existed different measures of the money supply, and knew even less about what distinguished them.)

Viewing the problems of monetary control through the eyes of those responsible for policy throws much light on the question of why, after 1971, so little effort was made to control the expansion indicated by the sharp rise in M3. Yet illumination is only partial, for two reasons. The first is historical: after about a year of CCC the authorities finally concluded that there had indeed been some excessive expansion of credit.[18] Making sense of the figures proved very difficult even after this realisation, but we still need another explanation to account for the weak and hesitant efforts at control after the late summer of 1972. The second reason arises from a more general problem of social explanation: is it sensible to explain how people act only in terms of the reasons which they offer for action? On the one hand it can be argued that accounts of human conduct are meaningless if disconnected from the perceptions of those whose behaviour is to be explained; against this is the consideration that such accounts only beg the question of why certain perceptions are formed in the first place.[19]

These abstractions intrude into the mundane problem of understanding why policy makers were so reluctant to raise interest rates after 1971. The established perception was that the money supply figures were unreliable; this was a bar to action. But the same could be said of most of the other available economic indicators. Yet in some cases unreliability induced extreme caution, as happened with the money supply statistics; in others, caution was over-ridden in the effort to change the indicators quickly. The twin cases of unemployment and output in the early 1970s are examples of the latter. So little is known about the accuracy of unemployment statistics that there is even disagreement about whether they greatly overstate or understate 'true' unemployment. Output statistics are also known to be unreliable, and are constantly revised in ways which greatly change our picture of how the economy has performed. All this was well known at the beginning of the 1970s; indeed in June 1970 the government's Chief Economic Adviser delivered a paper emphasising the uncertain quality of all economic indicators.[20] The problem in summary is thus as follows: from 1971 government hesitated to act on unreliable monetary statistics, but responded very quickly to unreliable figures about unemployment and output. There is a double significance in the different responses: they point up the peculiarity of official hesitations about controlling the money supply; and they emphasise that in facing a choice between controlling the growth of the money stock and controlling the growth of unemployment government unhesitatingly chose the latter.

The story is well known. The Conservatives came to office in June 1970 believing that by cutting taxes, reducing union power, increasing the influence of the free market and offering the prospect of EEC entry they could change the outlook of businessmen, and so produce increased investment, output and employment. Within a few months the official statistics, especially those for registered unemployed, suggested that this was not happening as quickly or completely as had been hoped. With measured unemployment rising, the Government introduced a series of increasingly expansionary measures. The two great steps in this process were the plans announced by the Chancellor in July 1971, and the Budget of March 1972 which planned for a deficit in excess of the (at the time) extraordinary figure of £3,000 million.[21]

The varying responses to the money supply figures on the one hand, and to the output and unemployment statistics on the other, are especially striking when viewed from the vantage point of the 1980s, for in the intervening years we have seen great changes in the relative political sensitivity of the different indicators. There was thus nothing natural about the choices made after 1971. They were of course formed in part by the fact that more faith was put in the accuracy of the unemployment and output figures than in the monetary statistics. Putting faith in some figures and doubting others is, however, precisely one of the ways in which policy makers endorse certain aims and reject others. Thus when Sir Keith Joseph concluded in 1974 that the Heath Government of which he was a member had paid insufficient attention to controlling the money supply, and too much attention to reducing unemployment, one of his first acts was to make a speech throwing doubt on the accuracy of official measures of the level of unemployment.[22] Apparently technical judgements about which indicators to rely on, and which to ignore, thus arise from assumptions about the proper objects of policy.

To recognise the full significance of such assumptions it is necessary to recall the part played by routine and by customary assumptions in policy making. Routine and custom are important in helping to solve problems created by the administrative complexity which is inseparable from modern government. The activity commonly labelled 'economic management', for instance, involves a myriad of separate and difficult decisions taken and implemented by numerous public servants. Only by relying on unthinking routine and custom is it possible to cope with the consequent problems of coordination. If every policy maker only acted after careful reasoning from first principles, economic management would be subject to even more delays and inconsistencies than is commonly the case. (Hence intellectuals who carry into administration the sceptical outlook suitable to a university seminar are often hopelessly disruptive.) The point is familiar to those who have practical experience of policy making. Christopher Dow, an academic economist who also made a successful executive career in the Bank of England, puts it as follows: actions and advice are necessarily based on some underlying ideas, but 'these have to be as far as possible a sort of distillation of the common form of wisdom, as far as there is one, which is usually accepted'; this is how institutions acquire, in Dow's phrase, 'operating modes of thought'.[23]

At the lower levels of government this need for routine uniformity is expressed in bureaucratic rules; at higher policy making levels, where the exercise of authority based on formal command is less common, the need is expressed in customary assumptions about the objects of policy, and how they should be pursued. These assumptions form a conventional wisdom widely and in part unthinkingly held. The assumptions are often challenged, and they can change with great suddenness; but the pressure to make decisions, and to make them in a way consistent with decisions already made elsewhere in the system, means that when one set of assumptions is discredited there are powerful influences favouring the creation of a new conventional wisdom.

The effort to cope with administrative complexity is thus an important reason why, without detailed and explicit consideration of the available choices, governments act on some indicators and ignore others. The content of the conventional wisdom about economic management in the early 1970s is well known. It can be labelled 'practical Keynesianism' to distinguish it both from the Keynesianism of academic economists and from Keynes's own writings.[24] For present purposes only some elements need be stressed. Certain values were widely held: the economy should be managed so as to simultaneously achieve a variety of objectives, notably full employment (variously defined), economic growth and stable prices. These beliefs were connected to empirical judgements about how the economy worked: levels of output and employment could, it was believed, be influenced by demand management, which in turn could be accomplished by changing the levels of taxation and public spending. When unemployment threatened to rise to what were conventionally agreed to be symbolically significant levels (the symbol in the early 1970s was one million on the register) demand should be increased. The prevailing influence of practical Keynesianism immediately explains why policy makers should have been so receptive to the notion that imperfections in the money supply figures counselled caution, while imperfections in other indicators were no bar to rapid action.

The customary assumptions which necessarily shape policy making are significant not only because of what they accept but also because of what they deny. Practical Keynesianism denied that one of its chief objectives – stable prices – could or should be achieved through tight control of the money supply. At the beginning of the 1970s this denial was openly voiced both by the Chancellor and by the Governor. In a speech to the Finance Houses Association early in 1971 Mr Barber argued that prices were rising excessively because of 'militantly-secured pay increases', not because of monetary expansion. His view was that a permissive monetary policy was necessary because even a 'neutral' policy (allowing the money supply to expand by just enough to match the growth in productivity) would be severely deflationary: 'Starting, as we did, from a position of high and increasing growth of incomes, quite out of line with the increase in productivity, this so-called "neutral" policy would in practice have meant very severe deflation indeed. That is not the aim of this Government.'[25] Sir Leslie O'Brien had expressed similar thoughts four months before: 'If we try to rely on the market place and on the strict operation of fiscal and monetary policies, we shall find, I think, that we can achieve price stability only at the cost of employment that might be on a very large scale indeed.' The Governor's was no passing remark. It arose from a rejection within the Bank of the monetarist account of the causes and the cure of inflation. Sir Leslie's Hodge Lecture in 1970 had sceptically reviewed monetarist arguments at length, and his scepticism echoed the conclusions of a paper written by one of his senior economic advisers which had examined the technical evidence for and against monetarism.[26]

If monetary policy could not and should not be the means of fighting inflation, stable prices obviously had to be achieved by other means. Practical Keynesianism traced inflation to 'militantly-secured pay increases', to use the Chancellor's phrase. The obvious conclusion was that keeping prices stable depended on controlling the rate of wage increases. The Governor recognised this by arguing publicly for a formal incomes policy almost as soon as the Conservatives were returned to office in 1970. The Government in the first instance put its faith in less formal means: in the N-1 policy, which was designed to drive each successive public sector pay settlement below the level of the preceding agreement; and in the effort to secure an informal arrangement on pay and price restraint with the representatives of labour and capital.

Attempts to get an informal agreement dominated talks within NEDC in the spring and summer of 1971, and decisively influenced the Chancellor's July measures, his most expansionary act to that date. The details of the measures closely resembled proposals contained in a paper tabled in NEDC by the TUC representatives, and in announcing them the Chancellor expressly linked the coming economic growth to the prospect of pay restraint.[27] The NEDC discussions produced an analysis which was to shape economic policy for the remainder of the Heath Government's life. Inflation, the analysis ran, was due to rises in costs, especially wage costs. By deliberately expanding the economy for a limited period, the Government could employ idle resources, reduce unit costs and push the economy on to a higher plateau of productivity. At the same time, faster economic growth would provide room for wage increases which were not inflationary. Price rises would be restrained to encourage low wage claims: four days before Mr Barber announced his July measures the CBI asked its members to limit price increases in the coming year to 5 per cent. The Government in turn had to pay for this cooperation: the Confederation made it clear that its members would limit price rises only if the growth rate of GNP were raised to 4 per cent and if price restraint in the private sector was matched by the nationalised industries.[28] This is how the Government initiated the misnamed 'Barber boom'. The need to secure the agreement of powerful interests on both sides of industry meant that it could not choke off demand by increasing interest rates; and the tax cuts, public works programmes and subsidies to pay for price restraint by the public sector all contributed to the extraordinary deficit which the Chancellor was forced to plan for in his 1972 Budget.

These events show how misleading it is to reduce the Heath Government's economic policy in general, and its monetary policy in particular, to a few simple images. The 'Barber boom' was not the Chancellor's special creation; it arose out of the practical Keynesianism whose assumptions were widely shared within government, by leaders of powerful economic interests, and by most influential economic commentators. The fact that these assumptions were widely held explains why the Chancellor's various expansionary measures were greeted at the time with approval; indeed it was a common complaint that he was too cautious.[29]

The public, polemical image of a 'Barber boom' is not shared by many of those with inside experience of those years. Among insiders an alternative image prevails, picturing the great expansion as a 'Heath boom', engineered by an unusually dominant Prime Minister abetted by Sir William Armstrong, an unusually assertive civil servant. The characteristic defect of external reconstructions of political events is a neglect of individual personalities; but the characteristic defect of reconstructions made by insiders is the converse, a tendency to magnify the significance of particular individuals. The 'Heath boom' image suffers from this latter flaw. The Prime Minister did indeed press hard for expansion, and was a powerful voice against putting up interest rates. The Chancellor, Treasury officials and the Bank did try to exercise a restraining hand, especially by arguing that rates should be raised.[30] But the voices favouring expansion won the argument so convincingly because their objectives and their analysis – that the rise in unemployment should be reversed, that inflation was caused chiefly by wage increases rather than by monetary expansion – coincided with the prevailing wisdom of practical Keynesianism.

A more sophisticated image of events after 1971 – that the economic boom and the failure to control credit were due to the electoral pressures of democracy – expresses some of the truth, but the image needs to be used with great caution. Electoral calculations did indeed influence policy. On a number of occasions the Cabinet rejected the joint argument of the Bank and the Treasury that interest rates should be allowed to rise moderately, and the primary motive in the minds of ministers was fear of the electoral consequences of a rise in the building society mortgage rate. Indeed Bank Rate was replaced by Minimum Lending Rate in October 1972 as a way of circumventing this political opposition – especially that of Mr Heath – to higher interest rates.[31] Bank Rate was, in the jargon, fixed by administrative decision; in other words, it resulted from a discretionary choice by policy makers. MLR was, by contrast, tied to rates set in the Treasury Bill Market; in other words, it could be presented to the politicians as the inevitable outcome of natural market forces. The presentation was a political ploy to implement the higher interest rates which officials believed to be necessary. MLR was never a 'natural' interest rate because the Bank could decisively influence market conditions by informal communications and by the terms on which it traded. The switch to MLR was nevertheless portentous, for it anticipated the now common practice of displacing the discretionary judgement of (usually elected) policy makers by supposedly automatic market forces.

The introduction of MLR prised some power away from the politicians, but the electoral stakes at risk in monetary policy impelled continuing Cabinet intervention. In particular, from the spring of 1973 Ministers wriggled desperately to find ways of keeping the building society mortgage rate in single figures. In April the societies were given a grant to help them keep the rate below 10 per cent. The decision was made in Cabinet despite Mr Barber's opposition: 'I warned my colleagues of the folly of subsidising a particular interest rate, but my view did not prevail.'[32] In September the Chancellor again opposed, and again lost, when Cabinet adopted an equally peculiar scheme, which instructed the banks not to pay more than 9½ per cent interest on deposits of under £10,000. The object – it failed – was to protect building societies from competition for funds, and thus to keep the cost of money for house mortgages below what was conventionally assumed to be the highly significant figure of 10 per cent.[33]

Despite the existence of particular decisions shaped by electoral calculations it is plain that the failure to control the money supply after 1971 was due to far more than electoral forces. Policy makers had to act in a world where accurate information about the economy was hard to come by, and where official indicators often had an uncertain connection with reality. To practise economic management in a manner at all decisive and consistent demanded that judgements be made about which inaccurate indicators to act on, and which to ignore. Practical Keynesianism supplied these judgements. It was an influential conventional wisdom because it offered the possibility of coping with the social complexity arising from the existence of powerful organised interests on both sides of industry. The argument developed here has a practical political implication: none of the key features which shaped policy – inaccurate indicators, the need to make customary assumptions to form consistent policies, the problem of managing social complexity – disappear if the institutional arrangements for making monetary policy are changed to reduce the influence of politicians and electors.

Failure to control the money supply after 1971 cannot be traced to the failings of particular politicians, and it can only be traced partly to the pressures of electoral democracy. Indeed there is an important sense in which the fiasco of the first two years of CCC reflects, not the excessive manipulation of credit conditions by policy makers, but rather their inability to exercise effective control over a sophisticated and inventive banking system operating under conditions of fierce competition. Two examples illustrate the point: the case of the reserve asset ratio, and the case of arbitrage.

The origins of the common reserve asset ratio which CCC applied uniformly to all banks lay partly in the authorities' desire to strengthen the clearing banks at the expense of the fringe bankers. The special cash and liquidity requirements observed by the clearing banks before 1971 put them at a disadvantage in competing in the wholesale money markets; the new ratio now gave them near equal treatment with their rivals.[34] But the reserve asset ratio was a makeshift affair, in part because it was simultaneously serving a variety of different purposes, and in part because of the great difficulty of devising rules which could be uniformly applied to a diversity of banks. The Bank's own description of the problems in devising a ratio illustrates clearly the intense intellectual and social complexity produced by a diverse and changing banking system.[35] In principle the new ratio limited the funds which any bank could raise in the markets, and thus the resources it had available to lend as credit. All banks were required to hold a fixed proportion of their liabilities (borrowings) in specified reserve assets; to expand borrowing, more reserve assets had to be acquired.

Even before CCC became fully operational technical commentators had noted that the reserve ratio was unlikely to be a serious restriction on the banks' ability to bid for business, since the authorities had no effective control of the varied collection of assets of which it was composed.[36] So the case proved. Studies of the working of CCC by professional economists document how the clearing banks and the Discount Houses, in particular, developed a complicated series of arrangements whose effect was to manufacture reserve assets and to put an end to the ratio as a constraint on the banks' efforts to bid for business. In some cases the effort was encouraged by the possibility of tax avoidance.[37] Gowland has estimated that in 1972 alone the volume of reserve assets created by the banks was sufficient to allow M3 to rise by 320 per cent, if conventional ratios were observed.[38]

The significance of the manipulation of the reserve asset ratio by the institutions operating in the money markets is twofold. It has a historical importance, because it disposes of the common polemical allegation that what happened after 1971 was simply the result of a calculated decision by government to 'print money' in order to stimulate economic growth.[39] 'Printing money' is in any case a highly misleading image of how credit is created in a modern financial system. The money which government literally prints and circulates – bank notes – plays no significant part in credit expansion; it is merely the small change of the economy. The great volume of credit lies in the assets and liabilities recorded in the balance sheets of financial institutions.[40] The government's contribution to what happened in the money markets after 1971 was passive not active; it lay in the inability and unwillingness to control money markets where the intensity of competition spurred operators to invent new ways of avoiding any restrictions on bidding for business.

This account also modifies the common – and highly influential – polemical argument that the great credit expansion was due to the growth of government debt after 1971. It is true that Mr Barber's Budgets did greatly increase the borrowing requirement, especially in the 1972 Budget. It is also true, however, that a large proportion of this debt was funded in a way most economists agree does not expand credit, by sales of debt to the non-bank public.[41] In addition, the calls for Special Deposits from the banks late in 1972 and early in 1973 were designed to cancel out the remaining effects on credit expansion arising from funding operations.

The historical importance of the episode of the asset ratio is reinforced by its analytical significance. In the manufacture of reserve assets between the banks and the Discount Houses we see the quintessence of complexity: powerful and sophisticated financial institutions, driven by the need to bid for business in fiercely competitive markets, ingeniously creating ways to circumvent official restrictions. There was no conspiracy in this, for nobody wanted to make a nonsense of the ratio. As with so many other policies a gap was merely noticed in the system of control and the financial institutions poured through.

Social complexity also lies at the source of the problem created by arbitrage. To engage in arbitrage is to take advantage of different rates of return in different markets by switching funds between them. In markets where prices adjust freely in response to supply and demand such differences are either eliminated, or represent a premium for some other element, such as varying levels of risk. Opportunities for arbitrage exist where differences in rates of return reflect other influences, such as political or other institutional restrictions. This was precisely the case with the money markets after 1971. The most instructive example concerns arbitrage in the autumn of 1973.[42] In July of that year the authorities had induced a sharp rise in interest rates, mainly in order to strengthen sterling. Since the clearing banks were now having to pay more for their wholeale funds, they might have been expected to correspondingly increase their base rate, which is the rate of interest used to calculate the cost of money to borrowers. The banks did not, however, increase base rates to match levels in the money markets. The reason in part was that raising base rates had certain administrative costs, and in conditions of great uncertainty about the future level of all interest rates it seemed sensible to delay taking any action. A second and more important reason was that base rates were politically sensitive. They were the conventional sign of the cost of money to the public. They also affected in turn the rates offered by the banks to borrowers, and thus could influence the rates offered and charged by building societies. (This was the Cabinet's reasoning when it ordered that the banks be forbidden to offer more than $9\frac{1}{2}$ per cent on deposits of less than £10,000.) In the autumn of 1973 the banks were especially sensitive to the political implications of base rates, for their high profits were already making them the object of politically embarrassing attention. All this was enough to make the banks hesitate about putting up the cost of borrowing to customers. These hesitations were apparently further intensified by direct political pressures from the authorities.[43]

The failure to increase rates by sufficient to match the cost of funds in the wholesale markets opened up a gap between the price the clearers' customers paid for funds drawn on overdraft, and the return which the same customers could receive by lending in the money markets. The gap was quickly spotted by the banks' big corporate customers. At any one time, big customers typically drew up to only about half of their agreed overdraft limits. As soon as a gap opened between base rate and money market rates, firms drew more on overdraft, and lent money (often back to the same banks) at a higher rate in the money markets. 'Round-tripping', as it was colloquially called, thus produced large, effortless profits for some of the biggest firms in the economy.

The analytical significance of the episode lies in the speed with which firms recognised and took advantage of the opportunities offered by arbitrage. It is a striking instance of how the rational, calculating character of the most highly developed markets has led to an increase in social complexity. Twenty-five years ago few big firms dealt in the money markets, let alone dealt in such a sophisticated way. Nowadays big corporations, with their corporate treasurers and their regiments of accountants and commercial lawyers, are organised to exploit every quirk in the money markets to profitable purpose.

The arbitrage episode thus emphasises the significance of social complexity, but it also has a historical significance, for it helped end the first phase in the life of Competition and Credit Control. The sharp rise in interest rates in the summer of 1973 should, according to the logic of CCC, have cut the rate of monetary growth. The figures suggested that the contrary was happening: in the last quarter of the year M3 grew at an accelerated pace reaching a rate, expressed in annual terms, of 36 per cent. Much of this renewed increase was due to arbitrage. Since it was a 'money-go-round' – to use a common colloquial description – no new credit was created, despite the fact that the indicator superficially suggested the contrary. It was nevertheless enough to complete the fiasco of the first phase of Competition and Credit Control. Faced with wild distortions in the main measure of the money supply the authorities, when compelled into the crisis measures of November and December 1973, retreated from some of the most distinctive 'market' principles of the 1971 reforms. Minimum Lending Rate was raised by administrative decision, and controls were set on the level of bank borrowing in the money markets. The 'corset', as the new system was commonly called, was a partial return to control by administrative decree. It stimulated ingenious efforts by bankers to do business outside its confines, and in this way revived many of the deficiencies in the old, pre-1971, system of control.

The measures of November and December 1973 did not abolish the reforms introduced under CCC. The changes which allowed intense competition in the money markets were irreversible, for too many powerful institutions now benefited from them. The modifications were nevertheless an important turning point. As well as introducing the corset the authorities reintroduced controls on hire purchase, thus abandoning the experiment with a free market in consumer credit.[44] The end of 1973 also saw the end of the great credit expansion: in 1974 M3 grew at less than half the rate recorded in the previous year. From December 1973 the problems of control in the money markets took on the different form of a banking crisis. This is the subject of the next chapter; there remains here the task of briefly considering the significance of complexity since 1974.

3 COMPLEXITY TRIUMPHANT: POLITICS AND MONEY SINCE 1974

No simple characterisation can describe what has happened to the politics of the money supply since the mid-1970s. The best that can be done is to note a paradox: politicians have become both more interested in the money supply, and yet more ready to hand the means of control over to others. The immediate effect of the great credit expansion was to make control of the money supply a 'political' issue as the term is conventionally understood; in other words, monetary policy moved from an esoteric to an exoteric arena. Arguments about the money supply became the common currency of partisan debate. Issues which a decade ago would have attracted attention only among a few specialists – such as the usefulness of monetary base control – now became questions on which even the Prime Minister formed a view.

At the same time politicians – indeed all policy makers – have been under pressure to give up discretionary management of the money supply. In 1976 the Chancellor was compelled, through the need for IMF assistance, to commit himself publicly to targets for monetary growth, and to shape fiscal and interest rate policies around that commitment.[45] After 1979 we had a Government whose leading members were intellectually convinced of the need to tie their own hands, by committing themselves to a Medium Term Financial Strategy which set targets for the growth of the money supply several years in advance.[46] The debate at the beginning of the 1980s about monetary base control was also part of the attack on discretionary management: all the different technical variants on the proposed new system had the object of displacing the discretionary judgement of the policy makers by rules which automatically triggered changes on signals from selected market indicators.[47] The technical changes in the means of monetary control introduced as a result of the debate were a partial concession to the advocates of monetary base control.[48] We have avoided what some opponents of democratic control wanted – an independent Currency Commission – but the discretionary power of policy makers has nevertheless been under attack.

The immediate reason for this paradoxical readiness both to recognise the political significance of monetary policy and to reduce political control of the money supply lies in the influence of monetarism. The most commonly noticed policy conclusion suggested by monetarist theory is that control of inflation depends on effective monetary control. This explains the greater political salience of monetary policy. A less commonly noticed conclusion is that the economy cannot be 'fine-tuned', as a Keynesian would have it. Monetary policy, it is argued, only works after a long lag of time. To be effective it must thus be non-discretionary: policy makers must bind themselves inescapably to such objectives as publicly stated targets for monetary growth.[49]

The influence of these notions does not spring merely from the intellectual force of an economic doctrine. 'Monetarism' has been propelled to political prominence by the rising power of the financial markets. In the attack on discretionary management the judgements of politicians and civil servants have been challenged by the 'automatic' workings of markets which are so capable of rapid adaptation that they quickly destroy efforts at control. The helpless attempts by Mrs Thatcher's Government to restrain the growth of the money supply show the extraordinary complexities hidden behind the mechanical images of control which have so influenced policy in recent years.[50] The statistical rock to which monetary policy was anchored turned out to be a flickering shadow: sterling M3, the main measure of the money stock, was an unstable and unreliable representation of monetary conditions. After two years in the Treasury Mr Biffen, one of the Government's original authentic monetarists, was confessing ruefully that M3 was a 'wayward mistress'.[51]

Examining the politics of monetary control in the early 1980s prompted a strong sense of *déjà vu*. The key problems – making sense of slippery financial statistics, controlling even more slippery institutions – were precisely those which afflicted policy makers a decade earlier. Mr Biffen's confession, coming from a convinced monetarist, carried a nice irony. In the early 1970s monetarists commonly criticised the attempt to operate an incomes policy by arguing that the power and ingenuity of institutions in the labour market turned the search for a 'fair' or 'just' policy into a futile quest for a philosopher's stone.[52] Efforts to control the money supply have the same chimerical quality, and for similar reasons: the tricky and inventive institutions in the financial markets are far too ingenious to be constrained by a simple set of non-discretionary rules. As in all other exercises in control – whether of wages, prices or crime – effectiveness demands that the inventiveness of the controlled be matched by the ingenuity of the controllers.

5 Crisis, Crash, Rescue

> Credit – the disposition of one man to trust another – is singularly varying. In England, after a great calamity, everybody is suspicious of everybody.

1 TRUST, CRISIS AND BANKING

Social calamities often have trivial immediate causes: an archduke assassinated, a message misunderstood or a chance indiscretion provoked. The reason is not difficult to fathom: peace and stability in social life rest on trust; where trust is weak a small mishap can destroy it. Bagehot put the point exactly in connection with banking: 'The peculiar essence of our banking system is an unprecedented trust between man and man; and when that trust is much weakened by hidden causes, a small accident may greatly hurt it.'[1]

Precisely such a 'small accident' began the great secondary banking crisis in Britain. On 22 November 1973 Mr Donald Bardsley resigned from London and County Securities, one of the numerous fringe banks which had grown up in London in the late 1960s and early 1970s. Bardsley was a respected City figure who had joined London and County only four months before from the merchant bankers Hill Samuel. The announcement of the resignation was delayed for four days, and in the intervening period London and County revealed superficially good profits in its half-yearly accounts. Any hope that these would restore confidence proved illusory: by 29 November so many depositors in the wholesale money markets had withdrawn their funds that the company was unable to meet its obligations. On the following day it was publicly revealed that a group composed of the company's clearing bank and its largest institutional shareholders were trying to devise a rescue. Four days later a consortium headed by First National Finance Corporation – the biggest and most successful of the fringe banks – took it over.[2]

The small mishap of a single resignation destroyed London and County because its soundness was already in doubt. The company had a history of public controversy, about the high interest rates charged on second mortgages, and about some unsatisfactory aspects of its published accounts. Public attention was heightened by the presence on the Board of Mr Jeremy Thorpe, then Leader of the Liberal Party. Mr Bardsley's appointment in March 1973 was designed to reassure the City that the company would be run prudently; his resignation confirmed suspicions to the contrary.

Just as a single resignation destroyed London and County, so the destruction of an insignificant fringe bank was the immediate cause of a greater crisis. During the first three weeks of December 1973 nervous depositors withdrew funds from fringe banks into the security of the clearing banks. This collapse of confidence was partly due to a wider sense of social and economic catastrophe. December was a cruel month. The international economy was still in turmoil after the Yom Kippur war. At home Mr Heath's Government was spending its dying days trying to fend off defeat at the hands of the miners. On 13 December the Prime Minister announced severe restrictions on electricity consumption, and the introduction in the New Year of a three-day working week. Four days later his Chancellor introduced a deflationary mini-Budget whose content marked the end of the experiment with expansion and portended the exhaustion of the great post-war boom. There was turmoil abroad, economic failure and class bitterness at home. A sense of apocalypse was everywhere. The financial markets, which at the best of times live on the verge of hysteria, were deeply affected: stock exchange prices fell 75 points in a few weeks.

The Bank of England responded to the initial collapse of confidence in the money markets by arranging confidential support for troubled banking institutions, but it avoided committing its own funds or establishing any formal machinery of rescue.[3] On 20 December it was forced into a more public commitment when Cedar Holdings, one of the troubled fringe banks, had its Stock Exchange quotation suspended. On the following day the Governor (Mr Gordon Richardson had succeeded Sir Leslie O'Brien in July 1973) called a meeting attended by himself, the Deputy Governor and the Chairmen of the clearing banks. At this meeting the Bank argued that combined action was needed to prevent a collapse of confidence. A press release on the same day announced that the Bank and the clearers would put resources into rescuing stricken fringe banks. Between that date and the end of the Christmas holiday the details were settled of a Control Committee which would guide all rescues. On 28 December the Committee met for the first time. It was chaired by the Deputy Governor, with a member from each clearing bank. Its immediate objectives were limited: to 'recycle' money withdrawn from the secondary banks and placed with the clearers back into the secondary banking system, and in this way to solve what was believed to be a short-term problem caused by nervousness among depositors in the wholesale markets.[4]

It very shortly became clear that the problems with which the Committee was coping were neither temporary nor on a small scale. Within three months it had committed nearly £400 million to recycling. By the end of 1974 the amount lent was almost £1,200 million.[5] Beyond this the clearers refused to contribute more, on the grounds that the rescue now accounted for 40 per cent of their reserves and assets. The Bank (which already contributed 10 per cent of the Control Committee's resources) was thus compelled to add another £85 million of its own money.[6] For a time in the summer and autumn of 1974 a large number of financial institutions were technically insolvent; numerous bankruptcies were only avoided because the Bank used all its influence to compel and cajole profitable institutions to support those in difficulty. The Control Committee itself helped twenty-six institutions, of which eight were eventually put into liquidation or into the hands of a receiver. The amounts used to provide support outside the Control Committee cannot be accurately calculated; the best informed financial journalist to follow the affair puts the total used in the whole rescue at about £3,000 million.[7]

The succeeding pages analyse this crisis. The problems revealed in 1974 were immediately economic in origin, so the next part of the chapter examines the connected mechanisms in the financial markets and in the property market which led to the difficulties. But the banking crisis was more than an economic failure; it was also a failure of supervision and regulation. It is an established duty of supervisory bodies to prevent banking failure and, should failure occur, to confine the consequences narrowly. Between the First World War and the 1970s these duties were carried out with almost complete success. 'Law, trust and supervision' (3 below) tries to account for the defects revealed so dramatically in 1973 and 1974. This leads naturally to an account of the rescue. Two simple questions are asked: why was the rescue mounted, and why was it possible to persuade stable and prosperous banks to support imprudent and often insolvent institutions? The answers illuminate the distribution of power in the banking community and emphasise once again the unique politics of banking.

2 BANKING, PRUDENCE AND PROPERTY

Rapid invention and swift adaptation mark modern financial markets. Invention and adaptation destroyed the controls which existed before 1971, and helped in the great credit expansion which occurred thereafter. The economic causes of the secondary banking crisis can likewise be traced to the links between inventive financial markets and equally inventive markets elsewhere, notably in commercial property.

The story of the property market before the crisis is itself a study in complexity. In post-war Britain the return on property investment consistently bettered the return on investment in manufacturing industry. The reasons varied in different parts of the property market. The high rewards of owner occupation, for instance, were the deliberate result of public policy, notably of a tax system designed to favour the private housebuyer. By contrast, the profitable returns on investment in office property were obtained partly in spite of public policy. High demand for commercial property was rooted in long-term changes in the economic structure, notably the proportional decline in primary and secondary industries and the rise of a tertiary (service) sector. Central government periodically fought both this trend and its manifestations in the property market. Before 1971, 'requests' to the banks concerning the allocation of credit persistently urged discrimination in favour of industrial investors and against those who wanted funds for commercial property development. The return of Labour to power in 1964 brought to office a party which was concerned about the land-use implications of office development and hostile to the speculative element in property dealing. In November 1964 the Government imposed a ban on further office development in London and shortly afterwards introduced a system of permits designed to control the pace of new developments in the South East.[8] This attempt at physical rationing immediately encountered problems of administrative complexity: while Whitehall was restricting the supply of office space the Bank of England was increasing demand by its success in attracting numerous foreign banks, which came to London to enjoy the freedom offered by the Bank's flexible system of supervision.

The economic results of these contradictions were unsurprising. The returns on existing property in the restricted area rose rapidly: between 1965 and 1970 office rents in the banking sector of the City rose over fourfold.[9] At the same time the restrictions led to intensive development just outside the forbidden zone. Summing up the experience of controls shortly before the introduction of Competition and Credit Control the chairman of a large property company remarked that 'almost every restriction, feared and resented at the time, proved to be a protection'.[10] The consequences for the banking system were just as significant. The attempt to divert lending from property hastened the rise of a secondary banking system, for many fringe banks prospered in the 1960s by lending to property developers who had been turned away by the clearers in obedience to official guidance.

When controls on bank lending were removed in 1971 manufacturing industry and property thus had very different post-war histories. The higher rates of return on property investment reinforced instinctive notions that in inflationary times the solidity of 'bricks and mortar' was the best defence against the declining value of money. In the two years after the introduction of Competition and Credit Control manufacturing industry either could not or would not match the demand for credit which came from the property market. The figures for bank lending tell the story: in the two years after November 1971 bank lending to property companies rose by over 400 per cent while lending to the manufacturing sector in the same interval rose by less than 50 per cent.[11]

These figures reflected increasing demand for all kinds of property. House prices nearly doubled in two years after 1971 because builders could not increase supply quickly enough to meet the new demand from buyers enticed into the market.[12] The problem of increasing the supply was even greater in commercial property: the supply of land for new development was fixed by obvious physical limits and by planning restrictions on land use; while the supply of new developments was delayed by the considerable complexity of translating a project from an architect's drawing board to a finished state. The result was that the great boom in commercial property after 1971 consisted largely of trade in existing property, rather than in new developments. The sudden injection of large sums of money into a market where supply could only slowly grow inevitably raised prices: by one index commercial property prices trebled between 1970 and 1973.[13] The rewards for speculation could be extraordinary: in one deal the Crown Agents and two private developers shared a profit of almost £34 million in a sale of shares to the Post Office Superannuation Fund.[14] It is little wonder that another developer recalled how 'we lived in a tremendous, a most optimistic world at that time. What you bought for a million pounds one day you sold for two the next, and that person sold for three the day after'.[15]

By 1973 property had the classic features of a market in a speculative mania: deals were being made, and loans to finance those deals raised, solely in the expectation that a continued boom would allow swift re-sale at a profit. The expectation is illustrated by the disparity between the trend of prices and rents: the near tripling of the former between 1970–3 was matched by only a 75 per cent rise in rents for City offices. It is thus not surprising that the borrowings of property companies grew out of proportion to their resources: in 1972 debt interest alone took half their income; in the following year the figure rose to two-thirds; by 1974 it was 90 per cent.[16]

Bank lending on these terms was a great departure from the traditional prudential rules of English banking. Some accounts of the secondary banking crisis have expressed this imprudence as the mistake of 'borrowing short and lending long'.[17] Although the stricken banks did indeed work in this manner, in doing merely this they were not acting imprudently. 'Borrowing short and lending long' is indeed an essential banking function, so much so that it even has the honour of a phrase in banking jargon: it is 'maturity transformation' where the bank is an intermediary between lenders who wish to part with money for a different span of time than borrowers wish to retain it. Imprudence enters when a bank fails to preserve adequate capital and reserves, and fails to organise its assets and liabilities so as to be able to meet calls to repay deposits.

These difficult tasks had been accomplished historically by evolving a variety of conventions and institutions: prescribed cash and liquidity ratios; the Bank of England as a lender of last resort; a large retail banking network providing a stable volume of deposits. The pace of change in financial markets made these prudential devices irrelevant for the fastest growing parts of the banking system. The new money markets – which after 1971 were the engine of credit expansion and a major source of funds for the property market – were cushioned by no stable base of retail deposits, worked without a lender of last resort and had to evolve new rules of prudent banking in conditions where novel financial practices and financial instruments were continually appearing. In the atmosphere created by the property boom there was no incentive to search for these new prudential rules. The commonest device practised by fringe banks to meet their obligations to repay depositors was 'liability management': an obligation to repay a deposit was met, not from the bank's own resources, but by raising elsewhere loans of comparable size.[18]

Liability management is yet one more sign of the extraordinary capacity for innovation which the financial markets display, but in the fierce competition for business which followed the introduction of CCC it seriously weakened prudential restraint. To be effective it demanded an efficient network by which potential depositors and lenders were put into contact. This service was provided by a new breed of money brokers who grew up with the wholesale markets. These brokers commonly arranged deals with scant attention to prudence. In the Governor's words: 'Deposits seem to have been placed in response simply to the offer of a higher rate of interest and without any closer relationship than the passing of a name, without commitment, by a broker.'[19]

By the height of the property boom in 1973 the secondary banking system was balanced in a highly delicate state. The secondary banks were deeply committed to the property companies. These commitments took the form of both loans and direct participation in projects. The money tied up in property was generally lent for longer periods than the banks were borrowing in the wholesale markets. The banks covered the difference by renewing deposits or, failing that, by creating new liabilities.

The first serious disturbances to this delicate balance came with the increase in interest rates engineered by the authorities in the summer and autumn of 1973. This had two disturbing effects. The immediate result was intense competition for money, making liability management an even more difficult business. The desperate lengths to which some of the weaker fringe banks were forced to go was illustrated by the subsequent discovery that 'window dressing' was widely practised: deposits were shifted between banks whose accounts were published at different times, merely in order to inflate balances for publicity purposes.[20] These immediate difficulties in retaining deposits and raising new money were compounded by the losses which the rise in interest rates now forced on many institutions. Banks which borrowed short term on the wholesale markets and lent on longer terms at fixed interest faced capital losses. The problem was not confined to fringe institutions: the respectable Discount Houses also incurred large losses in this way. But the newer secondary banks, unlike the Houses, did not have the Bank of England behind them as a lender of last resort.

These difficulties were intensified by the blows to confidence administered in the wider economy. The autumn of 1973 brought the

Yom Kippur war, the rise of oil prices and the consequent international recession. At home, it was increasingly clear that the British economy was incapable of sustaining the spurt of economic growth which had begun in 1972. In the City it was commonly rumoured that some of the weaker fringe banks were finding it difficult to raise deposits; the public collapse of London and County helped confirm the rumours. Subsequent investigations showed that London and County's problems were due to imprudence compounded by dishonesty.[21] That the bank was atypical in its dealings mattered not at all. Its failure revealed the weakness of a whole group of secondary banks operating risky businesses with no lender of last resort. Depositors experienced 'a fit of collective prudence' in the Governor's phrase:[22] money was withdrawn to the safety of banks that clearly did have the Bank of England behind them. The safest institutions of all, the clearing banks, benefited most. In some cases 'collective prudence' looked very like panic: one institution lost the bulk of its money market deposits in six hours of trading.[23]

These difficulties, though severe, seemed only a crisis of confidence. This reasoning suggested to those concerned with the rescue in its early stages that mere knowledge of support for stricken banks by the clearers and the Bank of England would calm depositors. It quickly became obvious that this was not so: the crisis of confidence was a first sign of a deeper disease whose origins were in the property market. At the end of 1973 the property boom ended when values finally reached their long-expected peak; but the sudden and steep fall in prices which soon began was unforeseen, probably because the market was now struck by an unusual combination of misfortunes. To the difficulties of declining demand for property the Government added other problems. The level of bank lending to property companies had long been viewed with disapproval by the authorities. In the autumn of 1972 the Bank breached the spirit of Competition and Credit Control – which urged lending on the most profitable terms – by asking the banks to restrain loans on property.[24] The request was to no avail: the pace of lending actually quickened subsequently. Whitehall then aimed a series of blows at the market: a freeze on office rents, and in December 1973 the announcement of an intended tax on developers. The market briefly kept its collective nerve, and then panicked. Early in 1974 prices began to fall steeply. By the end of the year commercial property values had been halved, and the FT index of property share prices had fallen nearly fivefold.[25] The immediate effect was to make it impossible for many companies to service debt, which had been raised in the expectation that interest could be paid out of speculative profits on sales. Repaying capital was of course out of the question.

Thus far, banks deeply committed to property companies resembled any other banker with a bad debt. Only the most recklessly incompetent lenders – such as the Crown Agents – had advanced money without security.[26] This security could theoretically be realised as a last resort. But the commonest forms of security were the shares of companies, the properties they owned, and personal guarantees from individual developers backed by their private wealth. The paper worth of all this security reflected valuations made at the height of the boom. Its collapse left banks holding security in all cases diminished greatly in value, in some cases worthless. Thus when the Stern group of property companies collapsed in the summer of 1974 Mr William Stern had given personal guarantees exceeding £100 million. With the collapse the paper wealth underwriting these guarantees vanished.[27] This tendency to place an excessive valuation on the worth of a security was not a mere isolated imprudence. It was produced by the drive to innovation in markets. The desire to maximise the return on assets produced in the property market a semi-profession of 'property valuers'. These valuers gave a stamp of objectivity to valuations which, especially at the height of the boom, were persistently over-optimistic. The effect of this excessive optimism was to inflate the book value of investments and to increase a company's borrowing capacity.[28]

The effects of the property crisis tied the secondary banks and the property companies together in misfortune. Developers could neither repay interest nor capital. The banks could not realise the security they held, because to do so would have pushed the property market into even deeper crisis, and would thus have intensified their own problems. The clearing banks had similar difficulties, though they were not as deeply involved. The clearers and the Bank of England nevertheless could not stand aside from the crisis, for any large default by a bank would damage confidence in the whole system. The Bank and the clearers were thus driven to organise a rescue. The immediate problems with which this rescue had to cope were economic in nature, but the crisis was also a sign of a major failure of public supervision and regulation. The sources of this I now examine.

3 LAW, TRUST AND SUPERVISION

The economic causes of the banking crisis can be traced to the changing structure of the economy, to the way public authorities responded to change and to the altered character of financial markets. These developments created the economic conditions for collapse; but the purpose of regulation was precisely to ensure that such economic conditions did not tempt bankers into imprudence. This is why the crisis signalled a failure of public supervision and control. The result did more than destroy a number of banks; it also fatally weakened the Bank of England's claim that traditional informal regulation successfully reconciled the demands of commercial freedom and prudent control.

The banking community thus lost twice by the crisis: it lost money, and it lost much of the freedom from legal and political restraints which went with traditional supervision. It is not surprising therefore that these losses prompted serious efforts to identify the causes of failure. Three common explanations are examined here: first, that the supervisory authorities, notably the Bank of England, were incompetent at their job; second, that the law on banking was such a chaotic tangle that numerous imprudent institutions were able to exploit legal ambiguities; and third, that the chaotic state of the law dispersed responsibility for supervision among a number of public bodies and thus created gaps in the supervisory system. The argument of the following pages will suggest that the first of these three accounts is true only as a tautology. The second and third illuminate particular kinds of failure which undoubtedly occurred, but they have to be supplemented by the recognition that another force was at work. This consisted in a disposition to place excessive trust in the independent capacity of bankers to act prudently. This excess was not due to a simple mistake, or to an aberration by particular individuals. Bankers had to be trusted in order to preserve the private, informal politics of banking. To this particular consideration must be added a more disturbing possibility: that the excessive tendency to trust those being supervised is inherent in numerous systems of supervision, and that this tendency constantly puts regulators at the mercy of the more ingenious of the regulated.

The first, simplest explanation for the failure to prevent the secondary banking crisis can, then, be described in an equally simple word: incompetence. There exists a long tradition of writing about the Bank of England, especially among professional economists, which pictures it as incorrigibly amateurish. In this view, the failure to recognise and to prevent what was happening in the money markets is in a long tradition of central bank incompetence. The Croom-Johnson inquiry into the Crown Agents also thought that the particularly large losses suffered by the Agents could be explained by the failure of some Bank officials – among others – to do their jobs competently.[29]

There is one sense in which this account is undoubtedly correct. The mere fact of failure on the scale which happened in 1974, and the evidence of imprudence and worse which failure revealed, showed that the job of supervision had not been done effectively. There is also evidence that the Bank's supervisory arrangements were organised in the way critics of its amateurism would expect: before the crisis, for instance, the Discount Office was attempting to supervise over three hundred institutions, and to carry out its many other duties, with a staff of fifteen.[30]

The incompetence theory nevertheless fails to carry the argument very far. It is at best incomplete because it begs the question of why the Bank, while highly competent at such tasks as organising a rescue, should have been incompetent at preventing the crisis which made rescue necessary. The Discount Office was indeed too small effectively to carry out close supervision; but then the Bank never wanted to practise close supervision, because to do so would have endangered the privacy and informality so central to traditional banking politics in Britain.

There is an even more serious defect in the 'incompetence' theory. Between the 1930s and the 1970s banking failures were rare in advanced economies; in Britain they had been almost unknown since the First World War.[31] From the start of the 1970s they became more common. The great crisis in the middle of the decade in Britain was part of an international wave of banking failures. Many of these had causes similar to the English case, notably excessive lending on the security of property values inflated by speculation. All the failures reflected the inability of supervisors to restrict imprudent dealings by banks.[32] These experiences do show that after 1970 supervisory authorities were in a literal sense not competent to regulate banks in such a way as to exclude the possibility of failure, a task which had previously seemed within their capacity. The international character of banking failure shows, however, that there is not much point in trying to locate the cause in some particular incompetence of the Bank of England, while the sudden banking failures in the 1970s make it necessary to understand what new conditions destroyed the long-established effectiveness of existing systems of supervision. One of the strengths of the argument that the crisis in Britain could be traced to the chaotic state of the law is that it throws light on these new conditions.

This second account assumes that the label 'bank' conveys powerful favourable impressions. The argument runs that any institution which can describe itself as a bank is therefore well placed to attract business. Before 1974, however, there existed very weak official controls over the use of banking labels. With little central control or supervision, various institutions were able to use the favourable impressions evoked by a banking label to do business in a highly imprudent way.[33]

This diagnosis should be treated with respect, if only because it describes the view of many financial experts who have looked at the secondary banking crisis. It was the explanation offered by the Department of Trade Inspectors who investigated the failure of London and County Securities.[34] It is also a view which has shaped banking regulation: much of the 1979 Banking Act is concerned to limit greatly which institutions may legally call themselves banks. The argument also has in its favour the fact that, when the crisis began, banking law was indeed a messy, incomplete patchwork. This was not the result of an accidental oversight. Like much else in the financial world it arose from a determination to preserve the esoteric politics of the City from the attentions of Parliament and Westminister. In practice this meant keeping the law to a minimum in banking regulations.

These efforts came into conflict with one of the results of social complexity, for in an economy where institutions were connected in numerous and often unexpected ways it was difficult to isolate one activity from the wider consequences of social change. As economic institutions became increasingly subject to legal licensing and control it was therefore inevitable that the statute book would enter even the world of banking. Over the years before 1974 there appeared a variety of statutes which allowed institutions to describe themselves as banks for a range of particular purposes. Some were comparatively unimportant and specialised – the Agricultural Credits Act, 1928, created a category of banks approved by the Ministry of Agriculture – but others helped the Bank of England to identify its own span of responsibility. Under the 1947 Exchange Control Act, for instance, the Bank used its administrative discretion to create a list of 'authorised banks' licensed to deal in foreign exchange. Other important categories of bank were created by the City's success in gaining exemption from restrictions applied to the rest of the business community: thus the most prestigious category defined those recognised banks exempted under Schedule 8 of the 1948 Companies Act from the full disclosure requirements of company law. The growing complexity of licensing and supervision meant that by the beginning of the 1970s there were seven different statutes under which an institution could be termed a bank.[35]

Of the different kinds of bank created by law, much subsequent attention concentrated on the so-called 'Section 123' institutions, since it was this group which provided most casualties in the crisis. The creation of Section 123 banks was a perfect miniature of social complexity, illustrating how legal regulation, economic change and social inventiveness combined to produce unexpected results. The story began with the complicated history of the Moneylending Laws. Since individuals usually turn to moneylenders (as distinct from banks) when their circumstances are desperate, the law on moneylending has long discriminated in favour of the borrower; pawnbroking and moneylending were two of the earliest parts of economic life to see legal consumer protection.[36] Moneylenders needed a licence, without which they could not legally reclaim debts. Only institutions of unambiguous and unimpeachable banking status were exempt from this requirement.

The simple distinction between banks and moneylenders was without difficulties when the banking industry had an uncomplicated structure dominated by the clearing banks and a few institutions drawn from the traditional City elite. But rapid change in the post-war years produced a wide range of enterprises which performed many banking functions without laying claim to traditional banking status. The finance houses which grew with the expanding market in consumer credit were a perfect instance of what economists called these 'other financial intermediaries'. In 1965 a customer of the largest finance house used the courts (in United Dominions Trust *v.* Kirkwood) to test the proposition that a finance house could not legally recover a loan since it was neither a bank nor a licensed moneylender. Kirkwood's particular challenge failed but the case revealed an alarming threat to both the consumer credit market and to the rapidly growing new wholesale money markets, where many of the operators were not banks as conventionally understood.[37] As a result the Board of Trade inserted Section 123 into the 1967 Companies Act. This gave the Board power to issue a certificate stating that an institution was, for the purposes of the Moneylending Laws, '*bona fide* carrying on the business of banking'.

The narrow scope and purpose of this power should be noticed: it was to issue a licence, not to provide for continuing supervision; and its purpose was only to ensure that an institution did not suffer the disadvantageous provisions of the moneylending laws. By 1970 there were over ninety institutions in the Section 123 category, of which only fourteen were on the list of banks making statistical returns to the Bank of England.[38]

The shape of the very influential argument that in the state of the law we will find the cause of the crisis is now clear. Banking regulation originally developed beyond the statute book. The pervasiveness of law in a complex economy forced the creation of various legal categories of bank for a number of limited purposes. This allowed numerous institutions not governed by the traditional prudence of bankers to acquire banking status, and to use that status to raise deposits from the unwary. The result, especially in the case of the Section 123 institutions, was to create a reckless group of fringe banks.

The peculiar state of banking law before the crisis is certainly important for it illustrates how complexity was already destroying the privacy and informality of the banking community. But to use the state of the law to explain why the crisis occurred is to confuse a consequence with a cause. The boundaries of the banking system were unclear precisely because change and adaptation in the financial community constantly produced institutions which could not be fitted to existing definitions and for which new categories had to be invented. This is exactly how the Section 123 group was created. The fringe banks were thus not the result of the chaotic state of the law; they were one of the causes of chaos. Nor is it easy to sustain the view that possessing the label 'bank' was a great help in attracting deposits. The argument has some credence where money was raised from small, unsophisticated depositors who might take the word 'bank' as a symbol of security. The great bulk of deposits at risk in the crisis were, however, raised in the wholesale money markets: in other words from banks, from other financial institutions and from large industrial corporations. It is literally beyond belief that such sophisticated depositors were misguided by the simple possession of a Section 123 Certificate into not recognising the risky nature of the business. The success of the Section 123 banks is explicable in more straightforward terms: in the battle for business which succeeded the ending of controls in 1971 they offered higher interest rates than competitors from the established banking sector. They were able to do this because they were lending in turn at higher rates in risky areas, such as on second mortgages and on property speculation.[39] The problems revealed in 1974 thus cannot be convincingly traced to the undoubtedly tangled state of the law, though that tangle does tell us a good deal about the forces which were destroying traditional supervision.

The third account examined here goes beyond the particular content of the law to analyse how supervision was conducted in practice. This explanation has been stressed by the Bank of England, and it is therefore no surprise that the diagnosis which it offers has influenced the remedies adopted since 1974. The argument is in essence a variation on the theme of administrative complexity. On this view, one of the consequences of the haphazard growth of different forms of banking recognition was that responsibility for licensing and supervision became fragmented, especially between the Bank and Whitehall. The Bank, through a variety of authorisations, conferred status on 'banks proper', to use the Governor's revealing phrase for what were more usually called 'primary' banks. Since the Bank of England could control who entered the primary system it supervised those institutions and acknowledged full responsibility for ensuring that they were prudently run. The secondary, or fringe, banks were by contrast licensed from Whitehall, principally by acquiring a Section 123 certificate. Since the Bank did not control the issue of licences it naturally did not feel responsible for supervision. In Whitehall, however, the exercise was defined – as with the issue of Section 123 certificates – as a limited exercise in certifying that an institution had various conventional banking features which allowed exemption from the Moneylending Laws.[40] The consequence was that in deciding whether or not to issue a certificate the Board of Trade only looked for 'a minimum level of banking characteristics', and felt no obligation to supervise the activities of certified institutions.[41] In this way many banks disappeared from the sight of supervision into the crevices between administrative agencies.

This account certainly makes sense of some important parts of the crisis. The failure to avoid the most politically embarrassing of all the casualties, the Crown Agents, was undoubtedly due in part to problems of communication and control created by administrative complexity. The Agents lived in that constitutional twilight inhabited by quasi-government agencies. In the late 1960s they began to supplement their declining traditional income (derived from providing technical and supply services to Commonwealth governments) by dabbling incompetently in the property and money markets. Not until May 1974 – when the Agents' losses exceeded £200 million – did the Bank and the Treasury step in to organise a rescue and try to salvage the wreckage. Yet since the late 1960s the Bank had been worried about the Agents' incompetence, imprudence, and in some cases impropriety.[42] The Bank had little direct control over the Agents' actions, however, and because it dealt with Whitehall largely through the Treasury its warnings had to go through a series of institutions – the Treasury, the sponsoring Department and the Agents themselves –

before any effect could be felt. The two major official inquiries into the Agents' problems do indeed show how this circuitous chain of communication both delayed and muted the transmission of warning signs. The evidence to the Croom–Johnson inquiry, in particular, shows that the Bank and the Treasury made very different assumptions about who was responsible for supervising the Agents' activities in the money markets: the Bank assumed that since the Agents were a quasi-public institution they were – like the Giro Bank – a Whitehall responsibility; the Treasury assumed that since the activities were taking place in the money markets they were a Bank responsibility.[43] The episode shows how far institutions are forced to rely on customary assumptions in demarcating responsibilities; but it also shows the defects of this inescapable reliance on custom, for by their very nature such assumptions conceal ambiguities in the way responsibility is divided.

These technical problems of communication and coordination were intensified by the rivalries which frequently spring up when different bureaucratic institutions have to accomplish common tasks. It has now been established, for instance, that there was a crucial delay of almost two years in appreciating the full enormity of the Crown Agents' incompetence, during which the Agents made further large losses. The delay occurred because although between them the responsible institutions – the Treasury, the Bank, the Foreign Office, the Exchequer and Audit Department – had ample signs that something was seriously wrong, these signs were never assembled together to spell out a message of alarm. The Croom–Johnson report into the affair portrays a world of intense institutional jealousies. Institutions fought subtle battles to control information, to establish jurisdiction and to obtain access to key committees; while the battles were fought the Agents went their incompetent, imprudent way.[44] Outsiders sometimes imagine that secrecy in British government is used only against those outside the machine; Croom–Johnson shows that supposed 'insiders' can be almost as much in the dark because control of information is a key weapon of the battles fought in conducting 'bureaucratic politics'.

Nor were problems of coordination confined to those areas where different agencies were engaged in common tasks; inside individual institutions there were also examples of failures to communicate and cooperate. In the Bank's case these problems were made worse by the informality which went with esoteric politics. The Croom–Johnson inquiry found that 'much of its work was done orally' and that decisions 'were either not recorded at all, or were recorded only in a brief manuscript note scribbled on the top of a minute, and often not copied to all concerned'. Consequently, 'when junior staff who had not been involved in earlier discussions were sent ... to represent the Bank at interdepartmental meetings, they were not familiar with the background or the Bank's views, and there was no file to which they could turn for a record of the Bank's previous involvement and thinking. Government departments looking for advice from those representing the Bank at such meetings had little idea of how inadequately informed they often were.'[45]

Problems of communication and coordination arising from administrative complexity thus give some clue to the causes of failure. Yet beyond the undoubtedly important case of the Crown Agents these problems have been overstated, in part because the argument that nobody was clearly responsible for the secondary banks absolves both the Bank and Whitehall from blame for lax supervision. The Bank's account in particular is a rationalisation after the event. It undoubtedly felt less responsibility for secondary banks than it acknowledged for the primary sector, but the clear dividing line which it has subsequently tried to draw is suspect. The Bank's case is that there were 'banks proper' which were effectively supervised, and an imprudent fringe, which slipped through the supervisory net. Yet some of the biggest casualties were within the Bank's acknowledged span of responsibility. The two most expensive occupants of the lifeboat were United Dominions Trust, not a fringe bank but the country's largest finance house; and First National Finance Corporation, which was close enough to the Discount Office to be asked to arrange the first rescue of London and County Securities.[46] The two victims which cost the Bank most money were its acknowledged responsibility: Slater Walker was rescued because it was on the Bank's list of institutions authorised to deal in foreign exchange and because its default on Eurocurrency dealings would have damaged London's standing as a financial centre; Edward Bates was rescued for similar reasons.[47] Indeed, so poor was the Bank's intelligence that Edward Bates was given 'authorised' status in December 1973, after the banking crisis had begun.

Nor is it the case that before 1974 the Bank left responsibility for Section 123 institutions entirely to Whitehall. To have done so would indeed have contradicted its style of supervision, which stressed flexibility and adaptation. This style meant that the Bank would take an interest in any institution operating in financial markets, whatever its formal status; that was why the financial community was encouraged to treat the Discount Office as a kind of confessional in which anyone connected with banking could informally pass on information. Indeed one of the enduring impressions left from reading the many public inquiries into failures and scandals in the City in the 1970s is the Bank's persistent presence behind the scenes: often advising, sometimes warning, always anxiously courted for approval.[48]

The Bank was thus closer to the fringe than its own account of the crisis suggests. It was also more involved in licensing the Section 123 banks than later official accounts indicate, for it had an effective veto over the issue of a certificate to any applicant. This is because the Department of Trade, in deciding on an application, demanded far more than that an institution exhibit certain structural banking features. Every applicant had to complete a detailed questionnaire giving details of its affairs, including the extent to which it was involved in such risky business as lending on second mortgages.[49] The Department always consulted the Discount Office before issuing a certificate. The exercise was thus much more than a search for certain nominal banking features. A certificate was issued only when the applicant was shown, in the Bank's own words, to be 'soundly based and operating fairly'.[50]

The defect with the system lay not in the Bank's inability to control the issue of certificates, but in the failure to check systematically either the information supplied by applicants or their subsequent dealings. British Bangladesh Trust's successful application in December 1973 for a Section 123 Certificate showed just how perfunctory official scrutiny could be. BBT was controlled by Mr John Stonehouse, MP, soon to be the subject of a bizarre scandal involving impersonation, disappearance and fraud. Long before the end of 1973 his business conduct was suspect: at the end of the previous year a highly critical article about Mr Stonehouse by reputable journalists on the *Sunday Times Business News* had prompted an inconclusive investigation by the Department of Trade. Yet when the Department's own Inspectors later investigated the ruins of Mr Stonehouse's business empire they found that false information in the Section 123 application was never uncovered because no official attempt was made to check its accuracy (by, for instance, requiring the corroboration of auditors).[51]

This failure was in part a product of the blindness which routine and custom impose on big organisations. The Department of Trade, in characteristic bureaucratic manner, processed the application according to fixed procedures; and in the Inspectors' words 'the procedures in use at that time did not provide for independent verification of the answers'.[52] The Bank, with its consciously anti-bureaucratic attitude, might have been more flexible; but it, too, was the prisoner of custom. The Bank's approach to supervision, originally evolved in regulating a small and socially homogeneous banking community, put trust in bankers and discouraged detailed scrutiny. The fear of 'bureaucracy' deprived the Discount Office of the administrative resources needed to practise close supervision; customary assumptions provided an alternative ideology of trust. As the Principal of the Office explained, in describing the failure to check details in Section 123 applications: 'for the most part I think we took those on trust... the basis being, of course, that it you ever found a chap out in a lie, he was finished for ever. You assumed nobody would be so stupid.'[53]

The failures of supervision revealed by the secondary banking crisis did not, therefore, arise chiefly from the confused state of the law nor were they mainly due to failures of coordination. They arose from the excessive trust placed by the authorities in the independent capacity of bankers to do business prudently. This excess was no aberration of one individual. It served powerful interests by allowing bankers to do business free of close bureaucratic controls and allowing the Bank of England to supervise the City with little interference from Whitehall or Westminster. In a phrase: it preserved esoteric politics.

The success of this kind of supervision caused its own destruction. Freedom from the close legal controls common in other banking systems gave London a great advantage, so that the history of the money markets in the 1960s and early 1970s was one of dazzling success and innovation. The consequent economic and social transformation destroyed the conditions which made it sensible to rely heavily on trust. The financial community increased in size and sophistication, but the Bank would not increase its regulatory staff in a corresponding way for fear of destroying the privacy and informality of its relations with bankers. The result was that at the very time when the banking community was becoming more diverse, was experiencing fierce competition and was pioneering new and risky practices, supervisors were forced to place an increasing weight on trust. The Discount Office's administrative resources were quite outstripped by the scale of the banking system: fifteen people supervising over three hundred banks could do little else but trust the supervised even when some of them – like Mr Stonehouse – had dubious reputations.

This excessive trust in the prudence of bankers arose in part from the particular history of financial regulation in Britain, but it also reflected a more general problem which commonly afflicts systems of inspection and control. Wilensky's study of failures of intelligence gathering in organisations – which in essence was the Bank's failure before 1974 – shows how far dependence on trust and routine inevitably shape inspection.[54] Conventional notions develop about how much scrutiny is adequate, and how much can be taken on trust. It is not difficult to understand why such conventions take root. Administrative complexity is one cause: predictable routine and custom help cope with problems of coordination. Social complexity is another. Supervisors find their task made immensely difficult if relations with the supervised are not amicable. Yet amity and feelings of trust are destroyed by unpredictability: supervisors who constantly demand fresh and unexpected information plainly have poor faith in the probity of those whom they supervise. This dislike of requests for new information is reinforced because collection is costly and because it delays decisions. The reluctance to spend time in scrutinising and verifying information is reinforced in highly competitive financial markets, which minimise collective responsibilities and emphasise swift decision. In the words of a leading figure in the early 1970s' boom: 'the wheels of commerce would grind to a halt if each party [to a bargain] was the other's keeper'.[55]

This necessary reliance on routine and trust makes all systems of inspection vulnerable, but particular problems are posed by complex and inventive financial institutions. Wilensky's analysis shows how great swindles can be executed very simply. This is because ingenious operators exploit the predictability and superficiality which routine and trust impose on systems of inspection.[56] In the events leading to the secondary banking crisis the reliance placed on audited accounts is a striking example of how routine and trust limit the effectiveness with which inspection can be conducted. A set of accounts signed and not qualified in any serious way by a reputable firm of auditors was conventionally accepted, both by the authorities and by the City, as a mark of financial health. This was not surprising: the influence of auditors as a professional group lay in their assumed capacity to simplify publicly the complexity of modern company accounts into clear, conventional signs of the financial soundness or otherwise of an enterprise.[57] But it has been clear since the mid-1970s that this customary trust in the significance of audited accounts was misplaced. The complexity of economic life, and the attendant complexity of company law, turned auditing into a highly subjective business. The public seal of approval in the auditor's signature often concealed fierce arguments between auditors and directors about how assets and liabilities should be treated and valued. In some cases these arguments occurred because directors were trying to conceal malpractices, but this was only part of a deeper problem: the pace of innovation in the financial system constantly created new practices and instruments, and created novel problems in making sense of accounts. Thus an auditor's signature, which was widely taken as a conventional shorthand sign that all was well, actually had a more limited and ambiguous meaning. As the guidance on principles of auditing issued to its members by the Institute of Chartered Accountants noted defensively: 'responsibility for the accounts and financial control of a company rests upon the directors ... If the directors have carried out their duty properly the detailed checking ... may extend to only a small proportion of transactions ... The auditors should aim to reduce the detailed checking to the minimum consistent with the system of internal control and the state in which they find the records.'[58]

The many official and unofficial inquests into the causes of the secondary banking crisis all assume that the failures of supervision which it revealed were a surprise requiring explanation. The assumption is in some respects perfectly reasonable, if only because the modern record of prudential supervision had until then been almost unblemished. Yet viewed in the light of what we know generally about the capacity of institutions to gather and act upon information the failures revealed in the crisis are no great surprise. In the specialist literature on information and intelligence there is ample evidence that organisations commonly fail to detect warning signals, or to take appropriate action when danger is apparent. 'Surprise despite warning' is a common feature of institutional life. It might be labelled 'the Pearl Harbor problem', after the famous failure of the American armed forces to take action despite ample signs that a Japanese attack was imminent.[59] Schelling called Pearl Harbor 'a supremely *ordinary* blunder of government';[60] likewise failure to detect and prevent the banking crisis was due to common, deep-rooted features of institutional life, perhaps strengthened by a particularly English reliance on trust.

'Pearl Harbor problems' recur because institutions are forced to a trusting reliance on routine and custom. Crises destroy this sanguine outlook. In the midst of disaster almost nothing is trusted; 'everybody is suspicious of everybody'. Afterwards, the search begins for new and more rigorous standards of surveillance and control. This is what happened in banking after 1974: the Bank of England placed less trust in the unchecked word of bankers, controlled more closely those who could enter the banking system, pressed for improvements in standards of auditing and accounting and imposed more detailed scrutiny on financial institutions. But these events were in the future. At the end of 1973 there existed a more immediate problem: how to cope with the crisis itself. This I now examine.

4 RESCUING AN INDUSTRY

Accounts of the events which toook place in banking during the mid-1970s conventionally speak of a single banking crisis and, correspondingly, of a single rescue. This is useful shorthand, but it is too simple for detailed description: just as there occurred not one but a set of connected crises, so there was mounted a connected set of rescues. Four different kinds of support should be distinguished. First in time came a group of individual rescues in the first three weeks of December 1973. At this stage it was believed in the Bank and in the City that the difficulties could be contained to a small group of institutions. The Bank put no funds into these rescues, but acted as an intermediary, bringing institutional shareholders and clearing bankers together and persuading them to support stricken institutions. The second set of rescues was organised by the Control Committee itself, beginning over the Christmas of 1973. The Bank provided slightly more than 10 per cent of the Committee's funds. A third group of rescues was carried out by the Bank alone, principally because after the autumn of 1974 it could not persuade the clearing banks in the Control Committee to provide more funds. The best known of these was the rescue after October 1975 of the banking and investment group Slater Walker following Mr Jim Slater's resignation as chairman. The bank has declined to reveal the cost of these rescues, but the independent accountants' report into Slater Walker calculated financial guarantees by the Bank of £70 million, and another £40 million in indemnities on bad debts.[61] The Deputy Governor at the time has said that rescues outside the Control Committee accounted for most of the Bank's losses.[62] The fourth set of rescues was the most informal and confidential: throughout 1974 the Bank was in effect rescuing stricken property companies. On these the Bank spent nothing, but lobbied government for changes in public policy to restore the fortunes of the depressed property market, and lobbied the creditors of property companies – which largely meant the banks – to persuade them not to call in loans which would have driven companies into bankruptcy.

(a) *Esoteric politics and industrial rescue*

To anyone acquainted with the politics of economic policy in Britain the most striking features of these rescues are that they occurred at all and that they took place with hardly any public argument. After December 1973 the Bank was practising large-scale industrial rescues in the financial and property markets. Except in particular cases where central departments were directly involved – as with the Crown Agents – it did so without consulting Whitehall, and without any ministerial interference. Indeed even in the case of the Crown Agents the Bank acted with remarkable independence: the Agents' sponsoring department in Whitehall only discovered from the newspapers that the Agents had been persuaded by the Bank to provide funds for the secondary banking rescue.[63] This is a remarkable contrast with the history of rescues in other parts of the economy. Industrial rescues have been common in recent years, but they have almost always been undertaken reluctantly. They have commonly aroused bitter public argument and fears – which even the authors of the rescues often shared – that supporting failed companies would damage healthy competitors and weaken the disciplines of a market economy.[64]

The immediate reason for this contrast between banking and other industries was that it never seriously occurred to any senior official in the Bank that in the crisis it could do anything but organise help. There was none of the agonizing so common to rescues elsewhere because, since at least 1890, when the Bank helped rescue the House of Baring from collapse, it had been a customary assumption in the Bank and the City that such a responsibility existed. This assumption was formed by the Bank's history. As it told the Wilson Committee: 'As a result of their experiences with the Overend Gurney crash of 1866, the Baring crisis of 1890 and the prolonged international crisis of 1929–33 the Bank – and the world at large – had come to regard the taking of prompt and decisive action to prevent a loss of confidence as one of the essential roles of a central bank.'[65]

This instinctive assumption of duty was vital to the success of the rescue. Had it been necessary for the Bank to work out a case for intervention from first principles the banking system would have been engulfed, such was the speed at which the crisis developed. The experience illustrates what Wilensky pointed out many years ago: the ideal of decision making favoured by academic theorists – reflective, searching, cautious – commonly produces less satisfactory results than come from hasty decisions forced out of policy makers in the press of crisis.[66]

The speed and ease with which the rescue was organised was thus in an immediate sense due to instinctive assumptions bred into the banking community. Why banking should have developed these unique assumptions is more difficult to understand. The Bank of England has traditionally argued that banking rescues differ from other industrial rescues because the demands of the financial system are special: since financial dealings depend heavily on trust between the parties the possibility that one side will default must be excluded. The knowledge that the Bank of England guarantees the stability of the banking system is thus essential to maintain confidence.[67]

There is plainly something in this argument. The history of banking in Britain in the nineteenth century was dominated by the effort to invent institutions – such as the lender of last resort – which would reassure depositors that their money was safe. Kindleberger has shown how, in the nineteenth century, the fear that rescuing imprudent banks might undermine market discipline was overcome by the argument that the confidence requirements of banking were special.[68] Yet the distinction between banking and manufacturing industry has been overdrawn, especially by the Bank of England in its anxiety to defend rescues. A major industrial collapse also damages confidence: among industrial investors, in the fragile world of trade credit and among employees everywhere. Nor was the Bank consistent in applying the argument, for in the crisis it supported only certain parties to financial transactions. Depositors in the stricken banks were fully compensated but no attempt was made to defend similarly the interests of shareholders, who lost both because of the collapse in prices and because of the very unfavourable terms on which the companies were reconstructed. The neglect of shareholders' interests was both damaging to investors' confidence and difficult to defend on grounds of equity, for it meant that while the Bank was defending the interests of large sophisticated depositors – such as big industrial corporations – it neglected the interests of numerous small, unsophisticated shareholders.[69]

These observations suggest that the Bank accepted an automatic duty to rescue depositors not primarily because banking had certain peculiar needs, but because of the special role which the Bank itself played in the British financial system. This suggestion is supported by the different behaviour of supervisory authorities in other countries when faced with collapse in the mid-1970s. Thus when in June 1974 the Bankhaus Herstatt suddenly ceased trading because of massive losses on the foreign exchange markets the West German authorities were only induced with the greatest reluctance to arrange some compensation for those who lost through Herstatt's default. (One of the most important pressures in overcoming reluctance came from the Bank of England, which was anxious to defend the interests of London banks that had lost by the Herstatt crash.)[70]

The conclusion thus seems inescapable that the rescue was launched not because of the peculiar needs of banking – though these existed in some degree – but because of the peculiar role of the Bank of England. The secondary banking rescue is the last great example of the esoteric politics of banking at work, before it was prised open by the consequences of the crisis and by other forces. Esoteric politics gave the Bank a key role as manager of the interests of the banking community. This involved regulating the banking system with the least possible interference from Whitehall or Westminster. In the case of banking failure this resistance to outside interference was strengthened by the argument that secrecy was necessary to preserve confidence in London as a great international centre. Many years before the secondary banking crisis, this had produced the doctrine that it was the Bank's job, when faced with an institution in difficulties, to 'do good by stealth', as Sir Leslie O'Brien put it. Speaking in 1970, Sir Leslie drew a pointed contrast between banking rescues and more conventional assistance to troubled manufacturing firms. 'Would you say', he asked rhetorically, 'that the well-advertised governmental help to industries which get themselves into trouble is as good as the kind of help which we give, preserving the fabric of the financial system without ... anybody knowing even that at one particular point of time a part of the fabric has become a bit shaky?' 'Doing good by stealth' led the Bank to help about a dozen institutions during the 1960s.[71]

The assumptions of esoteric politics thus almost automatically made the Bank organise a rescue. These assumptions were also the reason why it was able to do so independently of Whitehall and Parliament. Any central department attempting to help a troubled industry cannot escape being involved in public, partisan argument, both because of the conventions of ministerial responsibility and because of Parliament's right to question public spending. Apart from the special case of the Crown Agents – where the Labour MP George Cunningham ran a persistent and shrewd campaign – parliamentary interest in the secondary banking crisis was spasmodic and ill-informed.[72] Backbenchers, for instance, confused the large amounts recycled as deposits with the smaller amounts actually lost in the exercise.[73] Nor was this surprising: the whole tradition of financial politics excluded Parliament and thus prevented MPs from acquiring the kind of expertise which would have made effective scrutiny possible. Those with a desire to scrutinise – such as the left-wing Labour MP Mr Dennis Skinner – were hampered by a lack of background knowledge; those with the capacity to scrutinise – such as the MPs on the Conservative benches with City connections – shared the assumption common in the financial world that the City was best left to deal with the crisis in its own way.

The assumptions supporting esoteric politics also sheltered the Bank from scrutiny of the money which it was committing to the rescue. One of the results of the Bank's long struggle to maintain its separation from Whitehall is that its resources have never been classified as public money. This narrow technical point had an important practical consequence, for the Bank required neither Treasury nor parliamentary sanction for the sums which it contributed, and in some cases lost, in the rescue. The technicality also allowed it to deny afterwards that it risked and lost public money in the affair. As the Governor put in in 1978:

> I am always a little at a loss when I hear the expression 'tax-payers' money' used in this connection . . ., the Bank has capital and it has reserves and it is a public institution owned by the nation; but it does its business, as a bank does its business, on the deposits which it collects; and by far the greater part of the deposits which it has are deposits from banks.[74]

The rescues thus took place because the Bank was able and willing to organise them. It possessed the ability and the will because esoteric politics gave it the power to act and created the assumption that it should so act to safeguard the interests of the banking community. It might be thought that this made the Bank the creature of private banking interests. The contrary is the case: one of the most fascinating features of the rescues was the persistent tension between individual banks and the Bank of England as guardian of the whole system. The Bank wanted unity in the crisis; individual banks, not surprisingly, wanted to defend their own sectional interests. That they did not destroy the system by individually self-interested behaviour is a mark of the Bank of England's power. The tension between collective and individual interests is perfectly illustrated by the history of the Control Committee.

(b) *The politics of the Control Committee*

It is a measure of the novelty of the problems created for regulators by the new money markets that it took three weeks of financial turmoil after the collapse of London and County Securities before the Bank realised that a formal rescue of the whole system would have to be organised. Like almost everybody else in the City the Bank's senior officials at first assumed that London and County's troubles were an isolated event.[75] Even when other institutions began to approach the Bank with difficulties in the first three weeks of December 1973 its reaction was to treat each case separately, to avoid putting in any of its own money, and to act only as a broker bringing together the clearing bank and the major institutional shareholders of stricken firms, with the object of encouraging them to provide support. This response lasted until the week before Christmas, but on 20 December the Stock Exchange suspended the quotation of Cedar Holdings, a fringe bank with borrowings of over £70 million. At 3 a.m. on the same morning the Bank of England had, after an exhausting and sometimes acrimonious meeting, persuaded and bullied Cedar's clearing bank and its institutional shareholders into putting together a rescue package.[76] But this was insufficient to stave off the alarm caused by Cedar's public failure. By 21 December the Bank believed that 'there was a threat of a collapse of confidence' which demanded an organised response.[77] In the morning the Governor called a meeting of London clearing bank chairmen. He stressed to them that there existed a crisis which threatened more than a few fringe banks, and that restoring confidence demanded united public action. In the afternoon a press release announced that the Bank and clearers were combining to organise a rescue of secondary banks that were in difficulties. The announcement was as important as the decision itself, for it was still commonly believed that the difficulties were due to nervousness among depositors; the hope was that the mere announcement that the Bank and the clearers now stood behind troubled institutions would restore confidence.

The 21 December meeting, and the events of the following week, shaped the course of all the rescues. The initial decision to call in clearing bank chairmen put the largest burden on the clearers' shoulders. The load was distributed in this way for reasons of economics and of power. Both the Discount Houses and the leading merchant banks might with justice have been asked to help, because they had dealt profitably with the fringe. The Bank certainly had the power to compel them to participate. At the end of 1973, however, many Discount Houses and merchant banks were themselves in difficulty because of the crisis. Indeed there are persistent rumours that the Bank was forced to give covert help to some Houses and merchant banks, though since the law allows both classes of institution to conceal their inner reserves this cannot be verified.[78] The financial institutions, especially the pension funds, probably did have the resources to help, but they were beyond the range of the Bank's power. Throughout subsequent rescues the Bank was forced to approach them for help in individual cases but they were never as compliant as the banks. Indeed the Bank of England had an early warning of resistance because two big industrial pension funds – the Coal Board and Unilever – had expressed most scepticism about the hectic rescue organised for Cedar Holdings.[79]

The Bank was thus compelled to depend overwhelmingly on the clearers because other institutions within its control could not afford to help, while those with resources were beyond its grip. The press of crisis and the force of customary assumptions meant that the clearers put up no significant resistance to being conscripted. (At the first meeting with the Governor the only doubts came from the Midland, of all the clearers the bank closest to manufacturing industry.)[80] It was even possible later to bring in the Scottish clearing banks which, as they observed to the Wilson Committee, thus had to provide funds to rescue banks whose troubles were largely due to property speculation in south-east England.[81]

The initial decision to rely on the clearers was also the result of a simple financial calculation. The banks' retail network gave them funds independent of the money markets, while the crisis itself further swelled their deposits because nervous lenders withdrew their money from the fringe into the security of the clearing banks. Financial considerations also shaped the form of the rescue. The first intention was to 'recycle' deposits back into the secondary banks: in other words, money withdrawn from the fringe and placed with the clearers would be lent back to selected fringe institutions. This was intended to have two effects: it would prevent banks from immediately collapsing, and in the longer term would encourage depositors to stay with the fringe by reassuring them that their money was safe.

From these original intentions flowed the administrative details of the rescue. Some mechanism had to be created to raise and distribute the rescue funds. Over the Christmas of 1973, therefore, the details of a Control Committee (colloquially, 'the lifeboat') were settled. The Bank was from the beginning the dominating influence. In the Deputy Governor's words it 'designed and directed' the Committee: provided a chairman (the Deputy Governor); a secretariat; a meeting place for sessions which at the height of the crisis were daily, and which later took place every Monday afternoon; and a Money Desk through which the funds were raised and distributed.[82] When the Committee first met on 28 December other important details had also been decided. The clearing banks each had one member, of Deputy Chairman or similar rank. The burden of cost had also been settled. Ninety per cent of the funds came from the clearers, apportioned roughly according to size. At the 21 December meeting the Bank had resisted the suggestion that it put in some of its own money, but over the Christmas holiday the suggestion was pressed with sufficient force to change minds, and the Bank now agreed to contribute 10 per cent of the total.[83]

The rapid establishment of the Control Committee was a mark both of the unity of bankers and of the great influence exercised by the Bank of England; the speed, privacy and informality exemplified the style of esoteric politics. But this smooth course was assisted by a misunderstanding about the crisis which was shared by the Bank and by almost everybody in the City. This misunderstanding, which was soon to complicate the rescue considerably, showed how the novelty of the new money markets misled both commercial bankers and those with responsibility for regulation. The clearing banks readily supported the rescue because they agreed with the common initial diagnosis that the crisis was caused only by loss of confidence: fundamentally sound institutions, it was believed, were finding it difficult to renew their loans in the money markets because the failure of a small number of atypical fringe banks had created nervousness among depositors. We have it on the authority of several of those closely involved with the Control Committee that when they first joined it they never imagined the scale of commitments and losses which were eventually incurred.[84]

The Committee's assumption that it was supporting fundamentally sound institutions shaped the way it first went about its business. Applications for assistance were occasionally made directly, but more often came through what the Committee called the 'related bank', in other words the clearing bank to which the applicant was most deeply committed. The related bank was then usually commissioned to examine the application, and to make a recommendation. The criteria used assumed that the operation would be commercially profitable. No institution was to be given support unless it was trading solvently. Money was only to be put in on commercially profitable terms: the Committee usually lent at between 0.5 and 2 per cent above the prevailing money market rate. Since the rescue was conceived with the object of restoring confidence in the banking system the Committee also determined from the beginning only to consider applications from institutions that it considered to be banks, thus ruling out direct help for property companies.[85]

The clearing banks were therefore persuaded to put their money and their name behind the rescue because they shared the common belief that it would be brief, limited and probably profitable. The first three months of 1974 destroyed these illusions, but by then the clearers could not draw back without very serious losses. The amounts demanded of the Committee rose quickly to frightening levels: within three months the figure exceeded £400 million; by September 1974 it exceeded £900 million and was rising rapidly. By the end of the year it was within £18 million of the £1,200 million which the clearers had specified as the limit of their contribution. Even then it continued to rise, and when the £1,200 million limit was approached the Bank put in more of its own money until the peak of £1,285 million was reached in March 1975.[86]

The immediate reason for these unexpected increases was that the public sight of a rescue by the Bank and the clearers failed in its initial object of restoring confidence: depositors continued to withdraw money as the term of loans expired. This failure to restore confidence could be traced to a change in the economic circumstances of the fringe banks; the change falsified the assumption that the Committee was rescuing fundamentally sound institutions. The key to the alteration lay in the very large loans to property companies made in the preceding two years of boom. At the end of 1973 property prices reached a peak, stayed in 'a state of suspended animation' (to use the Bank's phrase) for a short time, and then began to fall sharply.[87] The economic mechanisms linking fringe banks and the property companies now plunged both into deeper crisis.

The rise in the volume of lending by the Control Committee hence signified more than an unexpected and alarming growth in the scale of the operation; it indicated a change in character, for the rescue was no longer a limited, commercially sensible support for solvent banks. The idea that the Committee would get a good return on its funds became notional: those in the lifeboat could not even pay interest on the loans, so the amount had to be added to the capital. The speed with which the crisis developed now meant that the searching examination which would have demonstrated an applicant's solvency could often not be carried out. The problem was intensified by the extraordinary complexity of many of the enterprises: for instance, one applicant for help had organised its affairs into 149 separate companies.[88] The Committee tried to cling to its initial rule that only the solvent would be helped, but in the circumstances – the speed with which decisions were demanded, the state of the property market and the internal complexity of many applicants – it is not surprising that the rule could not always be observed. The eight occupants of the lifeboat eventually put into liquidation or into the hands of a receiver understate the extent to which hopeless cases were helped; many of the other eighteen survivors only escaped the same fate because the Committee made the tactical decision that perseverance and reorganisation was a less expensive option.

The swift and unexpected transformation of the Control Committee's task created serious tension inside the support group. The clearing banks had divided interests: they had a collective interest in preventing the collapse of the banking system but individual interests in minimising their own contribution to the cost of rescue. The Bank of England was the defender of collective banking stability, but it, too had narrower interests since it wanted to put a limit on the costs it was forced to bear.

These tensions showed themselves in varying ways. There was discontent within individual banks. As the rescue grew larger and the crisis became more intense the Control Committee was often faced with the need to respond almost instantaneously to requests for loans. It was thus common for a bank to find that its representative on the Committee returned from a meeting having pledged his bank to provide yet more millions.[89] Tensions also existed over the allocation of the burden between the clearing banks. The operating rule was that banks would provide funds in proportion to a measure of their size, but there were numerous ways in which individual banks were compelled to give extra support: the Committee insisted, for instance, that before any applicant received help it had to exhaust existing credit with its clearing bank; and in some cases the Committee refused to bear any risk, thus compelling individual members to furnish the whole cost of a rescue.[90]

These divisions, though important, were not as significant as the line which divided the clearers from the Bank of England. As the crisis deepened and the cost mounted the clearers looked about for ways of limiting their own commitments. Two possibilities were seriously advocated in the Committee: restricting the range of banks to be rescued; and throwing more of the cost of the rescue on to the Bank of England. The Bank successfully resisted the first of these; it was forced to give way a little on the second.

The first option involved publishing a list of about seventy banks (in effect the most respectable institutions) which the Committee and the Bank would publicly pledge to defend under all circumstances. The knowledge of such a list, so the reasoning went, would create confidence in those named banks and would also exclude from rescue the costly, hopeless cases. The idea also had the subsidiary advantage of not requiring the clearers to rescue some institutions that they considered to have been run in a dubious way.[91]

The Bank candidly admitted that the unrestricted range of the rescue meant that help was indeed sometimes given to what it called 'undeserving' cases. It nevertheless strongly and successfully resisted pressure to publish a list of those that would in all circumstances be saved.[92] The Bank's object was to preserve the stability of the whole system, not to give salvation to a particular class of institution. It took the view that stability was indivisible: any bank excluded from the list of the saved would have met almost certain extinction; these failures would have damaged confidence in all banks. In this reasoning it was almost certainly correct: in November 1974, for instance, the difficulties of the fringe created such persistent rumours about the soundness of the National Westminster Bank, itself a member of the Control Committee, that the Nat West Chairman had to issue a public statement denying that it was receiving support from the Bank of England.[93]

Differences about the range of institutions to be rescued strikingly illustrate the tension between the sectional interests of the clearers and the Bank's commitment to defending the stability of the whole system. The differences about the size of the Bank's cash contribution to the rescue were more complex in origin, since they also involved the Bank's own sectional interests. The original agreement committing the Bank to provide 10 per cent of the funds had been made in the hurried events over Christmas 1973, when it was believed that the rescue would be limited and profitable. Even this contribution was, we already know, only conceded reluctantly. The Bank's official account is that the arrangement lasted until the Committee had lent £1,200 million, at which point the clearers declined to go further. This fortunately coincided with the peak of the crisis, so there was no need to make more claims on the clearers.[94]

This official account glosses a complicated history. Even before the £1,200 million limit was reached, the Bank had been compelled to put money beyond the 10 per cent limit into rescues, for in some of the cases where the Control Committee refused help the Bank joined individual clearing banks in giving assistance.[95] Nor is the coincidence between the £1,200 million limit and the peak of the crisis fortuitous.

The figure was set in August 1974, when the Committee's lending was then approaching £900 million. But it was not the first effort to put a limit on the clearers' contributions and to force the Bank to carry all the remaining burden. In previous months, one banker privately recalls, efforts had been made to 'knock in pegs' defining the limits of the clearers' share; each time the intensity of crisis swept the pegs away. The £1,200 million figure was thus not a limit on which the banks suddenly fixed; it was only the latest attempt to knock in those pegs. They happened to hold on this occasion because, the Bank having put in £85 million more of its own money, the demands on the Committee at last began to diminish in the spring of 1975. The success of this last effort to limit the size of the clearers' commitment meant that when in October 1975 the Slater Walker banking and investment group was rescued the Bank had to bear the full cost.

Despite these internal tensions, the Control Committee is an impressive example of the Bank of England's ability to compel individual institutions to subordinate their sectional interests to the Bank's conception of the wider needs of the banking community. Only the Bank could enforce the discipline needed for collective action; without this discipline the individual pursuit of self-interest would have produced an even graver crisis. It was helped in the task by initial underestimates of the cost of a rescue, and by fear when the full magnitude of the disaster became clear. Beyond these particular advantages, however, the Bank had deeper sources of influence, deriving from its key position in the financial community. It exploited these advantages ruthlessly. It was of course the dominating influence in the Control Committtee: chairing it, controlling the flow of paper, constantly able to intervene in the separate rescues. In short, it wielded conventional and highly effective sources of bureaucratic power.

It reinforced this power by using its special place in the financial community and in government to exercise influence more informally. The burden of rescue on the clearing banks was lightened by persuading those financial institutions that owned shares in striken fringe banks that they had a duty to help. Before the Control Committee gave any assistance it had to be convinced that there did not exist an institutional investor that could shoulder the burden instead. Even when an applicant was helped aboard the lifeboat the Bank used its influence to cajole money out of the institutions. As the Deputy Governor told the Fay Committee which investigated the Crown Agents: 'If there were responsible institutional investors that had put their money in and lent the support of their name as well as their money to a fringe banking operation we pressed upon them the argument that they therefore had a responsibility to rectify the problem, and not just leave it to ... the Control Committee to step in and, as it were, release them from responsibility'. By such arguments put informally the Bank persuaded the Agents to support the rescue to the tune of £60 million and got undisclosed amounts out of a wide range of pension funds and insurance companies.[96]

This informal influence also went into parts of the banking community not directly involved in the rescue. If the operation was to succeed it was vital that large depositors be dissuaded from withdrawing their money from risky fringe banks. This was a tricky exercise in persuasion, for it meant inviting capitalist concerns to put the collective good of banking stability over their individual short-term interests. Only the Bank's power and contacts could carry them along. Thus one internationally famous merchant bank which tried to put its own interests above the needs of the rescue by withdrawing deposits from one of the Control Committee's clients soon returned the money under pressure from the Bank of England.

The informal exercise of influence was not confined to the domestic banking system. In the summer of 1974 the crisis took on a frightening new shape when a series of banking failures in Europe and North America indicated that the difficulties were not confined to Britain. The development was alarming to London in part because some foreign failures – such as Herstatt – defaulted on debts owed to English banks. To this problem was added a more general cause of alarm: as a great centre of branches and subsidiaries of foreign banks, and as the major centre of Eurocurrency dealings, London would be peculiarly vulnerable in an international crisis. This was why the Bank of England took the lead in using the central bankers' network to try to cope with the international character of the crisis. At the July 1974 meeting of the Bank for International Settlements – the club of leading central bankers – Mr Richardson persuaded his colleagues from other countries to agree on the doctrine of parental responsibility.[97] This meant that any branch or subsidiary of a foreign bank which encountered difficulties would be its parent bank's responsibility. The Bank followed this up by requiring 'letters of comfort' from the foreign parents of banks operating in London; the letters were a written guarantee that the parent would assume responsibility in any difficulties.[98]

The letters were important because so many foreign institutions operated in London, but they also had another less obvious significance. The pace of change in international banking had produced novel and complex forms of ownership – such as consortium banks – where traditional lines of responsibility established by conventional forms of ownership were obscured. 'Letters of comfort' were designed to clarify this obscurity. Thus even at the height of the crisis we can see attempts being made to adopt new methods of public regulation to cope with the changed shape of banking.

The Bank's influence in the crisis also went beyond the boundaries of the banking system. The Control Committee's activities, and the Bank's numerous informal efforts to support the Committee in other ways, were all overtly directed to supporting the fringe banks; but since the fringe and the property companies were tied together in misfortune the rescue was indirectly a way of supporting the property market, for if the afflicted banks had not received deposits they would have been forced to call in their property loans. This in turn would have bankrupted many firms and put large amounts of property on to an already depressed market. The Bank initially tried to persuade other members of the Control Committtee to help property firms. When they declined it worked hard behind the scenes throughout 1974 to prevent companies collapsing, by lobbying creditors such as the clearing banks to persuade them not to call in the debts of property firms. For the most part it was successful in these efforts, but even where a company was a hopeless case the Bank did not give up. When the Stern property group collapsed in the summer of 1974 owing over £100 million the Bank used its influence to help work out a special scheme of arrangements, which meant that the liquidator did not have to dispose of £200 million worth of property when the market was weak.[99]

These activities shored up property from total collapse; re-establishing its secure foundations depended on a change in the public policies which had helped destroy confidence at the end of 1973. During the following year the Bank therefore lobbied Whitehall for some relaxation of the restrictions on the commercial property market. The urgency of the Bank's arguments is indicated by its willingness to take the case to the very highest levels. Thus on 8 May 1974 the Governor and his Deputy went to the Chancellor to request help for the property market. 'The Bank', they told him,

> feared that both the Stern Group and another property company were about to collapse and that such a crash would affect the banking system as a whole. Mr. Richardson argued that the main inhibition in the market was the freeze on commercial rents; if the Government gave an early indication that the freeze would be relaxed, a rescue operation would be easier.[100]

The Chancellor declined to help, but the Bank continued its advocacy throughout the summer, even carrying the argument to the Prime

Minister.[101] This persistence would doubtless be interpreted by radical critics of the Bank as further evidence that it is the tool of the City interests, and indeed it is not difficult to think of worthier objects of the Bank's attention in the stricken British economy of 1974. But the shape of the crisis dictated the Bank's behaviour. It is clear from numerous official statements that it looked with distaste on much of the property market. Yet, just as it was compelled to save some undesirable fringe banks, so it was compelled also to try to restore the fortunes of property, since only in this way could numerous financial institutions be hauled out of insolvency. The Bank's persistence was finally rewarded in December 1974, when the Government ended the freeze on business rents which had been introduced by its Conservative predecessor. The effect was immediate: property shares began to rise, and within two months the FT Property Share Index had doubled over its low of the previous November, outstripping the growth of all equities by 25 per cent.[102]

(c) *Costs and consequences*

By the beginning of 1975 the worst of the crisis was over, though this was far from clear at the time to those who were in the middle of the turmoil. Not until March did the Control Committee's lending finally peak at £1,285 million; not until the autumn of 1975 did it drop below £1,000 million.[103] Many difficulties still lay ahead: the expensive and embarrassing rescues, like the help for Slater Walker, which the Bank was forced to mount alone, and the even greater embarrassments of public inquiries into the losses made by the Crown Agents. By the end of 1974 some attempt was nevertheless being made to reorganise the stricken banks, and to count the cost of the affair.

Any narrative of the rescue might reasonably conclude with an estimate of these costs. The task is impossible: the monetary costs have been hidden, the other costs are literally incalculable. It is the last great triumph of esoteric politics that the Bank has without difficulty declined to reveal the full size of its involvement. It acknowledged making provision for losses exceeding £50 million in connection with its contributions to the Control Committee, but this published figure has been arrived at after offsetting losses against other profitable activities.[104] The figures also omit completely the cost of the rescues which the Bank carried out alone; and as the Deputy Governor, Sir Jasper Hollom, has said, the Bank's biggest losses were incurred outside the Control Committee, in such separate rescues as the Slater Walker affair.

The refusal to reveal true costs was entirely in keeping with the tradition of banking politics in Britain. The Bank took the view that the money used was from its own resources, and that details about losses were sensitive banking issues best dealt with confidentially. It carried the argument because backbench MPs who questioned Bank officials about the rescue were ready to accept this traditional assumption. The only precise figure for losses by a public body is the Fay Committee's estimate that the Crown Agents lost £212 million as a result of the combined crises in banking and property. The full costs of the clearing banks cannot yet be calculated, since even now all support operations are not at an end: the latest official estimate at the time of writing put the Control Committee's remaining lending at about £300 million.[105]

The incalculable wider costs include the damage done to confidence in the financial system at a time when the stability of the whole economy was in any case uncertain. The rescue also consumed scarce time and skill at a period in the mid-1970s when manufacturing industry's financial problems already demanded close attention. Against this loss must be set a considerable gain for the clearing banks: the crisis, in destroying part of the fringe, destroyed some of their most successful rivals. In this way, ironically, one of the original aims of Competition and Credit Control was achieved: the fringe was 'contracted' (the Bank's word), though the ferocity of contraction almost caused the whole system to expire.

The economic historian will want to compute the exact monetary cost and to estimate the wider financial consequences of the secondary banking crisis. Anyone interested in the politics of British banking will fix on a different set of results. The crisis altered banking regulation, and the inevitable consequence was an alteration in banking politics. The system of prudential regulation subsequently developed to control banking had marks which the City traditionally disliked: legality, bureaucratic detail and open argument. The rise of novel kinds of regulation, and the problems of prudential control in the new, risky world of banking are examined in the next chapter.

6 Rules, Risks and the Law

Men of business have keen sensations but short memories.

1 MARKETS, REGULATION AND FORMALITY

The events of 1974 were a crisis in the everyday sense of causing great danger for banking, but they were also critical in a more exactly clinical way: they marked a moment of fevered change after which the condition of the system was irreversibly altered. The immediate effects were cathartic: individuals, institutions and practices were purged from financial life. The effects in the longer term were immensely complicated. By destroying part of the banking system the crisis weakened the customary assumptions on which prudential regulation rested. Yet to alter the rules was to change more than the technicalities of financial surveillance. Banking regulation and banking politics were entwined. Devising new methods of control appropriate to the growing scale and complexity of financial markets opened banking to influences customarily thought undesirable: Whitehall, Westminster, the courts. The major theme in regulation since 1974 concerns the problem of choosing between new means of regulation and preserving esoteric politics.

This dilemma has been made even more uncomfortable by the continuing development of financial markets. Complexity was the root of the secondary banking crisis, but its effects did not end with the crisis. Financial markets still show an extraordinary capacity for adaptation and invention. Thus the authorities face the twin problems of responding to the conditions revealed in the mid-1970s and matching the continuing inventiveness of markets. Difficulties have been further intensified by the growing scale of financial institutions. The crisis of 1974 was primarily a national affair; in the 1980s the prudential regulation of supranational banks and markets is an increasingly pressing concern. The history of regulation since the crisis is therefore marked by conflicting forces: a drive to greater formality, but a fear that formality will destroy the traditional character of the City and weaken the ability of the authorities to match the inventiveness of financial markets. These conflicting influences are evident in three areas: the immediate attempts by the Bank of England to remedy defects in the system of supervision when the crisis became plain; the introduction of a comprehensive legal framework for regulation in the form of the 1979 Banking Act; and the search for some means of control to match the scale and ingenuity of supranational markets. Each of these areas is examined in turn in the following pages, but most space is given to the Banking Act. This is because the contradictions and ambiguities in that law illustrate to perfection the dilemmas of banking regulation in the 1980s.

2 CRISIS, CHANGE AND REGULATION

To its victims the secondary banking crisis was a disaster. Yet crises also have benefits, because they hasten reform and innovation. This is partly because imminent disaster acts, Johnsonian fashion, to concentrate the mind wonderfully in the search for remedies, and partly because the realisation of crisis shifts the existing distribution of power by discrediting those associated with old ways of doing things. The crisis in banking worked in exactly these ways. The Bank of England's efforts to remedy defects in the system of supervision were consequently inseparable from the hectic crisis management practised in 1974; but it was a measure of the power of the established ideas that the crisis was over six months old before it shifted attachment to traditional methods. It took the increased force of events in the summer of 1974 to destroy powerful institutions and deeply embedded practices.

The first victim was the Discount Office, the symbol of the Bank's old way of gathering information through the informal City grapevine. In July it was replaced by a new Banking Supervision Division. The Principal of the Office, James Keogh, became an adviser to the Governor, and later retired early to work for the Singapore Monetary Authority. In his place the Bank appointed George Blunden as Head of the new Division.[1] These changes signalled that the Bank was publicly discarding the long-established notion that supervision could be conducted as a by-product of intervention in the money markets. This renunciation in turn destroyed the belief that it could be practised by a small number of people using chiefly their personal knowledge to form judgements about who could be trusted in the banking community. The rapid increase in numbers employed in supervision measures the change which occurred: the Discount Office had a staff of fifteen; eight months after it was established the new Division had seven principals and over thirty other staff; within three more years the numbers had grown to seventy.[2] These changes in organisation showed that the intense crisis in the summer of 1974 had altered both outlook and influence in the Bank. Traditional doctrines strongly resisted the creation of a separate class of bank supervisors, yet here was the Bank publicly creating precisely such a group. The Discount Office's abolition also indicated the rise in influence of the regulators. The simple signs of this were the greater resources and status given to supervision, marked both by the rapid increase in the number of staff and by the fact that whereas Keogh was a Principal his successor was a Head of Department.

These institutional changes were stimulated by the fact that the crisis destroyed customary assumptions about the kind and amount of information which was required of banks. More staff were needed because closer and more complex supervision was to be conducted. A month after the Supervision Division was founded the Bank requested more frequent and more complete returns from the non-clearing banks. On 20 August it asked those from whom it already received statistics to supplement existing returns with more complete figures submitted quarterly. In addition it asked all the 'Section 123 Banks' – the group containing most of the casualties – to begin submitting information. The close connection between these requests and the problem of coping with the immediate crisis is illustrated by the speed with which the Bank was asking for the new information: having delayed for over seven months since the difficulties of the fringe first became clear, it now wanted the new statistics in the September banking returns. The kind of new information which the Bank asked for was also plainly influenced by the horror stories which were being uncovered as the Control Committee examined the stricken secondary banks: the details included information about the maturity patterns of sterling deposits, loans to associated companies and standby facilities.[3]

This new information was asked for in the traditional language of 'requests', but the politeness hid the fact that the crisis had also increased the Bank's power to require statistics from the banking system. The old style of supervision inhibited the Bank's ability to require information because of the high value placed on confidentiality. The authorities were thus never able to simply demand extra information, nor did banks feel obliged to supply it. Confidentiality was bound up with esoteric politics, since it was a powerful justification for keeping public regulators out of the detailed business of banking. As a result, the Bank had historically extended its right to request information only in exchange for offering privilges to such institutions as Discount Houses and leading merchant banks. The crisis of 1974 compelled the Bank to breach this conventional assumption that information only in exchange for offering privileges to such institutions as Discount Houses and leading merchant banks. The crisis of 1974 assertive way. As the Head of Banking Supervision remarked about the episode: 'Before the traumas ... smaller deposit takers would probably have been unwilling to participate in such a supervisory scheme without the benefit of a greater degree of recognition from us; but because of those traumas the extension of supervision has seemed natural and desirable and has been accepted by them'.[4]

A separate supervision division, a large group of specialised supervisors, demands by the Bank for more detailed statistical returns: all these endangered the privacy, informality and autonomy which banks had enjoyed under the old order. Salvaging something of the traditional system has been a difficult business, for the Bank is impaled on the horns of a dilemma: the new markets are too large and inventive to be supervised in the old ways, but too capable of swift change to be effectively regulated by formal rules.

The desire to escape this dilemma has deeply affected both banking regulation and banking politics. The effort at escape is partly rhetorical. The official Bank of England account is that the changes introduced since 1974 mark only the continuing evolution of the old system, and no official speech is complete without a tribute to the merits of traditional regulation. This rhetoric is important in reassuring the City that new rules will be administered with the flexibility demanded by markets. The City's sense of reassurance also has more substantial foundations, for since 1974 a determined effort has indeed been made to graft the new detail and formality on to the old informality and trust. Even in its request for new information at the height of the crisis the Bank stressed that prudential regulations would not be uniformly applied to all banks and that any requirements would be 'tailored to suit particular cases'.[5] This preference for individual discrimination over uniform regulation has marked the way the Bank has used its greatly improved statistics since 1974. The returns submitted are analysed in the Supervision Division, where certain key ratios (covering, for instance, capital adequacy and liquidity) are worked out. This statistical exercise is, however, only a preliminary to a more important stage, regular discussions with senior management of the individual institutions. These discussions are, in the Bank's words, 'the cornerstone of the ... system of supervision'. Their style is designed to recreate the intimacy and informality of the old approach to regulation. Thus the Bank emphasises that it looks for 'a relaxed two-way exchange not for an inquisitorial examination'.[6] The discussions also try to retain the traditional practice of exercising control through influencing key individuals rather than through applying fixed rules. In George Blunden's words: 'Frequent discussion between senior management of banks and senior officials of the Bank of England are more conducive to the maintenance of good banking practices than the technique adopted in many other countries of sending in teams of inspectors to examine the banks' books.' The Governor puts it more pithily: 'It is more useful to seek to influence a bank's policy from the top than to try to monitor its procedures from the bottom.'[7]

This is the official, benign view of what has been happening since 1974. Yet the great increase in the range and diversity of the institutions monitored, in the amount of information gathered and in the administrative resources devoted to supervision all transformed the system of regulation. The ambiguities and paradoxes in the Bank's attempt to graft the new formality on the old privacy and trust were especially clear in the unique treatment given to the clearing banks. The clearers (and the British Overseas Banks) were exempted from the 1974 request for more frequent and more detailed statistical returns. The formal reason for exemption was that the clearers' businesses were sufficiently complicated to require separate arrangements.[8] This argument allowed them to negotiate exemption from much of the formality and detail introduced elsewhere after 1974. At the end of that year the Bank and the clearers established a Working Party to consider 'the capital and liquidity adequacy of banks', especially in the light of the changes in banking practice produced by the new wholesale money markets. The report of the Working Party (which established the subsequent pattern of regulation for the clearing banks) emphasised the extent to which the clearers managed to negotiate especially favourable arrangements. In place of the quarterly examination by the Supervision Division to which all other banks were subject, the clearers were to hold only annual 'discussions' with the Bank. These discussions with the Supervision Division gave the Bank's supervisors no power of direction. Any matters of substance were to be referred to higher managerial levels culminating, if necessary, in 'particular topics being submitted to the Governor and to individual Chairmen'.[9]

The special arrangements devised for the clearers after the secondary banking crisis had an importance beyond the immediate circumstances in which they were worked out, for the idea of creating two classes of institutions distinguished by their prestige and by the strictness with which they were supervised reappeared in a much more elaborate way in the 1979 Banking Act. The passage and implementation of the Act revived doubts about how far the formality demanded by growing scale and complexity could be reconciled with traditional preferences for more informal supervision.

3 LEGISLATING FOR COMPLEXITY

Banking in Britain has long been influenced by the statute book, but not until 1979 did bankers work inside a consciously constructed legal framework. The law had previously impinged in unintended and often chaotic ways; indeed this was the legal background to the secondary banking crisis. This chaos was the result of esoteric politics, which resisted the conscious and systematic introduction of the statute book into regulation. The 1979 Banking Act thus did more than alter the law; it changed banking politics.

(a) *The puzzle of the Banking Act*

The Act introduces two main provisions: banks and other institutions taking deposits from the public have to be either recognised or licensed; and all 'recognised banks' and 'licensed deposit takers' have to contribute to a Deposit Protection Fund designed to give depositors 75 per cent compensation for any sum up to £10,000 lost by the failure of an authorised institution. The legal powers to administer the law are vested almost completely in the Bank of England, though under certain circumstances appeals against the Bank's decision can be made to a tribunal established by the Treasury.[10]

This comparatively short Act is revolutionary in British banking. The conscious introduction of the law on this scale is very different from the piecemeal and often unexpected legal intrusions experienced in the past, and it reverses powerful traditional expectations that banking can be regulated informally and privately. The two classes of institutions – licensed deposit taker and recognised bank – supersede the multiplicity of previous kinds of banking recognition and discard the notion, so central to traditional regulation, that there should be a ladder of recognition with numerous rungs which an institution could gradually ascend by expanding its services and improving its status in financial markets. The debates on the Act also exposed the banking community to an unprecedented amount of parliamentary attention; its implementation was accompanied by an unusual kind of formal lobbying and open argument. All these factors explain why the Act may be said not only to have changed the system of regulation but also to have altered the politics of British banking.

The official reasons given for introducing this legislation were straightforward. They were expressed summarily in the White Paper which outlined the original proposals in August 1976, and were repeated persistently thereafter.[11] The secondary banking crisis, the justification ran, had shown that there existed gaps in the system of supervision. The purpose of the new law was to close those gaps, and in doing so to give adequate protection to depositors; indeed according to Mr Denzil Davies, who as Minister of State at the Treasury had parliamentary responsibility for the proposals, the Bill had 'a single objective and that is the protection of depositors'.[12] Notwithstanding this single objective, official explanations for introducing the legislation also added a subsidiary reason. When Britain entered the European Economic Community efforts were already afoot to 'harmonize' – in Common Market jargon – banking regulation throughout the Community. Since Britain's banks were subject to a uniquely small amount of legal control any move towards common standards was almost bound to increase the significance of law in British banking. The first EEC Directive on credit institutions, which was adopted in December 1977, did indeed require a system of prior authorisation of all banking enterprises.[13]

These straightforward explanations actually make almost no sense of the legislation. The notion that our entry into Europe had much relevance can be quickly dismissed. It is true that the 1977 Directive did make it necessary to clarify the legal status of banks, but it demanded none of the key features of the Act, such as the two-tier system of authorisation or the Deposit Protection Fund. Indeed after Britain's entry into the EEC the Bank and the British Bankers' Association had already lobbied successfully in Brussels to reduce the amount of legal detail required by the Community's harmonisation measures.[14] The conclusion is inescapable: the demands of Europe could have been met with a simpler piece of legislation, or with no legislation at all.

Picturing the Act as remedying defects in supervision and deposit protection revealed by the events of 1974 is similarly incomprehensible. We know that the key changes in supervision had already been made by the Bank of England before the 1976 White Paper was published. The parts of the Act which protect deposits are irrelevant to the crisis which occurred in 1974, and to the most important problems of prudential regulation in modern banking. The events of the mid-1970s were the first great crisis of modern banking: that is, the problems were confined largely to the wholesale money markets, and were magnified because inter-bank borrowing in the markets transmitted the difficulties of a small number of institutions throughout the system. Developing rules to eliminate this risk of system failure is now the greatest problem in banking regulation.[15] The Act says nothing about this problem. The Deposit Protection Fund – the part of the legislation which provoked most parliamentary argument – is largely irrelevant to the wholesale markets, since it secures only 75 per cent of the first £10,000 of a deposit. The size of the Fund is also quite insufficient to cope with a crisis in the wholesale markets. The levy is designed to raise between five and six million pounds initially, and additional contributions cannot exceed 0.3 per cent of an institution's deposit base.[16] Yet, at the height of the secondary banking crisis the clearing banks had 40 per cent of their deposits and reserves committed to the Control Committee's activities alone.

The puzzle of the Banking Act may thus be briefly described: it purported to reform banking supervision many years after the substance of reform had actually been carried out by the Bank; and the deposits which it protected were only a small part of the money endangered in 1974, or at risk in any future crisis. This apparent irrelevance led some Conservative critics of the Bill to conclude that it resulted, in Mr Peter Tapsell's words, from 'the fashionable preoccupation with consumer protection'.[17] There is something in this view. During the 1970s the notion that economic activity was now too complex for consumers to be able to make free, rational decisions became a customary assumption in many parts of Whitehall. This assumption produced a considerable body of consumer protection laws. Parts of the Bill were plainly borrowed from these laws: thus the Deposit Protection Fund is very like the protection given to insurance policyholders by the Policyholders' Protection Act, 1975.[18] The influence of customary assumptions favouring consumer protection was also plain in official contributions to the parliamentary debates: the Minister, Mr Denzil Davies, explicitly contrasted the doctrine of 'caveat deposito' (sic) which shaped traditional banking regulation with the greater protection given by the new Act.[19]

Yet to picture the Act as only the product of custom and fashion would be unjust to its authors, especially those in the Treasury. The Minister and his advisers were undoubtedly influenced by consumerism, but they were aware that consumer protection as conventionally understood was a minor issue in both the 1974 crisis and in the wholesale money markets generally. The stress on protecting small depositors did not reflect an unthinking extension of consumer protection into banking; it reflected rather the effort to solve problems of political management which had been created by the resort to legislation. To understand why it was necessary to turn to the law the attitudes and interests of the Bank of England need examination, for it was given the key role in the legislation.

(b) *'New policy, new politics'*

In the parliamentary debates on the Bill, critics of the legislation sometimes implied that it had been wished on a reluctant Bank.[20] The implication was half true: the Bank wanted legislation; it did not want much of the Banking Bill. It was the first important institution to be driven to the conclusion that some new law was needed, but the conversion was grudging because using the statute book faced the Bank with a familiar problem: how to reconcile legal control with its traditional preference for privacy and informality. The Bank's ambivalence was the key influence in shaping the Bill.

Traditional regulation worked by excluding from the banking system those with excessively competitive appetites. The revolution in banking during the 1960s and early 1970s destroyed the effectiveness of these exclusions and showed, to use the Governor's words, that 'self-regulation can be put to too great a test if competition from the less-regulated and less-disciplined is too easily permitted'.[21] The crisis of 1974 helped the Bank to regain control over the existing institutions but offered no guarantee that it could in the longer term exclude the 'less-regulated and less-disciplined'. To ensure this the Bank needed to gain control over the scattered statutes which allowed a wide range of institutions to use the banking label.

From 1974 the Bank therefore had a consistent attitude: banks and similar deposit takers should be authorised by a single statute which the Bank of England would administer with wide discretionary power. The statute would give it control over entrants to banking; wide discretion would minimise legal and political intervention in the affairs of the banking community. The conventional distinction which the Bank traditionally made between banks proper and other deposit takers provided the germ of a solution to the problem of reconciling legal powers and flexibility, for recognised banks would form an upper tier exempt from the full details of legal control. In November 1975 the Governor publicly defined what was now the Bank's established doctrine. Extending effective regulation to deposit takers beyond 'banks in the full sense', he observed, probably required giving the Bank statutory authority; but full legalism was not appropriate to banks because 'it would foster a more legalistic attitude in other areas of their business'.[22]

Here is the public justification for the first proposals for legislation which the Bank was now privately communicating to the Treasury. These initial proposals differed in important details from what appeared in the White Paper of August 1976. The Bank initially wanted a system of authorisation which gave it very great discretionary powers: a two-tier system of recognition and licensing; no lists of criteria to be used in distinguishing between the two tiers; no appeal from the Bank's decision about where to place applicants; and no Deposit Protection Fund.[23]

'Policies determine politics', says Lowi's well known aphorism.[24] By extension, new policies create new politics: change the substance of policy and you change the range of interests and institutions who participate in its making. The Bank was now to learn this lesson. If it wanted a new law, it was in the hands of the Treasury, which would have to manage the legislation in the Cabinet and in Parliament. The Minister of State in charge of the Bill, and his advisers, had a presumptive right to comment on the proposals, since they would be responsible for publicly defending them. Thus the Bank surrendered its monopoly of control over the details of banking supervision. The points made by the Treasury on the Bank's first proposals could be said to confirm the traditional fear of bankers that introducing the law only opened the way for the formality and rigidity of the civil service and the statute book. An alternative way of putting the same point is to say that the Treasury expressed a concern for accountability which has traditionally been greater in the Civil Service and Westminster than in the City. The Treasury disliked the vagueness which surrounded the distinction between the two tiers of institutions, and it wanted those aggrieved by the Bank's decision to be able to appeal against them in the courts. To this the bank replied with a familiar defence of flexibility and the observation that it wanted to keep lawyers out of banking. (The latter was a slightly tactless point: the Minister was a lawyer.)

The compromises necessary to reconcile these different views were sketched in the White Paper and developed more fully in the Bill which eventually became law. The Bank conceded a right of appeal against its decisions, but to a Tribunal appointed by the Treasury rather than to the courts. It proved impossible to exclude lawyers completely, however, for appeals to the courts on points of law were also, inevitably, allowed. The Bank recouped some of this loss of administrative discretion (or flexibility, as it would put it) in the compromise over spelling out the criteria distinguishing the two tiers, which were drawn up in such a convoluted way as to give the Bank great freedom of action. The upper tier of recognised banks was designed to allow the Bank to preserve its traditional relations with 'banks proper'. Thus the criteria for recognised banks included providing a 'wide range of banking services' (which let in the clearing banks) or a 'specialised banking service' (which let in the Discount Houses). To exclude further any challenge to the Bank's discretion the Schedule also declared: 'Any question whether an institution is to be regarded ... as providing at any time either a wide range of banking services or a highly specialised banking service shall be determined by the bank.'[25]

The two-tier system, and the considerable discretion allowed in allocating applicants to the tiers, was a great victory for the Bank and for those institutions that it traditionally considered to be 'banks proper'. Recognised bank status is a rich prize: only institutions in the top tier can use the banking label, and most of the Bank's legal powers to intervene in the detailed management of an institution are applicable only to the lower tier of licensed deposit takers. In the past 'banks proper', subject as they were to official control, had often been at a disadvantage in competing with the 'less-regulated and less-disciplined'; the two-tier system decisively redressed the balance of advantage. It is little wonder that the commercial banking establishment welcomed this part of the legislation. In Lord O'Brien's words, speaking of the problems posed by fringe banks, 'Many of these institutions purported to be banks and took deposits while at the same time doing business which was far removed from banking proper. The purpose of this legislation now is to distinguish between such institutions and proper banks.'[26]

The fact that the second major provision in the legislation, the Deposit Protection Fund, in some degree qualified these advantages explains why 'banks proper' so fiercely opposed it. The DPF was largely a Treasury invention.[27] The Bank of England, in using the statute book to regain control over the banking system, had now to concede to Whitehall some say in the details of regulation. The Treasury in turn was influenced by the customary assumption in Whitehall that regulation should protect individual citizens who dealt with large, complex institutions, especially when those institutions were given a public seal of approval through recognition and licensing. This belief that the Bill should contain a measure of consumer protection was strengthened by the problems of securing Cabinet and parliamentary assent to the legislation. In some pessimistic accounts of parliamentary democracy the actual passage of legislation is treated as a trivial interlude between the bargaining which precedes drafting and the implementation which follows enactment. But legislation itself consumes scarce resources, and before any Bill is sponsored by government it must claim a share of those resources.

One of the scarcest of all resources is time, especially parliamentary time. The proposals in the August 1976 White paper could only become law if the Cabinet was convinced that they were important enough to merit a prominent place in the Government's legislative timetable. Recall the immediate circumstances: the Government could never be certain of majority support in Parliament; Labour was instinctively suspicious of bankers and had a left wing in Parliament which was hostile to the City; the Prime Minister (Mr Callaghan) and the Chancellor believed the Bank was incompetent, following the sterling crises of the mid-1970s.[28] The chances were therefore slim that time would be found for a Bill which only gave the Bank extensive, unfettered powers. The DPF was thus needed in bargaining for a place in the legislative queue. In both Cabinet and Commons the Bill was presented as a measure to protect small depositors. Even then difficulties remained: eyebrows were raised in Cabinet at the notion that £10,000 was a small deposit. The Bill had a hard struggle for parliamentary time, being crowded out of the 1977/78 session.[29] The great powers which it gave to the Bank of England were also questioned: the Prime Minister, who was particularly disillusioned with the Bank, apparently asked whether it was the best body for supervision. The question was pertinent, for in other countries it is common for regulation to be carried out by a specialised institution, not by the central bank. The query nevertheless still came to nothing: it would have taken more than a passing Prime Ministerial interest to prise responsibility for regulation from the Bank's hands.

(c) *Lobbying from Lombard Street*

The problems of political management which produced the Deposit Protection Fund were symptomatic of more general changes in the politics of banking. The growing scale and diversity of the banking system, and the growing impact of central government on the financial community, had even before the introduction of legislation encouraged bankers to seek ways of influencing policy outside informal contacts with the Bank of England.[30] The abolition of the clearing bank cartel in 1971 led the clearers to turn the Committee of London Clearing Bankers into a formally organised pressure group. In the following year, at the Bank's encouragement, the British Bankers' Association, previously an institution of little importance, was reorganised as a formal pressure group to lobby for the whole banking community, particularly in Brussels. In the mid-1970s the London Clearing Banks, faced with a threat of nationalisation by the Labour Party, appointed Mr Brendon Sewill, a former head of the Conservative Party's Research Department, to mount an ambitious public campaign against Labour's threat.

The consultations over the Banking Bill accelerated this shift away from the private and informal exercise of influence to presenting the corporate view of the banking community through formally organised groups. The detailed preparation of the legislation led to particularly close contacts between, on the one hand, the teams of Bank and Treasury officials concerned with the Bill and, on the other, officers of the British Bankers' Association and the Committee of London Clearing Bankers.[31] These direct contacts between Whitehall and Lombard Street had both an immediate and a long-term importance. They immediately allowed the banking community, in a way characteristic of organised pressure politics, to trawl through the details of the proposals.[32] In the longer term they encouraged the further development of open and formal interest representation. In some measure this latter change was welcomed by bankers, who found the Bank of England an increasingly unsatisfactory substitute for formal lobbying.[33] But entering the mainstream of pressure group politics also had costs: differences which had once been expressed privately now became open, while questions which traditionally were the subject of esoteric argument were exposed to the blast of adversary politics.

These costs are well illustrated by the parliamentary lobbying which took place between the autumn of 1978 and April of the following year, when the Bill finally became law. The detailed consultations which preceded the parliamentary debates meant that by Second Reading in the Commons the big banks were opposed only to one major part of the legislation, the proposal for a Deposit Protection Fund. The British Bankers' Association and the Committee of London Clearing Bankers thus concentrated their resources on fighting the DPF. The introduction of the Bill into Parliament had now shifted banking politics to a new arena. For almost the first time bankers were compelled to lobby in Westminster, and were thus faced with assumptions about the appropriate way to express political differences very different from those to which the City was accustomed. The Parliamentarians – especially of course the Opposition – treated the Bill in the manner usual to the Commons: it was one more means of fighting the adversary battle between the parties. The bankers, by contrast, saw Parliament only as a last chance to fight the DPF and a few less important items in the proposals. The bankers were thus rather a disappointment to the Opposition, which wanted to be supplied with ammunition for wholesale criticism of the Bill. The Opposition in turn were a disappointment to the bankers, for fighting the adversary battle in Parliament confronted the Conservatives with a familiar dilemma: they had to criticise the legislation trenchantly, but needed to temper this with a judgement about the substantive merits of the Bill, bearing in mind the prospect that electoral victory might make them responsible for its implementation. The dilemma was solved in a customary way: in the Commons the weight of parliamentary rhetoric was thrown against the consumer protection philosophy in the DPF, but when the issue came to a vote the bankers could not persuade the Conservatives to go into the Division lobby against the Fund. The Opposition prudently told the bankers that a vote against would look foolish if a small bank subsequently collapsed with the loss of depositors' money.

The intensity with which the big banks disliked the DPF shaped the parliamentary arguments over the Bill. The Opposition in the Commons, anxious to carry on the adversary battle, had to rely on the banking pressure groups to brief it with informed arguments against the legislation.[34] The bankers, by contrast, were uninterested in the partisan battle, and had a serious objection only to the DPF. The ammunition supplied to MPs thus chiefly concerned the Fund. The result made the debates on the DPF the longest and most heated during the passage of the legislation through the Commons. In the Lords also the BBA and the CLCB assembled a phalanx of banking peers to condemn the Fund.

This intense dislike is at first sight surprising, for the direct costs of contributing to the Fund were trivial to the largest institutions. Although payments were levied in rough proportion to the size of a bank's deposits, during consultations the big clearers had succeeded in placing an upper limit of £300,000 on any single contribution.[35] A bill of this size was insignificant for a big bank, especially as it could be offset against tax. Opposition arose in part from a simple reluctance to hand over even modest sums of money; but the intensity of that opposition was due to the uncertainties produced by the changing and unpredictable nature of banking politics. For the first time Lombard Street was coming under control from Whitehall and Westminster. The Fund itself set a particularly dangerous precedent by allowing central government to put a levy on the banks. Who knew where it might lead? The fear had a good foundation: in 1981 the Chancellor imposed a levy on bank profits to help reduce the Government's borrowing requirement.

The most important cause of opposition to the scheme, however, lay in the fact that it contradicted a central aim of the first part of the Act. The two tiers of recognition consciously discriminated in favour of institutions which had traditionally been close to the Bank. Recognised banking status was a sign to depositors that an institution had full approval from the Bank of England; no Fund was needed to tell depositors that their money was safe. By contrast, for those consigned to the second tier of 'licensed deposit taker' the Fund could help considerably in reassuring anyone with up to £10,000 to lend. In the debates about the Fund the problem was expressed as one of imprudence: the Fund, it was argued, would encourage depositors to lend to risky institutions at rates of interest higher than prudent banks could offer.[36] The big banks which would pay most were thus offered the galling prospect of contributing to a Fund which encouraged smaller competitors to take away business by engaging in high risk practices, safe in the knowledge that depositors would be reassured by the existence of the DPF.

The campaign against the DPF emphasised how resort to the statute book had altered the politics of banking, by changing the conventions of argument and the range of interests which could intervene in the argument. Differences which could once have been suppressed or discussed privately were now openly voiced. It was obvious, for instance, that in opposing the Fund the British Bankers' Association was voicing the views of its leaders, who were drawn from the banking establishment. But the BBA also had a large membership, some of whom might benefit from the reassurance which the DPF gave to depositors. This explains why, despite invitations from Whitehall, the BBA never managed to produce an alternative to the kind of deposit insurance provided by the Fund.[37] Even the clearing banks began to divide in public when it became obvious that the DPF would become law. The heaviest proportional burden was on medium sized banks, such as the Scottish clearers, because the large London clearing banks benefited from the upper limit of £300,000, while small deposit takers could pay as little as £2,500. In the Committee stages in the Lords, therefore, the Scottish clearers broke ranks by (unsuccessfully) pressing an amendment designed to alter the balance of contribution in favour of the medium sized banks.[38] Open lobbying likewise occurred against the first part of the Act. The finance houses, anticipating correctly that they would be consigned by the Bank to the second tier of licensed deposit takers, lobbied (unsuccessfully) up to Cabinet level for a third, intermediate tier into which they could be slotted.[39]

At the root of all this disturbance to the traditional pattern of banking politics lay social complexity; even the most trivial episodes in the passage of the legislation showed its destructive effects on esoteric politics. Thus in the Banking Bill, as in much legislation, the amendments conceded by government were only in a few cases a retreat from the intention of the original proposals. Most redrafting was designed to remedy unforeseen consequences of the original wording, particularly to exclude institutions and practices never intended to be subject to the legislation. This is a classic outcome of complexity, for interdependence between institutions in an advanced economy constantly produces such 'surprises'.[40] The political consequence of these surprises was to widen the range of institutions interested in lobbying to influence the legislation. During the Bill's passage banking regulation thus become the interest not only of the traditional elite in the City, but also of municipal and 'penny' banks, of the Law Society, and even of travel agents.[41]

Complexity destroys the esoteric politics of banking not only by drawing in a wide range of new interests, but by forcing the banks to pay attention to parts of the statute book not nominally concerned with the regulation of banking. This is exactly illustrated by the way the 1979 Act was used for the apparently irrelevant purpose of amending the 1974 Consumer Credit Act. The story of the amendment illustrates

Rules, Risks and the Law 129

why the banks have been increasingly forced to abandon the Bank of England as an instrument for exercising influence in Whitehall, and to turn instead to more orthodox lobbying. The 1974 Act required those who gave consumer credit to state the true rate of interest charged on loans. When the legislation was originally proposed the clearing banks realised that if the new law were applied to bank overdrafts, calculating and publishing true interest charges would be very burdensome. In the established manner of esoteric politics the Committee of London Clearing Bankers put the point to the Bank of England, which gave an assurance that the Bill would be amended to exclude bank overdrafts. The assurance was not fulfilled, the Bill was not amended, and the banks were unexpectedly left to make complicated and expensive calculations. This grievance surfaced persistently in the House of Lords' debates on the Banking Bill four years later.[42] As the Bill reached its final stages in March 1979 the bankers saw their chance. The original failure to find a space for the legislation in the 1977/78 session now fortuitously meant that the Bill was one of those measures whose progress was halted by the fall of the Labour Government on 28 March. To save the measure it was necessary to pass it quickly through the final stages in both Houses. The CLCB lobbyists told the Treasury that if the Consumer Credit Act were not amended as part of the new legislation they would ensure that banking peers in the Lords talked the Bill out. The amendment was conceded.

This example might suggest that bankers have adapted effortlessly, indeed ruthlessly, to the decline of esoteric politics. The banking lobby, especially the CLCB, is indeed an impressive operation. Its growing sophistication can be measured fairly precisely, in the transformation of the CLCB into a large and highly organised pressure group, and less precisely by comparing the perfunctory evidence which the clearing banks supplied to the Radcliffe Committee at the end of the 1950s with the massive and impressive documentation submitted two decades later to the Wilson Committee. Yet this move into more public and partisan areas has great dangers which bankers themselves are quick to realise. The danger is epitomised by the paradox at the heart of the Banking Act, a measure designed to protect the institutions which traditionally practised esoteric politics, but which used the law to give that protection. The waning of esoteric politics produced hesitation and contradiction. Thus the clearing banks favoured the 1979 Act because most of it was plainly in their interests, but in the parliamentary debates it was Lord Selsdon (the Midland) and Lord Seebohm (Barclays) who voiced most clearly the fear that the law would have destructive effects. As Lord Seebohm lamented: 'If we go on chipping away at the flexibility and the old customs of the City ... we shall sooner or later find that the City loses its paramount position as the financial centre of the world'.[43]

(d) *'A little misunderstanding'*

The first years of the new Act have been dominated by the task of considering applicants for recognition as banks and as licensed deposit takers. It is too soon to offer a decisive judgement about how far the legislation has allowed the Bank to retain its old relations with the banking elite while controlling other deposit takers in a more formal way. The present evidence nevertheless suggests that the growing scale and complexity of banking continues to work destructively on the old ways of doing things. Recognition and licensing have greatly increased the scale of the supervisory task. When the Bill was first introduced the Bank acknowledged responsibility for about three hundred institutions; by the time most of the first flood of applicants had been dealt with it had authorised 279 banks and licensed 259 deposit takers.[44]

Nor has it been possible to implement the Act free of legal entanglements, for some of those whose applications were rejected have, inevitably, appealed against the Bank's judgement. The disappointment of those placed in the second tier of licensed deposit takers – it includes large finance houses – has compelled the Bank to modify its original argument that there are 'banks proper' and the rest. In May 1980 the present Governor referred, with some understatement, to a 'little misunderstanding and misapprehension' in the banking community about the Bank's responsibilities. He argued that recognised banks were distinguished from licensed deposit takers by the range and kind of services provided. Consequently, 'classification as a licensed deposit taker is not to be seen of itself as impugning the status of an institution ... I should regard the market as failing in professional expertise if it were to base its assessment on this distinction alone'.[45]

The licensed deposit takers do not take this sanguine view. Recognised banking status is a highly sought prize, a fact emphasised by the now common practice of referring to the two-tier system as first and second division banking.[46] The difference was emphasised in 1981 by a proposal – presently postponed – to limit membership of the British Bankers' Association to recognised banks. Whatever the Bank now says, the common picture of licensed deposit takers as 'second division bankers' is no misunderstanding; it is the direct consequence of the original desire to preserve traditional, informal regulation by keeping small the community of 'banks proper'. In some degree the two-tier system has been a success: the comparatively light prudential supervision enjoyed by recognised banks obviously helps preserve informality, and economises on resources by minimising the numbers who have been employed in supervision.[47] But the contradictions between the effort to preserve traditional ways, and the growing scale and complexity of banking, produce numerous tensions. The Bank has created two-tier banking, but cannot fully acknowledge the fact because to do so would further offend the interests in the second tier of licensed deposit takers. The Bank wants to practise the old esoteric politics of regulation with the recognised banks, but finds that the size and diversity of this group makes it very difficult to settle issues privately and informally. Traditional regulation was built in a banking community dominated by a small number of aristocratic families and owner-controlled institutions. The banking system in the 1980s is increasingly dominated by foreigners: three-quarters of banks in London are foreign, mostly American. (There are more American banks in London than in New York.)[48] Even many British banks are multinational corporations trading in what is to an increasing degree a single world banking market. Esoteric politics cannot survive these changes: the Bank is increasingly forced to consult bankers using the kind of formal procedures – public consultation documents, negotiations with highly organised pressure groups – common elsewhere in the world of pressure group politics.

This formality has in turn encouraged open argument between different banking interests. The consultative document on bank liquidity issued in 1980 illustrates the problem perfectly. The Bank originally circulated the document to a restricted group in the British Bankers' Association. The BBA in turn circulated it to a limited number of institutions. Here was an attempt to solve problems in the old way by involving a small elite in confidential discussions. But the very existence of written proposals – a sure sign of bureaucratisation – doomed the attempt. The document was leaked, and a fierce public argument occurred. The cause of the argument – and probably the motive for the leak – was that the proposals clearly favoured the clearing banks. This was hardly surprising, for the document drew on the discussion in the working party set up by the Bank and the clearers in 1974 to examine liquidity and capital adequacy. The proposals favoured the clearing banks over those in the wholesale markets by offering especially favourable treatment to the clearers' retail deposits. This prompted the American banks in particular to openly lobby for changes.[49] The Bank has now withdrawn the document and promised an amended version. The case of the liquidity proposals nicely illustrates some key problems in banking regulation: issues which are of immense intellectual complexity are made even more difficult by the tugging and hauling of different banking interests.

Even the Bank's traditional relations with the clearing banks are now under pressure, as the clearers' operations become increasingly multinational. The takeover battle in 1981 illustrates the problem. Standard Chartered (a British Overseas Bank chaired by Lord Barber, the former Chancellor of the Exchequer) made a takeover bid for one of the Scottish clearing banks. The Bank informally approved the bid, only to find that a significant rival to Standard Chartered appeared, in the form of the Hong Kong and Shanghai Banking Corporation, a large multinational based in the Far East. The Bank resisted the Hong Kong and Shanghai bid, on the grounds that foreign ownership of a clearing bank would endanger the close and informal control which it exercised over the clearers in conducting monetary policy. The bid was referred to the Monopolies Commission, itself a sign that the Bank had lost control of the issue. When the Bank began to sense that it might lose the argument before the Commission, it lobbied in Whitehall for legislation to give it statutory power to regulate takeovers. The lobbying was unsuccessful, principally because in the bureaucratic conflict aroused by the request the Foreign Office sponsored the claims of the Hong Kong and Shanghai.[50] The request highlights the extraordinary contradictions involved in the new politics of banking in Britain. The paradox of the Banking Act reappeared: here was the Bank resorting to the statute book to try to preserve its traditional, informal arrangements. (The result of the Monopolies Commission report was that neither bid went ahead.)

Critics of the bank's behaviour in 1981 also pointed to another oddity in its actions: here it was, trying to prevent foreign control of a British clearing bank at the very time when the clearers were themselves developing as multinational enterprises, principally by the kind of acquisitions abroad which the Bank was resisting at home. The point connects to an important change in banking and in financial markets. The 1970s saw the rise to prominence of supranational markets and institutions. The problems of prudential supervision raised as a result have concerned central bankers since the great crisis of the mid-1970s.

4 COMPLEXITY MAGNIFIED: SUPERVISING SUPRANATIONAL MARKETS

The distinctive feature of the banking revolution which took place in the 1960s was the rise of the domestic wholesale markets; the distinctive feature of the next decade was the extraordinary growth of supranational wholesale markets. This second change compounded the problems of regulation created by the original rise of wholesale banking. British banks took a disproportionate share of this growth: between 1967 and 1978 the international liabilities of banks in the UK rose fifteenfold, while those for banks of other 'Group of Ten' countries rose tenfold.[51] The disparity reflects London's continuing success as an international financial centre; it also puts the Bank of England in the forefront of the search for effective means of regulating these markets.

The new supranational markets magnify every problem of complexity posed by the regulation of domestic banking. They are themselves in part a product of social complexity since their rapid growth has been stimulated by 'the exemption of Eurocurrency deposits from monetary controls in the form of minimum reserve requirements'.[52] Their regulation presents daunting problems of intellectual complexity. The elementary task of surveillance is complicated by the absence of any supranational equivalent of a central bank or supervisory authority, while the international differences in reporting and accounting conventions make the interpretation and comparison of banking statistics extremely difficult. The absence of a supranational supervisory authority means that such regulation as takes place rests on cooperation between institutions in different countries; securing this in turn means surmounting formidable problems of administrative complexity. The lack of a supranational lender of last resort, and the novel character of the business conducted in the markets, intensifies the problem of assessing risk and devising appropriate prudential safeguards. As in domestic wholesale markets, lending between banks forms a significant proportion of business: by one authoritative estimate, over one-third of international banking liabilities are the result of such deposits.[53] This creates the risk of an international magnification of the problems experienced domestically in Britain in 1974: the failure of one bank acting, domino fashion, to cause others to fall and thus endanger the whole system.

The danger of failure has in turn been increased by the vast scale of loans advanced in the markets. Since the great rise in oil prices at the end of 1973 the markets have been important in recycling the deposits of oil-rich states, especially to poor countries: between 1973 and the end of the decade Euromarket lending to non-oil exporting, less developed countries (the most impoverished) rose nearly ninefold, to account for over 40 per cent of all loans.[54] A market where much business consists of deposits between banks, and where large loans are made to impoverished countries, faces serious problems of prudential regulation. In domestic markets laws governing bankruptcy act both as a deterrent against default on a debt and as a way of salvaging some of the loan if the worst occurs. Though countries are sometimes loosely spoken of as 'bankrupt' there exists no comparable legal framework governing loans to states in the supranational markets. When a country defaults on its debt payments, as Zaire did in the mid-1970s, the banks have little option but to try to reschedule the debt. When the default is huge and the defaulter occupies a strategic position in the international political system — as was the case with Poland which in 1981 owed about £14 billion to commercial banks — problems of prudential control become an adjunct to power politics.[55]

This litany of complexity might make the reader wonder at the very survival of the international banking system, but the likelihood of failure is determined not simply by the complexity of the circumstances but by the speed and effectiveness with which banks and regulatory authorities adapt to those circumstances. The history of banking regulation has been a history of (partly) successful adaptation to the problems created by change. Since each individual bank has an obvious incentive to avoid its own failure, the new forms of business have stimulated the search for ways to assess and minimise novel risks. Thus since the late 1970s both the banking literature and the big banks themselves have put considerable effort into searching for some reliable means of measuring 'country risk'.[56] But the nub of the problem in banking, as in other forms of regulation, is that the individual search for safety cannot ensure the safety of the whole system; the task of managing collective security in supranational markets has therefore fallen to the national supervisory authorities.

Just as crisis played a significant part in reforming domestic regulation in Britain after 1974, so it similarly stimulated regulation in international banking. If one event could be said to have destroyed the sanguine belief that the old ways of practising prudential regulation were effective it was the failure of the Bankhaus Herstatt in June 1974. The Herstatt failure, which involved a default on obligations in the foreign exchange markets, immediately transformed separate domestic banking difficulties in different countries into an international banking crisis. The first attempts at international cooperation arose out of the attempt to cope with the Herstatt failure. The initial problems of coordinating between different countries were eased by the existence of a well-established central bankers' network based on the Bank for International Settlement at Basle. At the regular meeting of BIS in Basle in July 1974 the Governor of the Bank of England managed to persuade his fellow central bankers (apparently with some difficulty) to agree on the doctrine of parental responsibility, according to which parent banks accepted responsibility for the obligations of their branches and subsidiaries operating in other countries.[57] In London the Bank followed up this general agreement by extracting 'letters of comfort' from the parents of banks operating in Britain.

An even more important result of the Herstatt failure was the decision taken by central bankers in September 1974 to establish a Committee on Banking Regulations and Supervisory Practices.[58] The Committee – which draws members from the leading capitalist economies – is served from Basle by a secretariat provided through the BIS. The Bank of England's key role is indicated by the fact that the first two heads of its Supervision Division were also the first two chairmen of the Committee (George Blunden 1974–7, Peter Cooke 1977–   ).[59]

The Basle Committee is not the first effort to coordinate the activities of banking supervisors. Within the EEC before the crisis of the mid-1970s there existed the Dondelinger Committee 'for fostering mutual understanding and for confidential exchanges of information'. More recently, the EEC Group of Bank Supervisory Authorities, for which the Bank of England provides a secretariat, has met regularly.[60] The Committee on Banking Regulations is, however, a recognition of the obvious fact that the new markets go well beyond the boundaries of the EEC. The Committee's most important functions have been to encourage the international spread of new techniques of control, and to pass on information about conditions in markets. Each of the quarterly meetings begins with reports on any new developments in the separate national supervisory systems. According to its first chairman virtually every country represented on the Committee revised its methods of supervision as a result of lessons learnt in these discussions.[61]

This conscious attempt to learn new techniques of control, and to spread them internationally, has accompanied another conscious, highly sensitive aim: the Committee has been used to give early warning of particular cases of prudential risk. This is a delicate matter because it endangers traditional banking confidentiality, but the privacy and informality of the Committee's regular meetings provide the ideal conditions for such an exercise. The Committee has also looked for longer term solutions to the problems created by the new markets, and has begun to tackle one of the most serious manifestations of administrative complexity, the problem of so demarcating national responsibilities that significant activities – such as managing off-shore funds – do not slip outside any national authority.[62]

The complexities of observation and understanding have also been a key concern. When banks operate world-wide in countries with very different accounting systems, formidable problems exist in obtaining an accurate picture of an institution's financial affairs. The Bank of England has responded to this difficulty by pressing for 'transparency', the maximum disclosure of their activities by international banks. (The point illustrates yet again how problems of regulation have transformed attitudes: little more than a decade ago the Bank was an extreme defender of confidentiality and secrecy in banking.) To increase 'transparency' the Basle Committee spent several years agreeing principles for composing consolidated accounts covering the worldwide operation of banks.[63] These developments parallel the efforts of the International Accounting Standards Committee to agree common accounting standards for use in different countries. The Committee has a fortuitous link with the Bank of England for its founder, Sir Henry Benson, is now an Industrial Adviser to the Governor.[64] These attempts to distil some clear financial data out of the mist of banking statistics have been reinforced by efforts to recreate traditional forms of self-regulation at a supranational level, in such forms as the International Association of Bond Dealers which was originally established in London in 1969.

These many developments usefully modify currently fashionable notions that supranational markets and enterprises (in banking or elsewhere) make national states helpless. Markets and firms certainly change in ways which create serious problems for regulators; but national authorities can likewise learn and adapt, particularly under the stimulus of a crisis such as occurred in banking in the mid-1970s. The great difficulty is that adaptation is a painful business which, if successful, may threaten powerful interests. Experience since the mid-1970s shows the limits to international cooperation. The greatest advances – such as establishing the principle of parental responsibility – occurred at the height of the 1974 crisis, when fear stimulated innovation and encouraged a concern with collective security. Since then advances have been discernible, but slow.

Members of the Basle Committee have from the beginning been forced to define their roles modestly: 'to learn from each other and to apply the knowledge so acquired'.[65] Early in its deliberations the Committee found that even the limited ambition of establishing a separate specialised system of reporting by international banks was impossible.[66] The obstacles include the obvious limits to most forms of international cooperation. Different political and legal systems define the powers of central banks and other supervisory authorities in very different ways, while there are also great variations in the organisation and economic role of banking systems in different countries. The many differences put a clear limit even on such agreements as have been worked out: thus while the principle of 'parental responsibility' has been formally accepted, not all national authorities accept it to the same degree.[67] Indeed, according to Dale, proposals produced in the United States by the Federal Reserve Board under the International Banking Act of 1978 threatened to supplant the principle of parental responsibility by the principle of control by the host central bank. The proposals drew objections from other central banks, including the Bank of England, who were fearful of losing control over the foreign activities of their own native banks.[68]

It is plain what is happening. The attempt to work out cooperation at the international level is encountering bureaucratic rivalries over the allocation of responsibilities similar to those which constantly occur within national governments; but at the international level these rivalries are sharpened because there exists no obvious arbitrator between disputing bureaucratic bodies, while the stakes in the battle are increased by considerations of national sovereignty. The crisis of 1974 clarified responsibilities for supervision; it did not produce any mechanism for future crisis management.[69] Future international banking crises will be managed, as in the past, by inventing solutions under the pressure of disaster.

The present modest efforts to improve the quality of surveillance in the new markets face particular difficulties because of their international scale. The agreement on the need for consolidated banking accounts is, for example, considerably limited in usefulness because there exist so many different national accounting systems, and because there exists little international agreement on common conventions. Narrow, highly technical accounting problems pose serious problems of regulation and control for public policy makers. Even within nations the rapid inflation of the 1970s created immense problems of intellectual complexity by destroying the utility of conventional accounting methods as guides to the profitability and financial soundness of businesses. In Britain the result was to provoke a set of fierce disputes in the accountancy profession about how standards of reliable reporting might be restored. The substance of the argument was technical, but the outcome deeply affected policy areas as different as taxation, fraud prevention and the prudential control of financial institutions.[70] The magnitude of the difficulties facing bank supervisors attempting to monitor international banking may be appreciated by realising that to the destructive effects of inflation on the reliability of accounting information must be added the variations in national accounting standards. In some descriptions of the impact of the supranational economy on the nation state these developments are presented as working wholly to the advantage of multinational corporations, but the lack of agreed accounting standards also faces individual enterprises with problems in assessing their true profits, in managing their tax liabilities and even in ensuring their own prudential soundness.[71]

The problem of agreeing accounting standards which would allow supervisors to obtain an accurate picture of the state of a bank's health is replicated in numerous other areas of banking supervision. In Britain since the mid-1970s the effort to work out some uniform measures of liquidity and capital adequacy has, we saw earlier, been hindered both by questions of great intellectual complexity, and by the conflicting interests of different parts of the banking system. Any attempt to establish internationally applicable standards encounters all these problems, compounded by variations in national standards and conventions.

Even this recital of formidable problems does not exhaust the difficulties created by the new supranational world of banking. The limited attempt to tackle the problems has so far been confined almost wholly to the eleven countries represented on the Basle Committee. The Committee has made some contact with about sixty other national supervisory authorities, while the Bank of England has also tried to widen the range of cooperation through its extensive bilateral contacts and through such initiatives as the international Conference of Supervisors which it organised in 1979.[72] It is plain, however, that widening the geographical range in this way diminishes further the prospects of achieving united action and common standards.

The problem has been intensified by a peculiarity of supranational banking. Traditional banking markets – such as the London Discount

Market – were located in a single geographical centre. The rise of the supranational markets has coincided with – indeed stimulated – the development of a worldwide system of almost instantaneous electronic communication. The new markets are organised on a global scale, and exist only as a set of points on a sophisticated communications network. This makes the most advanced banking markets highly mobile: it is now technologically possible to organise financial markets from almost any country on earth.[73] This considerably increases the ease with which operators can shift business from the more regulated to the less regulated centres. The phenomenon accounts for the rise in recent years of financial centres outside the great traditional metropolitan banking locations. It also helps account for the rapid growth of the supranational markets, for an environment free of the regulations constraining domestic banking has been one of the greatest attractions of the new markets.

These limits to regulation pose many problems for bank supervisors. The contrast between tightly regulated domestic banks and the freer supranational environment has revived some traditional problems of consumer protection. In any markets, swindlers go to the less regulated parts; thus the greatest financial frauds of the 1970s took place in the market for offshore funds.[74] Though such swindles do not endanger the stability of banking systems they affect banking politics by raising embarrassing questions about the adequacy of existing means of regulation. More serious problems are posed by the scale of lending and borrowing, by the significance of inter-bank borrowing and by the problem of coping with defaulters. Even if the markets can survive a default by a large national borrower such as Poland, the act of coping with default changes the politics of banking, for negotiations with the debtor inevitably become entangled with wider issues of international politics.[75] For over a generation central bankers have been used to the notion that the control of interest rates and of exchange rates was bound up with the wider politics of economic management; in the new world of supranational banking the prudential control of banks is acquiring a similarly political character.

7 Complexity, Trust and Policy Making

> In political activity ... men sail a boundless and bottomless sea; there is neither harbour for shelter nor floor for anchorage, neither starting-place nor appointed destination. The enterprise is to keep afloat on an even keel.[1]

1 THE PROBLEM OF OPPORTUNISM

Case-studies throw light on old arguments and illuminate new ones. Therein lies both their strength and weakness: the light of a single study shines brightly, but its beam is always narrow. Case-studies work best when they are exemplary, displaying in an especially clear way characteristics common elsewhere. The examination of banking policy and politics conducted in the preceding chapters has this exemplary quality. Even a fleeting acquaintance with policy making shows that the problems encountered in banking are not unique: the battle with complexity fought in financial markets is part of a continuing war waged whenever policy is made and applied. The following pages therefore extend beyond banking into the wider politics of complexity. They begin by recalling and extending my argument about its nature. Opportunism – an aspect of social complexity – is identified as the heart of the policy problem. In 'Capitalism and Complexity' (2 below) two radical ways of coping with opportunism are examined and rejected. The concluding section describes some less ambitious solutions.

The war with complexity is in part a battle with nature, for intellectual complexity arises from what Oliver Williamson calls the 'neurophysiological limits' of human intelligence.[2] In more homely English, 'the dull brain perplexes and retards': policy makers suffer from the normal human limitations of observing little and understanding less.

This battle with nature is made considerably more difficult because it is entwined with a contest of a more social character: policy making and application is a battle of wits between controller and controlled. In financial markets, in labour markets, in levying taxes, public institutions make rules; private individuals and institutions commonly evade or avoid those rules; public bodies try to change the rules in consequence. This is part of what is expressed in the idea of social complexity. Problems of observation and understanding are thus magnified because, in pursuing self-interest, individuals and institutions constantly manipulate and conceal information. Williamson's notion of opportunism aptly describes this behaviour. Opportunism is more than the pursuit of self-interest; it is its pursuit with guile, by subtle and devious means.[3] Who could deny its common existence in policy areas as diverse as the application of tax law, the control of gambling, the regulation of financial markets, the control of dangerous addictive drugs and the regulation of the property market?

The greatest literary fantasies of authoritarian control, such as Orwell's *1984*, imagine that in mass industrial societies opportunism can be extinguished by a combination of high technology and thought control. The imaginative force of such fantasies is greater than their sociological accuracy. The most effective systems of authoritarian control occur in societies organised on a small scale, where problems of observation are eased and where social pressures discourage opportunism.[4] By contrast, the scale of industrial societies magnifies the task of observation, while the anonymity which goes with scale reduces the effectiveness of social pressures designed to discourage opportunistic behaviour. La Porte's work offers the additional insight that under industrialism social complexity becomes formally organised. In the modern economy in particular opportunism is increasingly practised by sophisticated institutions rather than by solitary individuals. Specialisation and the division of labour make these institutions dependent on each other in numerous subtle ways. These subtle links are one source of the 'surprises' of which La Porte speaks, for the multiplicity of institutional connections combine in many unexpected ways.[5] To the policy maker surprises show themselves as unexpected results of public policy. These surprises not only result from the statistically numerous outcomes possible when many institutions are joined in relations of dependence; they are also the product of the conscious, opportunistic manipulation of dependence relations. Policy is full of surprises because rules designed to influence one kind of human conduct are manipulated to affect conduct elsewhere. Consider as an example the following anecdote.

Since the early 1970s British industry has increasingly preferred to lease rather than to buy capital equipment. Leasing has been called the most remarkable phenomenon to hit the British financial scene since the growth of secondary banking in the 1960s; in the decade after 1970 it increased thirtyfold in volume. The change has considerable implications for policies designed to influence the level of investment, and even for interpreting official indicators of what investment is taking place. Yet this momentous boom is a policy 'surprise', an unintended outcome of a minor tax reform. Since 1972 it has been possible to off-set much of the cost of leasing against tax. The search for 'tax efficiency' – as modern management accounting describes the opportunistic arrangement of assets to minimise tax liabilities – has lured in numerous large firms. In the mid-1970s opportunism produced a particular boom in clothes leasing. This was because the pay guidelines established in various phases by the Labour Government after July 1975 put especially severe limits on increases for the higher paid. Firms therefore began to cast around for ways of giving their managers benefits outside the guidelines. A small amendment to the 1976 Finance Act allowed the cost of clothes leasing to be off-set against tax, and companies began leasing clothes to their executives at advantageous rates. Recognising the opportunity for new business, bespoke tailors in turn offered wardrobes of specially made clothes to companies.[6]

This anecdote nicely illustrates the irrepressible ingenuity with which sophisticated institutions circumvent official controls. To put the point more analytically, the episode displays the key elements in social complexity: the 'surprise' in the way rules for one policy area are manipulated to affect rules elsewhere; the learning which occurs between opportunistic institutions; and the joining of apparently distinct policies in unexpected ways.

It will be plain that one of the added inconveniences of social complexity is greater administrative complexity. As in the classic case of tax law, opportunism persistently finds a way through the regulations. These in turn are constantly modified, continually growing in complexity. These complex rules demand correspondingly complex means of implementation. Large beuraucratic machines have to be created, funded and kept in some kind of working order. The opportunistic manipulation of rules intended for one policy area to a different purpose in another area makes it imperative that public institutions with different responsibilities cooperate with each other; thus is intensified the search for Siedman's 'philosophers's stone' of coordination.[7]

This complex machinery of policy making and execution compounds the problem of opportunism, for the individuals who run the machine are also capable of pursuing interests with guile and subtlety. Thus Hall's study of *Great Planning Disasters* on three continents identifies the opportunistic manipulation of issues and information by those concerned with policy making and execution as a major reason for the existence of expensive and ill-advised projects as different as the Anglo-French Concorde, the Sydney Opera House and the Bay Area Rapid Transit System in San Francisco.[8] The battles conducted in making and applying policy are thus not only struggles with nature and with the human objects of control; they are battles inside government about allocating bureaucratic responsibilities, about status and about controlling economic resources.

The three faces of complexity – intellectual, social and administrative – exist in some degree independently of each other. In a world without opportunism policy would still be a battle against Williamson's 'neurophysiological' limits to human intelligence. Problems of administrative coordination are likewise universal: even in conditions where full hearted cooperation is common – as in many team games, or in efforts to cope with natural disasters – considerable attention has to be given to coordinating the activities of different individuals.[9] It is nevertheless plain that the social capacity to adapt and change in the opportunistic pursuit of self-interest greatly increases intellectual and administrative complexity. Opportunism produces unexpected adaptations, leads to information being manipulated and concealed, and forces the evolution of complex rules and a complex machinery of enforcement. That is why social complexity, and opportunism in particular, is the heart of the policy problem.

The difficulties produced by complexity are numerous, the solutions commonly proposed equally so. In examining the latter I begin with a gross simplification by distinguishing two broadly contrasting remedies which have recently attracted much attention: the first urges a change in social morality; the second proposes both a considerable restriction in the range of social life which government seeks to influence, and a change in the rules governing the exercise of public power. These latter prescriptions are often offered by robust defenders of the market economy. The argument for a change in social morality, by contrast, arises from a critical analysis of the moral foundations of capitalism. This criticism has been put most eloquently in that elegy on the spirit of capitalism, Hirsch's *Social Limits to Growth*. Hirsch's argument plainly resembles criticisms of market morality offered in England in recent years by Titmuss, by Goldthorpe and by Fox.[10] In the following section only a small part of a subtle and careful case is considered.

2 COMPLEXITY AND CAPITALISM

The key part of Hirsch's argument concerns the problems created by the opportunistic pursuit of self-interest. He notes that, when the effort is made to control behaviour, those who try to exercise control begin with a 'standing handicap', for they first have to identify and measure the activity to be controlled. In other words, they encounter the complexities of observation and understanding. Hirsch argues that, except where control is attempted in small communities, this gives the controlled ample scope to manipulate information so as to escape restrictions. He concludes that controls can therefore only be effective where there exists a moral consensus between controllers and controlled which will lead the latter to cooperate voluntarily: 'while ... cooperation can, in some cases, be replaced by coercive rules, or stimulated through collectively imposed inducements to individuals' private interests, this will rarely be as practicable and efficient as when it is internally motivated ... restraints on individual behaviour imposed in the collective interest can be enforced most effectively when the sense of obligation is internalized'. Hirsch's view is that the capitalist ethic destroys the conditions for this cooperation, by emphasising the primacy of individual interests over collective obligations. Rules are consequently manipulated for individual gain: 'the law has to be obeyed; the spirit of the law does not'. In the early stages of capitalism individual appetites were restrained by religion, but the very advance of the rationalistic spirit of capitalism destroys these bonds: 'The market system was, at bottom, more dependent on religious binding than the feudal system, having abandoned direct social ties maintained by the obligations of custom and status. Yet the individualistic rationalistic base of the market undermined the unseen religious support.'[11]

This Durkheim-like analysis throws a revealing light on the opportunism revealed in the story of leasing in the 1970s, and on much more. The modern history of banking regulation, for instance, conforms strikingly to Hirsch's analysis: the way in which the rise of rational calculation and fierce competition fatally undermined the restraints present in the private world of traditional banking regulation; the extraordinary difficulties encountered in establishing new rules whose spirit would not be destroyed by the ingenuity of banks and their customers; the Bank of England's apparently vain attempts to recreate traditional kinds of trust and informality in the new banking markets. The problems in banking are in turn a mirror of problems elsewhere: in financial markets generally, in the markets for property and for labour, and in many areas where the state attempts to regulate non-economic behaviour. The growing sophistication with which rules and regulations are frustrated drives governments forward to devise more complex and more coercive means of control. If the Hirsch argument is correct this drive towards more technically efficient controls is futile. The controllers always work under their 'standing handicap'; the controlled use this advantage to escape restriction opportunistically. Government is thus pushed into applying rules of an increasingly convoluted character by administrative means of such complexity that great resources have to be devoted merely to maintain the institutions of enforcement. The proper remedy lies not in the search for more technically effective machinery to make and implement policy, but in reforms designed to replace the amoral individualism of capitalism with an ethic of social restraint. Accomplishing this, says Hirsch, involves substantial economic and social reforms.[12]

At the heart of Hirsch's arguments are two assumptions: that cooperation stimulated by moral commitments is, wherever possible, preferable to either coercion or reliance on self-interest; and that creating moral commitments is increasingly obstructed by the calculating, self-interested spirit of capitalism. The first assumption I accept; the second I question. Take the history of banking regulation. Though the last two decades conform to the pattern suggested by Hirsch, it is much less certain that his interpretation can be sustained over a longer period. The history of British banking is not simply one of steadily declining restraint as capitalism developed. There existed unrestrained (often fraudulent) competition at the height of the Industrial Revolution. The crises produced by fierce competition stimulated the development of restraints. These in turn were undermined by the rise of new financial markets and new banking institutions. The recent history of regulation is the story of attempts to cope with these novelties.

Nor is it generally obvious that as capitalism advances moral restraint declines. If the calculating spirit of capitalism causes a 'moral lacuna', we ought to find that morality is weakest where capitalism is most highly developed. The reverse is the case; the most advanced capitalist institutions, big corporations, are more restrained in their behaviour than are its less advanced parts. It is true that big companies opportunistically practise tax avoidance; but illegal tax evasion is actually commonest among the historically backward sections of capitalism such as small firms and the self-employed. When we look beyond taxes the pattern is even clearer. In consumer protection, pollution control, regulating health and safety at work, enforcement problems are concentrated disproportionately among smaller firms. In the market for credit the borrower is much more likely to be charged usurious rates of interest by that pre-capitalist survivor, the pawnbroker, than by a big capitalist bank. Clarke's study of recent business scandals likewise identifies entrepreneurs in the mould of the traditional capitalist as most likely to disregard moral or legal codes.[13] Nor is it the case that big corporations obey only the letter and not the spirit of the law. In consumer protection, for instance, the biggest companies have generally been in advance of legal requirements.

The opportunistic manipulation of rules and regulations is common in our society. In the field of tax law it is practised with great sophistication by large capitalist concerns. But Hirsch's argument that capitalism destroys restraint would lead us to expect opportunism to be greatest where capitalism is most advanced socially and technically. This is not so: small firms – the less advanced part of capitalism – are the most opportunistic. The conclusion must be that coping with the opportunism which is the heart of social complexity need not await a major reform of capitalism.

Hirsch's solution to the problem of complexity was to reform the moral basis of our society. A very different remedy is offered by the argument that in a variety of spheres government should give up the effort at control, and should guide its remaining activities by clear, non-discretionary rules. The case is clearest when advanced by economists such as Friedman. Transferring social tasks from the sphere of political administration to the domain of the market is presumed to alleviate numerous problems of complexity. Administrative complexity is reduced by restricting administration; social complexity is diminished because the rules of the market are presumed to harness the self-interested energies of social actors which would otherwise be consumed by the opportunistic evasion or manipulation of controls; intellectual complexity is lessened because the price system is presumed to offer a highly efficient way of signalling information. The best known example of the argument is the case for a 'monetary rule': the suggestion that economic management should rest largely on a public obligation to keep the growth of a specified monetary indicator within an agreed range.[14]

It is plain that there is a connection between arguments for less government and for a government more closely bound by non-discretionary rules. If this were not so the argument against discretion would be unexceptionable for, all other things being equal, it is perverse to prefer a complex, discretionary guideline to a simple, non-discretionary rule. The choice is a hard one because reducing discretion has numerous other consequences. It is an open part of the monetarist argument that relying on a monetary rule involves sacrificing numerous existing policy objectives. This presents no analytical problem for anyone intellectually convinced of the need to reduce the scope of government, but it creates serious difficulties of political management. Take the case for abolishing many of the complex existing tax regulations and allowances in favour of uniform rates of taxation set at lower levels than is presently the case. Those who have opportunistically manipulated the present system to lower their tax liabilities (such as property owners who have managed their mortgage commitments with this in mind) will oppose change if it threatens to raise their tax bill. Such considerations can be ignored by the market economist. They cannot be ignored by those in government who have to make and implement policy in a political system where pressure groups and bodies of electors act opportunistically to defend their interests.

Even supposing this opportunism were overcome, there remains an even more serious difficulty in relying extensively on non-discretionary rules. Private individuals and interests manipulate and evade complex regulations. Why should they not act in the same opportunistic way with simple, non-discretionary rules? The presumption of self-interested action means that such behaviour is to be expected. The standard answer is that non-discretionary rules can be framed so as to be proof against opportunistic manipulation. Anyone who believes this should read Hood's comprehensive study of the 'limits of administration', which is full of examples of non-discretionary rules turned to unexpected uses by the ingenuity of the controlled.[15] The heart of the Friedmanite case, the argument for a 'monetary rule', shows the difficulties, for monetarists have been singularly unsuccessful in specifying the lever which could control a sophisticated banking system so closely that it would be unable to expand credit beyond the rate desired by the authorities. Numerous other instances exist. What could have been simpler and less open to discretionary interpretation than, for instance, the rule laid down in July 1975 that nobody earning in excess of £8,500 per annum should receive a pay increase in the first stage of the Government's new pay policy? To give the higher paid more ought to have meant breaking the rule. Yet as the example of clothes leasing showed it was perfectly possible with a little ingenious manipulation of tax laws to pay more in the form of fringe benefits. Those who favour confining self-interested behaviour inside non-discretionary rules have yet to counter the most powerful part of Hirsch's argument: to invite the working of self-interest inside the rules is also to invite the opportunistic manipulation of those rules.[16]

Since even non-discretionary rules founder in complexity, the more radical option of disengaging government is commonly suggested. 'De-regulation' – the abolition or relaxation of rules – has been proposed and tried in numerous areas. It is an extremely attractive way of apparently abolishing complexity: attractive to economic liberals because it removes illegitimate state controls; to radical libertarians on the left because it allows private individuals to make free choices in matters conventionally defined as involving personal morality; attractive to policy makers because it abolishes tasks which often seem impossible to accomplish. De-regulation has been offered as a standard solution to the complexities of exercising public control over financial markets and labour markets, while in Britain since the 1960s areas as different as gambling, land use, abortion and obscene publications have all been de-regulated.

This apparent remedy for complexity is illusory. By retreating from intervention governments can certainly give up searching for solutions to particular problems of intellectual and administrative complexity, but they cannot, in doing so, abolish the opportunism which is the heart of the policy problem. The four very different examples of industrial relations, gambling, abortion and obscene publications all make the point.

Industrial relations is the best known instance. Taking the state out of the labour market when collective bargaining is well established merely frees organised workers and organised employers to compete or to collude opportunistically, at the expense of such third parties as consumers. Gambling is a less well known but even more striking example. Gaming in private houses and clubs was permitted after 1960, in part because detecting and preventing illegal gaming was impossible. In other words, the old restrictions were destroyed by a mixture of intellectual and social complexity. The relaxed rules were in turn opportunistically exploited by gambling interests to spread commercial gaming establishments widely. This led in 1968 to the setting up of the Gaming Board, which was given wide discretionary powers. In turn the Board has been faced with numerous scandals caused by the opportunistic manipulation of its rules by the gambling industry.[17] (The pattern is extraordinarily like the experience of banking after 1971: de-regulation, in the hope of bringing covert activity into the open; the opportunistic exploitation of new freedoms; the imposition of fresh controls by giving wide discretionary powers to a regulatory body; and the opportunistic adaptation of the new rules by the regulated.)

The recent history of abortion law likewise shows the paradoxes of de-regulation. The 1967 Act which considerably eased the rules under which abortions could be legally conducted was prompted by a variety of considerations. One of the most important was that the attempt to ban abortions faced considerable complexities of observation, as in the well known difficulty of detecting numerous 'back street' abortions. But de-regulation could involve nothing so simple as a retreat by the state. To prevent the opportunistic exploitation of new freedoms at the expense of the unborn it was necessary to specify a complex (and highly contentious) set of rules under which abortion was allowed. The 1967 Act also allowed the demand for abortion to be legally met through the free market, and thus created an industry operating privately-run clinics. Opportunistic competition between clinics in turn has prompted a system of licensing and control, to safeguard the health of patients, to guard against evasions of the law, and to prevent 'excessive' competition, such as the practice of using taxi-drivers to canvass for business.[18]

The control of pornographic publications is, finally, a striking case of an activity in the middle of a bout of de-regulation. Critics of the obscenity laws have generally pointed to the intellectual complexities involved in their making and application. It has manifestly been beyond the wit of policy makers to produce a definition of the obscene which is not uncertain and arbitrary. In addition, whenever definitions of obscenity have connected it to the power morally to corrupt the argument has come up against the limits of human understanding: even when there is agreement on the nature of moral corruption not enough is known about the springs of human behaviour to allow a conclusive demonstration that consuming pornography causes corrupt thought or action. In the 1970s juries were evidently increasingly impressed by these arguments, for they showed a growing reluctance in many places to convict when individuals were prosecuted for selling obscene publications.[19] The opportunistic use of this liberality by dealers in pornography to expand the boundaries of the acceptable has in turn created a new set of regulatory difficulties. These include the problem of preventing the use of children for pornographic purposes, preventing the sale of unsuitable material to young people, and even controlling shop use so that communities (such as Soho in London) are not totally dominated by the pornography industry.

These arguments do not imply that it is impossible to give up all public controls which are difficult to operate: it is easy to imagine completely unfettered banking, just as it is easy to imagine unfettered gambling, the free sale of heroin or the absence of any restraints on the publication of pornography. But the opportunistic use of these freedoms in the pursuit of profit would soon lead to demands for control, since the results would be offensive to widely held values, such as the need to protect children from exploitation. Nor does the argument lead inevitably to what are often called 'illiberal' conclusions. Granted certain premises (moral and otherwise) it can be perfectly rational to prefer the controlled provision of abortion to the state of affairs existing before 1967, or a regulated industry supplying pornography to the present state of the law. Such alternatives cannot, however, be sensibly presented as choices between being committed to all the complexities of control, or retreating away from complexity; they are choices between different kinds and combinations of intellectual, social and administrative complexity. That is why the commonly canvassed remedy of restricting the range of activities regulated by the state is no solution. In a world of sophisticated opportunists governments have to live with complexity. In the next section I consider how they can live tolerably.

3   LIVING WITH COMPLEXITY

The opportunism which is part of social complexity is also the heart of the policy problem. If people are to live tolerably with complexity opportunism must either be tightly controlled, or it must be harnessed, or its influence must be diminished by appealing to more altruistic motives. To simplify greatly, these three possibilities correspond to three kinds of practical solution. The first demands that government be made a more efficient instrument of surveillance and control. This means more technical rationality. Government is treated as a machine for gathering and analysing information, and for acting swiftly on that information in the light of clear, agreed objectives. By contrast, harnessing opportunism means going a different way, towards more competition and incentives within government. The hierarchies of conventional public administration are 'uncoupled'. Public services are contracted out by competitive tender, and public agencies are encouraged to compete. The objects are twofold: competition is presumed both to stimulate the search for more efficient government, and to control bureaucratic institutions more effectively than do conventional political procedures for ensuring accountability. The common argument for more open discussion in policy making is a milder version of this case, since it is presumed that open government will stimulate intellectual competition and expose poor arguments. The third alternative, diminishing opportunism, involves creating a set of moral assumptions uniting policy makers and those with whom they deal. These shared assumptions would then allow policy to be made and implemented in an atmosphere of trust where neither private institutions nor public servants opportunistically exploited rules.

These three choices – more technical rationality, more competition between policy makers and more trust – are not mutually exclusive; indeed it is impossible to see how government could work effectively without a high level of technical competence, some system of incentives and an extensive reliance on trust. In some circumstances different options may reinforce each other: thus it is easy to imagine how competition may stimulate the search for more technical rationality. But I will suggest that there exists an optimum combination of the three. Beyond the optimum we enter the familiar world of dilemmas where painful choices must be made. Nor in practice do we know how to recognise the optimum combination in any particular case, and even if we could there is no guarantee that people and resources could be controlled so as to approach it. This connects to an additional difficulty. Opportunism has to be controlled, harnessed or diminished within two separate groups: among those who make and apply policy, and among those private individuals and institutions who are subject to it.

(a) *More technical rationality*

The immediate impulse behind the search for greater technical rationality lies in the desire to acquire better information in order to understand the past more fully and to forecast the future more accurately. This effort to cope with intellectual complexity is entwined with another problem: understanding is made especially difficult because individuals and institutions opportunistically adapt and change in unexpected ways. The search for greater technical rationality is thus not only an intellectual search for better knowledge and understanding; it is also a quest for ways in which this knowledge and understanding can be used by government to exercise more effective control. Acquiring more technical rationality thus means both acquiring better information and designing institutions better capable of acting swiftly on new information. These two different problems prompt two different responses: equipping government with better technology, and fashioning organisations which can quickly learn and adapt to changing circumstances.

The simplest manifestation of the desire for more technical rationality can be seen in the great increase in the amount of data collected by government in recent decades. The growing size of the state, combined with the invention of electronic systems for storing and retrieving information, have vastly increased the amount of data which can be handled. Through what J. B. Rule calls 'symbiosis' information can also be transmitted from one storage system to another. The most immediate benefits can be gained in crime detection by, for instance, giving the police access to computer-filed information about car registrations.[20]

Rule has identified an important dilemma which puts a clear limit to the usefulness of such technologically based improvements. There is a choice to be made between storing in simple statistical form large amounts of easily assimilable data and storing smaller amounts of 'fine grained' information which is more revealing, but is correspondingly difficult to interpret and understand.[21] The dilemma is made the more acute because the tendency to rely on simple, predictable indicators is often seized on opportunistically as a way of avoiding controls. This is one of the commonest experiences in economic management, where using a particular measure in controlling wages or bank lending quickly produces evasion and avoidance, in turn diminishing the usefulness of the indicator.[22] We saw the Bank of England struggling with this dilemma in its effort to steer a course between applying common statistical rules of banking prudence and judging the prudential soundness of each bank by individual examination.

The drive to acquire better data fuses with the search for techniques which allow government to use resources more efficiently and to exercise control more effectively. Carley has written a sensitive account of these efforts. They include cost-utility techniques, such as cost-benefit analysis, which are designed to raise the efficiency with which resources are allocated; studies of impact, designed to help in evaluating the results of policy; more open evaluation research, involving controlled experiments; and forecasting techniques ranging from the simple extrapolation of past trends to the use of intellectually complex computer-based models such as are common in economic management.[23]

This search for more technical rationality has been objected to on a number of grounds. Some of the difficulties raised refer to particular methods rather than to the general search for better techniques. Thus social experiments – such as the famous New Jersey negative income tax experiments – raise important ethical problems, since by its nature experimentation means manipulating in a discriminatory fashion the lives of citizens who are its subjects.[24] In a different way Self has assailed the intellectual assumptions of many techniques imported from economic analysis.[25] Even the most committed defender of technical rationality will have to admit that any particular technique has to survive close scrutiny of its intellectual foundations, ethical and otherwise.

A more general objection has come from those who fear a threat to liberty from governments increasingly equipped with the capacity to gather and act on information. Particular concern has been expressed about the growing bank of data accumulating in government.[26] Anyone who rejects these fears risks looking complacent whenever a particular abuse of privacy is revealed. Yet the remarkable feature of the modern state is not how much it knows, but how sketchy is its information about the activities which it tries to control. There are good reasons for this. Because of the dilemma identified by Rule, government continually faces the choice between amassing crude and limited data easily expressed statistically, and gathering more 'fine-grained', sophisticated information which is harder to store and analyse. The dilemma is intensified because, as Hirsch observed, controllers always work under the handicap of having first to observe and understand before they can control. This allows individuals ample scope opportunistically to manipulate or escape the means of detection.

A different though equally general objection to the search for technical rationality has come from those who support the incrementalist theory that policy is best made by 'muddling through' piecemeal. Wildavsky, in his highly influential studies of budgeting, has argued for the primacy of what he calls 'political' rationality, and has documented how the effort to introduce many rational techniques into budgeting clogs up the system with paper and allows participants to manipulate techniques in the opportunistic pursuit of their interests.[27] Opportunism has indeed dogged the attempt to use rational techniques. Studies as different as Hall's comparative examination of disastrous physical planning decisions and Sapolsky's study of the Polaris missile development show public servants manipulating information and techniques in the opportunistic pursuit of individual and institutional interests.[28]

This kind of opportunism gives good grounds for looking sceptically at any claims that particular policy options are dictated by technical rationality, but it hardly destroys the case for continuing to search for technical improvements. As Carley observes, objections commonly assume that the aim is comprehensive rationality, but there is no reason why the search for better data and techniques should not go with the realisation that any improvement will be limited. Wildavsky's alternative, 'political rationality', is especially unconvincing: it looks like a polite name for the outcomes produced by opportunistic bargaining between interests in and outside government.[29] As long as government attempts administratively complex tasks and intellectually complex judgements it is difficult to see why the search for better technical rationality should not continue.

The limited usefulness of particular techniques helps explain the attraction of an alternative way of searching for rationality. One of the key problems in government is created by the ability of private institutions to adapt and change. It thus seems sensible to emphasise, not the technology of policy, but the design of public institutions capable of matching this capacity to change and adapt. Empirical studies of bureaucracy show that, contrary to Weber's classical argument, bureaucratic organisation is often far from the most technically rational means of organising collective action. Bureaucracies suffer well known diseases including a fixation with rules and an inability to change. Cybernetic theories attempt to understand the conditions under which learning and adaptation can occur quickly and accurately.[30]

The study of 'government as a learning system' – to use Schon's phrase – has produced long lists of reasons why public institutions do not learn and adapt easily.[31] We know from the history of banking regulation that crisis is a great aid to learning, but that it is also a very painful and costly one. The cybernetic study of government has, however, yet to provide any useful general rules of institutional design which go beyond platitudes about the importance of remaining open and adaptive. This is not surprising, for since the pioneering work of

Burns and Stalker the lesson of modern organisation theory has been that the appropriate design for an institution is contingent on a wide range of factors both inside the institution and in its environment.[32] There are indeed good contingent reasons why change and adaptation in government actually need to be limited. The modern state is, among other things, a very large organisation. In big organisations settled routines and ways of solving problems – 'standard operating procedures', as the organisation theorists would put it – are vital aids to consistent and coordinated action; in other words, they deal with administrative complexity. In a similar way shared customary assumptions – Schon's 'ideas in good currency' – allow policy makers to communicate and cooperate with each other and to produce decisions consistent with what has happened in the past and with what is presently happening elsewhere in government.[33] In liberal democracies cultural expectations reinforce this preference for routine, since it is expected that the powers of public policy makers will be constrained by general rules and that like cases will be treated alike. The practical consequence of this is seen in tax administration, where authorities constrained by rules are generally a step behind opportunistic tax avoiders and evaders. Were the tax authorities fully capable of rapid learning and adaptation they would be a danger to democracy and to the rule of law.

The problem of how to encourage learning is also tackled by those who argue for more incentives and competition within government. One of the attractions of their argument is that it seems to promise improved learning and adaptation without sacrificing the rules which limit public power.

(b) *More competition*

That competition inside government aids learning and responsiveness is conventional wisdom in Britain. Public corporations, for instance, compete both with each other and with private firms in supplying goods and services. Many goods and services are also supplied to government by competitive tender. The principle of competition is therefore not at issue; the argument is about how far it should be applied. The possibilities are well illustrated by models for the economic analysis of government originally developed in the United States by Tullock, by Downs and by Niskanen.[34] These models in turn draw on reasoning common in economic analysis. Public servants are assumed to be motivated by the desire to maximise some measure of their own utility, such as their income, the size of the budget they control or the size of their department. Their unrestrained pursuit of self-interest leads to a socially wasteful level of services and, more concretely, to little serious effort to contain costs. The remedy is to encourage more competition, both intellectual and economic. The former opens up the policy debate, supplies different sources of information, and thus prevents bureaucrats from using their special expertise to control the terms of debate about policy options. Economic competition (for instance in the form of competitive tendering) likewise increases the flow of information, encourages efficient use of resources and makes public servants more responsive to the needs of consumers.

The influence of such ideas has been growing. Hall has drawn on economic models in his explanation of planning disasters, while Hartley has applied them rigorously to British defence policy, and has recommended an experiment in which rival branches of the armed forces bid for the contract to provide particular defence services, rather as bidding occurs for franchises to operate commercial television stations. Henderson's analysis of prediction 'error' in the development of Concorde and in nuclear energy policy also plainly owes much to the application of economic reasoning.[35]

Since the principle of intellectual and economic competition is well established the only argument is about how far it should be extended. The case for more open discussion in policy making (such as is advanced by Henderson) looks particularly unexceptionable, especially to intellectuals who after all live by the free exchange of ideas. Yet the argument that more open policy making is better policy making is an untested and dubious hypothesis. It is dubious because in making policy more openly we do more than increase the free flow of information; we also introduce new actors and interests whose demands have to be accommodated. The point was well understood by bankers who struggled to separate the esoteric politics of the City from the exoteric politics of Parliament and party. More open policy debate encourages partisan controversy and the adversary style of argument which goes with it. It is entirely rational to prefer open, adversary conflict to private, esoteric policy making, for instance on the grounds that powerful interests should be subjected to control by elected politicians; but it is not clear that where the adversary system deeply influences policy (for example, in education) it results in more efficiency or effectiveness than where policy is made esoterically. A judgement about when more intellectual competition would in any particular case produce more technically efficient policy is a fine one. By contrast, the arguments against introducing economic competition on the scale proposed by writers like Hartley seem very clear. The limits to using competition are set by three considerations: opportunism, the limits of consumer sovereignty and the problem of administrative complexity.

Opportunism is a difficulty because in the economic model of bureaucratic behaviour public servants are presumed to manipulate information in a self-interested way. By actually encouraging self-interest, more competition encourages this manipulation and lessens the normative restraints exercised by professional values. Hirsch has pointed to a striking example in American education. Performance contracting in schools involves paying teachers by output rather than by input: in other words, payment depends on results measured by pupils' attainment in certain standard tests. But the objective is defeated by 'the incentive such a system also gives to teachers to neglect those aspects of educational output that fall outside the tests and to manipulate the tests themselves by teaching how to pass tests or how to cheat without being penalised'. Similar but more gruesome difficulties were experienced in the efforts to use 'body counts' as a measure of output for American forces in the Vietnamese war.[36]

Even supposing this kind of opportunism to be controllable there exist limits set by the extent to which consumers should have sovereign choice. The aim of introducing more competition is undoubtedly to make policy makers highly responsive to those who pay for and consume public services. Yet there are many policy areas where a rational case can be made for unresponsive paternalism. Competition in broadcasting, for instance, is only to be preferred if Reithian conceptions of the proper functions of a broadcasting service are abandoned; otherwise the influence of competition from commercial television and radio in Britain in recent years must be judged a disaster.

To opportunism and the limits of consumer sovereignty must be added the problem of administrative complexity. Achieving effective cooperation between different public agencies is already made difficult by bureaucratic rivalries and suspicions. Competition will intensify these. The navy's knowledge that its 'franchise' to supply nuclear defence is to be challenged by the RAF is hardly likely to help cooperation between the two services; indeed, there will be a strong incentive to conceal information in case it gives advantages to future rival bidders.

Competition increases suspicion; in doing so it conflicts with the effort to raise trust as a way of coping with complexity.

(c) *More trust*

Hirsch has eloquently put the case for relying more completely on trust in organising collective action. Opportunism can be neither effectively repressed by tight hierarchical controls, nor effectively harnessed through competition; neither hierarchy nor competition can prevent rules being manipulated by those responsible for making them and by those for whom they are designed. Only when behaviour is constrained by moral codes can individuals be trusted to follow the letter and the spirit of rules and regulations. Hirsch believed that the culture of capitalism destroyed this necessary morality. Much modern economic analysis is even more pessimistic: working from utilitarian asumptions it presumes that opportunism is an unalterable natural disposition.[37] My argument is a middle way between these: that the sense of obligation can be created, but that doing so is a desperately difficult business plagued by dilemmas.

These dilemmas appear as soon as we consider the ways in which public institutions commonly try to create a sense of obligation among their members not to act opportunistically. In public bureaucracies (as in all large organisations) socialisation and training are commonly designed to create moral commitments; much manifestly technical training has this important unspoken function. Yet the practical experience of socialisation in an organisation is known to have two sides: it involves being taught those codes of an institution which discourage opportunism; and less officially it involves learning how to manipulate the institution and its rules in an opportunistic way.

Almost every way of creating and sustaining moral codes has this double-edged quality. The growing significance of professionalism in the public services is a striking example. Professionalism is notoriously an instrument of opportunism: it is used to manipulate markets so as to raise the price of professional services, and to manipulate information so as to mystify outsiders and increase the power and authority of practitioners.[38] Bureaucracies which employ professionals in large numbers also find professional loyalties a considerable obstacle in securing effective coordination and control.[39] But it is also plain that in so far as those who supply services like education and health care can be trusted not to behave opportunistically their restraint is guaranteed, not mainly by bureaucratic controls, but by a professional sense of obligation. The benefits of professionalism are increased because in fields as diverse as medicine and accountancy acquiring technical skills goes with learning moral obligations. Although professionalism in the public sector has to be treated with caution it offers a promising way of discouraging opportunism by public servants. Aspirants to professional status should be cautiously encouraged, however incongruous the aspirations may look by conventional standards. Thus claims by those who empty dustbins to be treated as 'refuse disposal operatives' are commonly treated with levity; but this search for occupational dignity is important because it indicates both a demand for respect and a willingness to take on professional-like obligations.

The restraints imposed by professional obligations shade into more diffuse obligations which can come from the sense of being a public servant. Anything which diminishes the distinctiveness of public service endangers commitment to these diffuse obligations. For this reason efforts to model the conduct of public institutions on the private sector need to be looked at sceptically. The fashionable search for entrepreneurial initiative in civil servants is a particular danger, because it is a direct incitement to opportunism. An even greater danger is posed by the spread of militant pay bargaining from private industry into the public sector. In the last two decades militant trade unionism and aggressive collective bargaining have destroyed many of the restraints produced by professional codes and the commitment to public service. The most obvious sign of destruction has been the growing willingness to take industrial action which harms the recipients of services. The opportunism of public sector employers has encouraged this destruction. The clearest instance is the case of nursing, where the restraint created by the obligation felt to patients has been exploited as a way of imposing limits on pay.

The prospects for reversing the spread of militant pay bargaining are not good; alternative ways of settling pay, such as arbitration and 'fair comparison', are being widely discarded. The difficulties are especially acute when inflation is high, for any method which removes the incentive to resort to militancy involves protecting public servants from some of the pain of rising prices. This in turn creates the understandable suspicion elsewhere in the community that public employees are manipulating policy to give themselves special privileges. In turn this diminishes the trust in government felt by private citizens. There is thus a connection between the problem of creating moral restraints among those responsible for policy and creating similar restraints elsewhere in the community.

Opportunistic behaviour by powerful private interests is a key problem in policy making, particularly in respect of economic policy: the state wrestles with opportunism in financial markets, in industrial relations, in tax collection and in a host of other areas. Attempts to foster moral codes reproduce dilemmas encountered in the public sector. For example, the ambiguous character of professionalism reappears. One of the most important reasons why large capitalist corporations often accept restraints more onerous than the bare letter of the law is undoubtedly that their behaviour is influenced by professional standards learnt by those who occupy positions of influence inside corporations. Yet professional skills also help corporations to practise highly sophisticated opportunism. The most obvious example of this dual effect is provided by the influence of professional standards in accounting and auditing. These standards, uncertain and contested though they often are, have been crucial in establishing some measures of consistency and truthfulness in financial statements. If there were no accounting profession, laws designed to ensure some prudence and honesty in business life would be even more imperfectly applied than at present.[40] But at the same time accounting skills are extensively used by corporations to manipulate rules, notably in the pursuit of 'tax efficiency'. The state is not helpless in the face of this opportunism, for by licensing an institution to control the entry to an occupation it can try to have some say over the terms of training, and in this way can influence the moral codes of the profession. This strategy is nevertheless fraught with difficulties. Granting what is effectively a public monopoly to practise a trade to a particular group gives wide scope for opportunism; the history of the medical profession illustrates the economic advantages which such opportunism brings.

State licensing of a profession is itself a particular instance of the more general resort to corporatism as a way of curbing opportunism. Corporatist controls have been widely tried: in particular industries; in industrial relations; and in financial markets. Under corporatism, the state either openly licenses an institution to control a particular sphere or tolerates privileges for those prepared to recognise restraints.[41] It works best when the public and private sectors are united in a close, small community, and where the rules and the spirit in which they are to be applied are clearly understood. Such circumstances described perfectly the regulation of financial markets in Britain until a couple of decades ago. The decline of that closed world also shows the limits to corporatism. Where markets are organised on a large scale with no binding of social homogeneity the understandings needed to rely on trust do not appear. This is essentially why corporatism failed in industrial relations. When institutions opportunistically break or bend rules – which describes the behaviour of both fringe banks and militant trade unions – the willingness of those inside corporatist institutions to observe restraint correspondingly declines. At this point the system is faced with the choice of dismantling controls and trusting to competition, or going forward to a more legally coercive set of restrictions. Both options face well known, if different, problems of complexity.

Even where corporatist controls can be maintained their existence sets very clear limits to the kinds of policies which can be pursued. The curbs on opportunism are purchased at the price of sharing policy making with affected interests. Hence in financial markets traditional regulation rested on esoteric politics: Whitehall and Westminster kept out of the City; numerous issues were removed from 'politics' as conventionally understood, in other words, from the control of law and of Parliament; and financial interests were able to exercise great influence over markets, and through markets over financial policy.

To all this must be added what, in the financial markets, is a fatal last problem. Corporatism is a system of national control. No supranational political authority exists even to attempt the task of creating in the supranational markets the kind of enclosed community so necessary for its success. The best that can be expected is what is observable at the moment in banking: the slow and painful growth of cooperation between different national authorities and the equally slow and painful progress towards establishing international professional standards.

Academic studies of particular policies, especially of government fiascos, usually conclude with a characteristic peroration. The writer, emerging briefly from the rational tranquillity of the library and the study, looks with horror on the chaos of government. He urges policy makers to pull themselves together: to be less secretive, to gather better information, to clarify their objectives, and to use more rational techniques. Peroration exhausted, he then disappears back to the comfortable obscurity of academic life. The temptation to deliver these sermons should be resisted. Our brief review of the imperfect and contradictory ways of living with complexity calls to mind Perrow's argument that most choices facing institutions have the quality of dilemmas. Every remedy brings its own disease, every benefit a painful loss.[42] Even the most attractive possibilities contain the seeds of their own destruction. Solutions are compelled by failure and crisis, and are then destroyed by more failure and crisis. Decisions are rarely produced by careful thought; they are invented half-consciously in the often desperate effort to cope with immediate dangers, or in calmer times they come out of the bovine power of custom. Thus do we all try to live with complexity; or at least to survive it.

Notes and References

Sources are referred to in full on the first occasion; subsequent references use a shortened version. *Bank of England Quarterly Bulletin* is referred to throughout as *BEQB*.

CHAPTER 1: THE POLITICS OF COMPLEXITY

1. Measurement problems are summarised in M. J. Artis, 'Monetary Policy – Part II', in F. T. Blackaby (ed.), *British Economic Policy 1960–74: Demand Management*, students' edition (London: Cambridge University Press, 1979) pp. 258–303 (280–5); Geoffrey E. J. Dennis, 'Money Supply and its Control', in W. J. P. Maunder (ed.), *The British Economy in the 1970s* (London: Heinemann Educational Books, 1980) pp. 35–60 (51–4).
2. The figures are derived from Margaret Reid, *The Secondary Banking Crisis 1973–5* (London: Macmillan, 1982) pp. 190–2. The figure for public institutions is arrived at by adding her estimate of the Bank of England's losses to those of the Crown Agents. The figure for the clearing banks is incomplete because the support operation is even now not finished. Problems of estimating losses are discussed in Chapter 5.
3. For instance Graham C. Hockley, *Public Finance* (London: Routledge & Kegan Paul, 1979) pp. 32–41.
4. The key changes occurred in September but others preceded and succeeded them. The relevant documents are: 'Competition and credit control: a consultative document issued on 14 May 1971', *BEQB*, 11 (1971) pp. 189–93; 'Key issues in monetary and credit policy: text of an address by the Governor', *BEQB*, 11 (1971) pp. 195–8; 'Competition and credit control: the discount market', *BEQB*, 11 (1971) pp. 314–15; 'Competition and credit control: extract from a Sykes Memorial lecture by the Chief Cashier of the Bank of England', *BEQB*, 11 (1971) pp. 477–81.
5. House of Commons (HC) *Debates*, vol. 817, cols 1064–5 (18 May 1971). Speaker: the Chief Secretary to the Treasury, Mr Maurice Macmillan.
6. Theodore J. Lowi, 'Four Systems of Policy, Politics and Choice', *Public Administration Review*, 32 (1972) pp. 298–310.
7. Notably David Gowland, *Monetary Policy and Credit Control* (London: Croom Helm, 1978) and K. K. Zawadzki, *Competition and Credit Control* (Oxford: Basil Blackwell, 1981).
8. For balanced criticism see W. I. Jenkins, *Policy Analysis* (Oxford: Martin

164   The Politics of Banking

   Robertson, 1978) pp. 19–20 and 90–2; Robert E. Goodin, 'Rational Politicians and Rational Bureaucrats', *Public Administration*, 60 (1982) pp. 23–41 (37) is more dismissive.
9. In Select Committee on Nationalised Industries (Sub-Committee C), *Minutes of Evidence*, HC 166–i (1977–8) p. 4.
10. It is not generally realised that internal targets existed before 1976: see 'Reflections on the conduct of monetary policy: the first Mais lecture given by the Governor', *BEQB*, 18 (1978) p. 978.
11. For a practical demonstration of exactly this point see William Greider, 'The Education of David Stockman', *The Atlantic Monthly*, December 1981, pp. 27–54. (I owe this reference to Anthony King.) The classic statements of intellectual complexity are H. A. Simon, 'Theories of decision making in economics and behavioural science', *American Economic Review*, 49 (1959) pp. 253–83; Charles E. Lindblom, 'The Science of "Muddling Through"', *Public Administration Review*, 19 (1959) pp. 79–85. A useful collection of papers is F. Castles *et al* (eds), *Decisions, Organisations and Society* (Harmondsworth: Penguin, 1976).
12. Todd R. La Porte (ed.), *Organised Social Complexity: challenge to politics and policy* (Princeton University Press, 1975).
13. A thorough study of the bureaucratic division of labour is Andrew Dunsire, *Implementation in a Bureaucracy* (Oxford: Martin Robertson, 1978).
14. Harold Seidman, *Politics, Position and Power*, 2nd edition (London: Oxford University Press, 1975) p. 190.
15. Anthony King, 'Overload: Problems of Governing in the 1970s' in F. F. Ridley (ed.), *Studies in Politics* (London: Oxford University Press, 1975) pp. 284–96; Richard Rose and Guy Peters, *Can Government Go Bankrupt?* (London: Macmillan, 1979); Richard Rose (ed.), *Challenge to Governance: studies in overloaded polities* (London: Sage, 1980).
16. This I take to be the lesson offered in the finest of all implementation studies: Jeffrey L. Pressman and Aaron B. Wildavsky, *Implementation* (London: University of California Press, 1973).

CHAPTER 2: THE POLITICS OF LOMBARD STREET

1. On Britain, S. G. Checkland, *The Rise of Industrial Society in England* (London: Longman, 1964) pp. 202–12; on the United States, Paul B. Trescott, *Financing American Enterprise* (New York: Harper & Row, 1963) pp. 64–87; on Germany, P. Barrett Whale, *Joint Stock Banking in Germany* (London: Frank Casss, 1968, original publication 1930) pp. 36–65.
2. On traditional preferences: R. S. Sayers, *Modern Banking*, 7th edition (Oxford: Clarendon Press, 1967) pp. 186–90; on change: The London Clearing Banks, *Evidence by the Committee of London Clearing Bankers to the Committee to Review the Functioning of Financial Institutions* (London: CLCB/Longman, 1978) pp. 98–113.
3. Committee on Finance and Industry (Chairman: Lord Macmillan), *Report*, Cmd 3897 (1931) p. 162.

Notes and References 165

4. Thomas Balogh, *Studies in Financial Organisation* (Cambridge University Press, 1950) pp. 230–41.
5. On Germany, Fritz Stern, *Gold and Iron* (London: Allen & Unwin, 1980), Part Three; on the United States, Seymour Martin Lipset and Earl Raab, *The Politics of Unreason* (London: Heinemann, 1970).
6. Sidney Pollard, *The Development of the British Economy 1914–1967*, 2nd edition (London: Edward Arnold, 1969) pp. 232–3 has details.
7. Michael Moran, 'Finance Capital and Pressure-Group Politics in Britain', *British Journal of Political Science*, 11 (1981) pp. 381–404.
8. Brian Griffiths, 'The Development of Restrictive Practices in the U.K. Monetary System', *The Manchester School*, XLI (1973) pp. 3–18.
9. The classic is R. J. Truptil, *British Banks and the London Money Market* (London: Jonathan Cape, 1936) pp. 191–7.
10. Michael Lisle-Williams, 'Continuities in the English Financial Elite, 1850–1980', paper given to a conference on 'Capital, Ideology and Politics', University of Sheffield, January 1981. I am grateful to Michael Lisle-Williams for permission to cite this interim report on his Doctoral research.
11. G. A. Fletcher, *The Discount Houses in London* (London: Macmillan, 1976) pp. 43–58.
12. Lisle-Williams, 'The English Financial Elite', pp. 54–5.
13. Committee on the Working of the Monetary System (Chairman: Lord Radcliffe), *Principal Memoranda of Evidence*, vol. 1 (London: HMSO, 1960) p. 52.
14. Griffiths, 'Development of Restrictive Practices in the U.K. Monetary System', pp. 4–8; Edward Nevin and E. W. Davis, *The London Clearing Banks* (London: Elek Books, 1970) pp. 73–83.
15. Fletcher, *The Discount Houses in London*, pp. 43–51.
16. The origins of the practice are in R. S. Sayers, *The Bank of England 1891–1944*, vol. 2 (London: Cambridge University Press, 1976) p. 537; and for its uses see Radcliffe Committee, *Minutes of Evidence* (London: HMSO, 1960) p. 260.
17. For elaboration: David K. Sheppard, *The Growth and Role of UK Financial Institutions 1880–1962* (London: Methuen, 1971) pp. 13–16.
18. Quoted in Sir John Clapham, *The Bank of England: A History*, vol. I (London: Cambridge University Press, 1944) p. 174.
19. J. E. Wadsworth, 'Banking Ratios Past and Present', in C. R. Whittesley and J. S. G. Wilson (eds), *Essays in Money and Banking* (Oxford: Clarendon Press, 1968) pp. 229–51; Fred Hirsch, 'The Bagehot Problem', *The Manchester School*, (1977) pp. 241–57.
20. Charles P. Kindleberger, *Manias, Panics, and Crashes: a history of financial crises* (London: Macmillan, 1978) p. 161. Kindleberger's is also an excellent study of how means of crisis management have evolved.
21. Clapham, *The Bank of England*, II, pp. 95–102, 199–211; 226–34; 263 ff; L. S. Presnell, 'Gold Reserves, Banking Reserves, and the Baring Crisis of 1890', in Whittesley and Wilson (eds), *Essays in Money and Banking*, pp. 167–228.
22. For a summary of the statutes see Committee to Review the Functioning of Financial Institutions (Chairman: Sir Harold Wilson), *Second Stage*

Evidence, vol. 4 (London: HMSO, 1979) pp. 101-2.
23. For the Discount Houses: Fletcher, *The Discount Houses in London*, p. 33; for 'market determined' recognition, Wilson Committee, *Second Stage Evidence*, vol. 4, pp. 96-7.
24. George Blunden, 'The supervision of the UK banking system', *BEQB*, 15 (1975) pp. 188-94.
25. The politics of industrial policy are examined in Wyn Grant, *The Political Economy of Industrial Policy* (London: Butterworths, 1982); for help to banks in the 1960s see Select Committee on Nationalised Industries, *Report*, Minutes of Evidence and Appendices, HC 258 (1969-70) p. 283. For an explicit defence of secrecy by the Governor, ibid., p. 146.
26. For practices as late as 1970 see HC 258 (1969-70) pp. 41-2.
27. Michael Artis, *Foundations of British Monetary Policy* (Oxford: Blackwell, 1965) p. 69. These arrangements were altered in 1981.
28. This measure is authoritatively described in Sir Norman Chester, *The Nationalisation of British Industry 1945-51* (London: HMSO, 1975) pp. 880-5; the Act's wording is reprinted in HC 258 (1969-70), Appendix 16.
29. For an example of how the system worked: Bank of England, *Annual Report 1966*, pp. 7-8.
30. For an elaborate account see HC 258 (1969-70) pp. xxv-xxviii.
31. On 'voluntarism' in industrial relations: Colin Crouch, *Class Conflict and the Industrial Relations Crisis* (London: Heinemann, 1977) pp. 143 ff.
32. Changes in the 1960s are well summarised in R. J. Clark, 'The Evolution of Monetary and Financial Institutions', in David R. Croome and Harry G. Johnson (eds), *Money in Britain 1959-1969* (London: Oxford University Press, 1970) pp. 131-49.
33. HC 258 (1969-70) p. 38.
34. Artis, *Foundations of British Monetary Policy*, pp. 83-93; Bank of England, *Annual Report 1962*, p. 3.
35. The quotation is from Artis, *Foundations ...*, p. 86; for Radcliffe see Committee on the Working of the Monetary System, *Report*, Cmnd 827 (1959) p. 74.
36. For a clear, succinct sketch of the system before 1914, Pollard, *Development of the British Economy*, pp. 14-18.
37. This paragraph draws on Sayers, *The Bank of England*, vol. I, pp. 1-17.
38. For early struggles see Sir Henry Clay, *Lord Norman* (London: Macmillan, 1957) pp. 290-9; Andrew Boyle, *Montagu Norman* (London: Cassell, 1967) p. 228. For 1950s Radcliffe, *Report*, p. 274.
39. The background is sketched in The Monopolies Commission, *Barclays Bank Ltd., Lloyds Bank Ltd. and Martins Bank Ltd.: a report on the proposed mergers*, HC 319 (1967-8) pp. 1-4.
40. Radcliffe Committee, *Minutes of Evidence*, p. 864.
41. E. Victor Morgan and W. A. Thomas, *The Stock Exchange: its history and functions* (London: Elek, 1962) pp. 185-9 has measures.
42. The first quotation is from Radcliffe Committee, *Principal Memoranda*, vol. 3, p. 47; the second from Radcliffe, *Minutes*, p. 876.
43. For the challenge: Samuel Brittan, *Steering the Economy* (Harmondsworth: Penguin, 1970) p. 388.

44. For problems with Lord Cromer: Sir Harold Wilson, *The Labour Government 1964–70: a personal record* (London: Weidenfeld & Nicolson/Michael Joseph, 1971) p. 34; Marcia Williams, *Inside Number 10* (London: Weidenfeld & Nicolson, 1972) p. 36; for complaints about his successor, HC *Debates*, vol. 753, cols 1241–4 (9 November 1967).
45. Note, for instance, the Bank's omission from a standard study of public expenditure politics, Hugh Heclo and Aaron Wildavsky, *The Private Government of Public Money*, 2nd edition (London: Macmillan, 1981).
46. Richard A. Chapman and J. R. Greenaway, *The Dynamics of Administrative Reform* (London: Croom Helm, 1980) pp. 100–14.
47. On Norman's aversion to politicians, Sayers, *The Bank of England*, vol. I, p. 160.
48. Clay, *Lord Norman*, p. 298.
49. Radcliffe Committee, *Minutes of Evidence*, p. 15.
50. Brittan, *Steering the Economy*, p. 79.
51. For a sceptical analysis see Radcliffe Committee, *Report*, pp. 272–3.
52. HC 258 (1969–70) p. lxxxvii.
53. Ibid., p. 131.
54. Macmillan Committee, *Minutes of Evidence*, vol. II (London: HMSO, 1931) p. 296.
55. Lord Cobbold in Radcliffe Committee, *Principal Memoranda of Evidence*, vol. 1, p. 52.
56. Ibid., vol. 3, p. 33.
57. Radcliffe Committee, *Minutes of Evidence*, p. 876.
58. W. J. M. Mackenzie, 'Models of English Politics', in Richard Rose (ed.), *Studies in British Politics*, 3rd edition (London: Macmillan, 1976) pp. 5–15. The paper originally appeared in French in 1965. I have excluded Mackenzie's third model of *dissent*.
59. Sir George Bolton, 'What the Bank of England Is', *The Banker*, August 1970, p. 821.

CHAPTER 3: THE POLITICS OF POLICY CHANGE

1. Graham Allison and Morton H. Halperin, 'Bureaucratic Politics: A Paradigm and Some Policy Implications', in R. Tanter and R. H. Ullman (eds), *Theory and Policy in International Relations* (Princeton University Press, 1972).
2. 'Competition and credit control', *BEQB*, 11 (1971) pp. 189–93.
3. 'Key issues in monetary and credit policy', *BEQB*, 11 (1971) pp. 195–8.
4. The best summary of control measures in the 1960s is 'The operation of monetary policy since the Radcliffe Report: a paper prepared in the Bank of England in consultation with H.M. Treasury', *BEQB*, 9 (1969) pp. 448–60.
5. HC *Debates*, vol. 799, cols 1233–4 (14 April 1970).
6. 'Key issues in monetary and credit policy', p. 196.
7. Committee on Consumer Credit (Chairman: Lord Crowther) *Report*, Cmnd 4596 (1971) pp. 146–51. The Report was published in March 1971 but was signed in the previous December.

8. 'Competition and credit control', p. 192.
9. For the theoretical background see, for instance, Andrew Crockett, *Money: Theory, Policy and Institutions* (London: Thomas Nelson, 1973) pp. 161-73.
10. 'Key issues in monetary and credit policy', p. 195.
11. Ibid.
12. Gowland, *Monetary Policy and Credit Control*, pp. 51-2.
13. The clearest description is in Zawadzki, *Competition and Credit Control*, pp. 40-1.
14. Gowland, *Monetary Policy and Credit Control*, p. 31.
15. Brittan, *Steering the Economy*, p. 157.
16. National Board for Prices and Incomes, Report No. 34, *Bank Charges*, Cmnd 3292 (1967) pp. 27-35; Report No. 40, *Second General Report*, Cmnd, 3394 (1967) pp. 36-7.
17. HC 319 (1967-8) p. 46.
18. Crowther Committee, *Report*, especially Part Three.
19. John Thompson, 'The Role of the Commercial Banks in the Economy', *Journal of the Institute of Bankers*, April 1968, pp. 96-105; John Hunsworth, 'Efficiency in the Banks', *The Bankers' Magazine*, April 1969, pp. 225-9; Brian Griffiths, 'British Banking: A Plan for Competition', *The Banker*, May 1970, pp. 491-9.
20. Patrick Dunleavy, *Urban Political Analysis: The politics of collective consumption* (London: Macmillan, 1980) p. 99.
21. These reflections rest on casual observation and on Erving Goffman, *Asylums* (Harmondsworth: Penguin, 1968).
22. Quoted in Paul Davidson, *Money and the Real World*, 2nd edition (London: Macmillan, 1978) p. ix.
23. On timing see M. D. K. W. Foot, 'Monetary Targets: Their Nature and Record in the Major Economies', in Brian Griffiths and Geoffrey E. Wood (eds), *Monetary Targets* (London: Macmillan, 1981) pp. 13-46.
24. The Governor, Mansion House Speech, *BEQB*, 11 (1971) p. 506.
25. Ronald W. Clark, *Tizard* (London: Metheun, 1965); Patrick Dunleavy, *The Politics of Mass Housing in Britain, 1945-75* (Oxford: Clarendon Press, 1981) pp. 133-41; on a historical lobby, S. E. Finer, 'The Transmission of Benthamite ideas 1820-50', in Gillian Sutherland (ed.), *Studies in the growth of nineteenth-century government* (London: Routledge & Kegan Paul, 1972) pp. 11-32.
26. Note especially Harry G. Johnson, 'Recent Developments in Monetary Theory – A Commentary', in Croome and Johnson, *Money in Britain*, pp. 83-114; and H. G. Johnson (ed.), *Readings in British Monetary Economics* (Oxford: Clarendon Press, 1972) pp. 151-200.
27. Sayers' most influential text was *Modern Banking*; by the late 1960s it reached its seventh edition.
28. The novelty is explicit in Griffiths, 'Development of Restrictive Practices in the U.K. Monetary System', pp. 17-18; and in Hirsch, 'The Bagehot Problem', p. 241. For micro-analysis, Harry G. Johnson, 'Problems of Efficiency in Monetary Management', *Journal of Political Economy*, 75 (1968) pp. 971-90.
29. Brittan, *Steering the Economy*, pp. 396-7.

30. Alan Walters, *Money in Boom and Slump*, 3rd edition (London: Institute of Economic Affairs, 1971).
31. Brian Griffiths, *Competition in Banking* (London: Institute of Economic Affairs, 1970).
32. See references in notes 26 and 28 for Johnson's specialist work. His higher journalism includes 'Observations on the Bank Merger Proposals', *The Bankers' Magazine*, September 1968, pp. 135–7; 'Current Issues in Monetary Policy', *The Bankers' Magazine*, November 1968, pp. 251–7.
33. On the last, HC 258 (1969–70) p. 272.
34. See Opie's article in *The Bankers' Magazine*, April 1969, pp. 230–2.
35. Printed in Croome and Johnson, *Money in Britain*, pp. 69–74 and 122–6.
36. The Governor, Mansion House Speech, *BEQB*, 11 (1971) p. 506.
37. S. E. Finer (ed.), *Adversary Politics and Electoral Reform* (London: Wigram, 1975); Michael Stewart, *Politics and Economic Policy in the UK since 1964: the Jekyll and Hyde Years* (Oxford: Pergamon Press, 1978) especially pp. 241–7.
38. HC *Debates*, vol. 814, col. 1372 (30 March 1971).
39. For a banker see Deryk Weyer, 'Competition and Credit Control', *The Bankers' Magazine*, March 1974, pp. 14–17. Mr Weyer was then Senior General Manager of Barclays Bank.
40. Stephen Young and A. V. Lowe, *Intervention in the Mixed Economy* (London: Croom Helm, 1974) pp. 121–46; Brendon Sewill, 'A View from the Inside', in Ralph Harris and Brendon Sewill, *British Economic Policy 1970–1974: Two Views* (London: Institute of Economic Affairs, 1975) pp. 27–63.
41. HC *Debates*, vol. 799, cols 1234–5 (14 April 1970).
42. 'Key issues in monetary and credit policy', p. 198.
43. One of the most interesting of recent Marxist accounts is David Coates, *Labour in power?* (London: Longman, 1980); more orthodox pressure group theory is well represented by Samuel Beer, *Modern British Politics*, 2nd edition (London: Faber, 1969) pp. 318–51; J. J. Richardson and A. G. Jordan, *Governing Under Pressure* (Oxford: Martin Robertson, 1979).
44. HC 319 (1967–8) pp. 4–6.
45. Calculated from Wilson Committee, *Report*, Cmnd 7939 (1980), Appendix 10, Table 10.7.
46. Cmnd 3292 (1967) pp. 13–14.
47. The first authoritative account of secondary banks is Jack Revell, *Changes in British Banking: the growth of a secondary banking system* (London: Hill, Samuel, 1968); for a more comprehensive view, Malcolm Craig, *The Sterling Money Markets* (Epping: Gower Press, 1976).
48. Calculated from the Wilson Committee, *Report*, Appendix 3, Table 3.70.
49. Committee of London Clearing Bankers, *Evidence to the Wilson Committee*, p. 134.
50. John Humble and S. G. Holliman, 'Management By Objectives – I and II', *Journal of the Institute of Bankers*, December 1970, pp. 400–18.
51. See the banks' arguments in HC 319 (1967–68) pp. 13–19.
52. On rapid growth of subsidiaries see *The Bankers' Magazine*, September 1971 p. 110.
53. Bank of England evidence in HC 258 (1969–70) p. 73.

54. Interview in *The Banker*, April 1970, pp. 354–60. For an earlier attack on ceilings by the chairman of Barclays Bank see Thompson, 'The Role of the Commercial Banks in the Economy'.
55. Deryk Weyer, 'Competition and Credit Control', *The Bankers' Magazine*, March 1974, pp. 14–17.
56. Committee of London Clearing Bankers, *Evidence to the Wilson Committee*, p. 49.
57. Harry Johnson, 'The Report on Bank Charges', *The Bankers' Magazine*, August 1967, pp. 64–8, reprinted in Johnson (ed.), *Readings in British Monetary Economics*, pp. 321–9.
58. Sir Cuthbert Clegg, 'Competing for Deposits', Presidential address to the Institute of Bankers, reprinted in *Journal of the Institute of Bankers*, June 1969, pp. 161–78.
59. For a sceptical review see James Q. Wilson (ed.), *The Politics of Regulation* (New York: Basic Books, 1980) pp. 357–94.
60. Ascribed to Price by Graham Allison, *Essence of Decision: Explaining the Cuban Missile Crisis* (Boston: Little, Brown, 1971) pp. 71 and 316.
61. Ibid., p. 167.
62. For two of many examples see Governor's speech to the Finance Houses Association, 21 March 1968, in *BEQB*, 8 (1968) pp. 173–5; and his 'Monetary management in the United Kingdom: the Jane Hodge Memorial Lecture', *BEQB*, 11 (1971) pp. 37–47 (40).
63. The Governor, Mansion House Speech, *BEQB*, 7 (1967) p. 382.
64. A principal theme of, for instance, 'The operation of monetary policy since the Radcliffe Report'.
65. The story is in Jack Revell, *The British Financial System* (London: Macmillan, 1973) p. 131.
66. Crowther Committee, *Report*, p. 362.
67. Mansion House Speech, *BEQB*, 7 (1967) p. 382.
68. Mr Richardson in HC 166–ii (1977–8) p. 31; the Wilson evidence is in 'The secondary banking crisis and the Bank of England's support operations', *BEQB*, 18 (1978) pp. 230–9. This paper (which uses the word 'contract', p. 131) was omitted from the volumes of evidence published by Wilson.
69. HC 319 (1967–8) p. 41. The quotation is the Commission's paraphrase of the Governor's evidence.
70. On this point: Committee of London Clearing Bankers, *Evidence to the Wilson Committee*, p. 49.
71. HC 319 (1967–8) p. 43.
72. This observation is documented in Michael Moran, 'Power, Policy and the City of London', in Roger King (ed.), *Capital and Politics* (London: Routledge & Kegan Paul, 1983).
73. Heclo and Wildavsky, *Private Government of Public Money*, preface to 2nd edition; Maurice Wright, 'Public Expenditure in Britain: The Crisis of Control', *Public Administration*, 55 (1977) pp. 143–69; for the public challenge to the private politics of nuclear power, Roger Williams, *The Nuclear Power Decisions* (London: Croom Helm, 1980) pp. 261–311.
74. Sir George Bolton, 'What the Bank of England Is', *The Banker*, August 1970, p. 821.

Notes and References 171

CHAPTER 4: THE POLITICS OF THE MONEY SUPPLY

1. The two-year average is in 'Reflections on the conduct of monetary policy', p. 32. Some other measures are in A. R. Prest and D. J. Coppock (eds), *The UK Economy: A Manual of Applied Economics*, 8th edition (London: Weidenfeld & Nicolson, 1980) pp. 302–11.
2. For this paragraph I have drawn on the 'Chronology' in Gowland, *Monetary Policy and Credit Control*, Appendix A.
3. The changes at the end of 1973 are clearly summarised in J. H. B. Tew, 'Monetary Policy – Part I', in Blackaby (ed.), *British Economic Policy 1960–74*, pp. 218–57 (256–7).
4. David Laidler, 'United Kingdom inflation and its background: a monetarist perspective', in Michael Parkin and Michael T. Sumner (eds), *Inflation in the United Kingdom* (Manchester: Manchester University Press, 1978) pp. 52–74.
5. The Government's early attempt at a strategy is described in 'The medium-term financial strategy', *Treasury Economic Progress Report*, April 1980, pp. 2–4.
6. The most influential modern argument for non-discretionary monetary management is Milton Friedman, *Capitalism and Freedom* (Chicago: University of Chicago Press, 1964) pp. 37–55. Two influential pessimistic post-Barber polemics are Peter Jay, *Employment, Inflation and Politics* (London: Institute of Economic Affairs, 1976); Samuel Brittan, *The Economic Consequences of Democracy* (London: Temple Smith, 1977). For a careful analysis of empirical evidence about elections and the money supply see Edward R. Tufte, *Political Control of the Economy* (Princeton University Press, 1978) pp. 48–52.
7. 'Memorandum by Professor M. Friedman', in House of Commons Treasury and Civil Service Committee, *Memoranda on Monetary Policy* (HC 720, 1979–80) pp. 55–61.
8. For the history of financial statistics see Wilson Committee, *Report*, Appendix 9.
9. HC 258 (1969–70) pp. 32–3.
10. 'The operation of monetary policy since the Radcliffe Report', pp. 451–3.
11. Problems of interpretation are put more theoretically by one of the Bank's senior economists in C. A. E. Goodhart, *Money, Information and Uncertainty* (London: Macmillan, 1975) pp. 152–69.
12. 'Goodhart's Law' is described in Charles Goodhart, 'Problems of Monetary Management: The U.K. Experience', in Anthony S. Courakis (ed.), *Inflation, Depression and Economic Policy in the West* (London: Alexandrine Publishing, 1981) pp. 111–132 (116).
13. 'The stock of money' *BEQB*, 10 (1970) p. 321.
14. Mansion House Speech, *BEQB*, 12 (1972) pp. 515–16. The Governor's speech was read in his absence by the Deputy Governor.
15. 'Does the money supply really matter?', *BEQB*, 13 (1973) pp. 193–202.
16. For the last two see, for instance, *Treasury Economic Progress Report*, December 1972, p. 7; and HC *Debates*, vol. 852, col. 251 (6 March 1973, the Chancellor's Budget Speech).
17. For instance, *The Banker*, November 1973, p. 1237; *The Economist*, 30 June 1973, p. 13.

18. Chief Secretary to the Treasury, HC *Debates*, vol. 842, col. 1731 (9 August 1972); the Governor, Mansion House Speech, *BEQB*, 12 (1972) pp. 516–17.
19. The classic argument is in Peter Winch, *The Idea of a Social Science and its Relation to Philosophy* (London: Routledge, 1958). The issue runs through Alan Ryan (ed.), *The Philosophy of Social Explanation* (London: Oxford University Press, 1973).
20. Maurice Peston, 'Unemployment: Why We Need a New Measurement', *Lloyds Bank Review*, 104 (1972) pp. 1–7; P. D. Balacs, 'Economic Data and Economic Policy', ibid., pp. 35–50; Sir Donald MacDougall, *Studies In Political Economy* vol. II (London: Macmillan, 1975) pp. 255–60.
21. For a summary, Tony Westaway, 'Stabilisation Policy and Fiscal Reform', in Maunder (ed.), *British Economy in the 1970s*, pp. 14–19.
22. Sir Keith Joseph, speech at Preston, 5 September 1974, printed in *Reversing the Trend* (Chichester: Barry Rose, 1975) pp. 22–30.
23. Ninth Report from the Expenditure Committee, *Public Expenditure, Inflation and the Balance of Payments*, HC 328 (1974) p. 106.
24. The standard reference in this discussion is Axel Leijonhufvud, *On Keynesian Economics and the Economics of Keynes* (London: Oxford University Press, 1968) pp. 3–48.
25. Speech to the Finance Houses Associations, printed in *The Banker*, February 1971, pp. 202–4.
26. The Governor, speech at the Mansion House, 15 October 1970, *BEQB*, 10 (1970) p. 474; 'Monetary management in the United Kingdom'; C. A. E. Goodhart and A. D. Crockett, 'The importance of money' *BEQB*, 10 (1970) pp. 159–98. For equally sceptical conclusions, A. D. Crockett, 'Timing relationships between movements of monetary and national income variables', ibid., pp. 459–68.
27. The details of negotiations and of trade union proposals are in Trades Union Congress, *103rd Annual Report* (1971) pp. 250–61; the Chancellor's statement is in HC *Debates*, vol. 821, cols 1035–50 (19 July 1971).
28. Trades Union Congress, ibid.
29. For instance, *The Economist*, 25 March 1972, pp. 11–14.
30. These assertions came from private conversations, but are partly corroborated by William Keegan and Rupert Pennant-Rea, *Who Runs the Economy?* (London: Temple Smith, 1979) pp. 71 and 120.
31. The point was made in numerous private conversations.
32. Lord Barber, 'Comments upon a commentator', *Financial Times*, 8 December 1977, p. 21.
33. *The Economist*, 7 April 1973, p. 83 and 15 September 1973, p. 101 has details of these measures.
34. Though not complete equity, for the clearers were required to hold special cash balances at the Bank of England.
35. Chief Cashier, Sykes Memorial Lecture, pp. 480–1.
36. D. F. Lomax, 'Competition and the Clearing Banks', *The Banker*, October 1971, pp. 1160–5; E. V. Morgan and R. L. Harrington, 'Reserve Assets and the Supply of Money', *The Manchester School*, XLI (1973) pp. 73–87; E. W. Davis and K. A. Yeomans, 'Competition and Credit Control: The Rubicon and Beyond', *Lloyds Bank Review*, 107 (1973) pp. 44–55.

Notes and References 173

37. D. F. Lomax, 'Reserve Assets and Competition and Credit Control', *National Westminster Bank Quarterly Review*, August 1973, pp. 36–46; Gowland, *Monetary Policy and Credit Control*, pp. 32–5.
38. Gowland, *Monetary Policy and Credit Control*, p. 32.
39. For instance, *The Sunday Times*, 12 December 1976.
40. I take this to be economic orthodoxy. See, for instance, E. T. Nevin, *Textbook of Economic Analysis*, 3rd edition (London: Macmillan, 1967) pp. 290–4.
41. For exposition see Zawadzki, *Competition and Credit Control*, pp. 61–73.
42. The episode is summarised in Tew, 'Monetary Policy', pp. 255–6.
43. For evidence of political pressure see Weyer, 'Competition and Credit Control', p. 15.
44. Details of changes are in *BEQB*, 14 (1974) pp. 37–40.
45. The best study of the episode is by Coates, *Labour in Power?*, pp. 38–43.
46. Announced, HC *Debates*, vol. 981, cols 1442–6 (26 March 1980, the Budget Statement).
47. The variants are succinctly summarised in *Monetary Control*, Cmnd 7858 (1980).
48. 'Monetary Base: Revolution in UK Policy', *The Banker*, December 1980, p. 10.
49. On the point, Griffiths and Wood, *Monetary Targets*, pp. 1–12.
50. The early wrecking of the Government's targets can be seen in HC 163-I (1980–1) Table 3.1.
51. Quoted in *The Times*, 22 October 1981.
52. Samuel Brittan and Peter Lilley, *The Delusion of Incomes Policy* (London: Temple Smith, 1977) pp. 184–211.

CHAPTER 5: CRISIS, CRASH, RESCUE

1. Walter Bagehot, *Lombard Street: a description of the money market*, 14th edition (London: John Murray, 1915) pp. 151–2.
2. Department of Trade, *London and County Securities Group*, Inspectors' Report (London: HMSO 1976) pp. 12–13.
3. 'The secondary banking crisis', *BEQB*, 18 (1978) p. 232; 'The story of the City crisis', *The Banker*, February 1974, pp. 87–9.
4. This account is drawn from the Governor's evidence, in HC 166-i (1977–8).
5. 'The secondary banking crisis', *BEQB*, 18 (1978) Appendix 1.
6. 'The secondary banking crisis', *BEQB*, 18 (1978) p. 235.
7. Reid, *The Secondary Banking Crisis*, pp. 190–2.
8. Oliver Marriott, *The Property Boom* (London: Hamish Hamilton, 1967) p. 11.
9. Committee on Invisible Exports, Economists Advisory Group, quoted in Michael Clarke, *Fallen Idols: Elites and the Search for the Acceptable Face of Capitalism* (London: Junction Books, 1981) p. 89.
10. Nigel Broackes, Chairman of Trafalgar House Investments, quoted in *Investors Chronicle*, 20 March 1970, p. 1007.

11. Calculated by me from figures in London Clearing Bankers, *Evidence to the Wilson Committee*, pp. 87 and 277.
12. David H. McKay and Andrew W. Cox, *The Politics of Urban Change* (London: Croom Helm, 1979) p. 143 has figures.
13. Gowland, *Monetary Policy and Credit Control*, p. 79.
14. Committee of Inquiry into the Crown Agents (Chairman, E. S. Fay) *Report*, HC 48 (1977–8) p. 95.
15. Statement to Department of Trade, *Ferguson and General Investments Limited*, Inspectors' Report (London: HMSO, 1979) p. 7. The speaker was Mr S. M. Van Gelder, joint Managing Director of Keyser Ullmann.
16. Gowland, *Monetary Policy and Credit Control*, p. 79; London Clearing Bankers, *Evidence to the Wilson Committee*, p. 242.
17. For example in Derek F. Channon, *British Banking Strategy and the International Challenge* (London: Macmillan, 1977) p. 96.
18. The organisation of the markets in the early 1970s is concisely described in Revell, *The British Financial System*, pp. 268–88.
19. Governor, speech to the Institute of Bankers, *BEQB*, 14 (1974) p. 54.
20. For example, Department of Trade Inspectors' Report, *London and County Securities*, pp. 80–1.
21. Ibid., pp. 239–51.
22. In HC 166–i (1977–8) p. 5.
23. Richard Lambert, 'Banks in Turmoil', *The Sunday Times*, 8 September 1974.
24. The text of the request is in *BEQB*, 12 (1972) p. 327.
25. *Investors Chronicle*, 6 December 1974, pp. 924–5; *Investors Chronicle Supplement*, 'Industrial and Commercial Property', 14 November 1975, p. 11.
26. Fay Committee, *Report*, pp. 147–51.
27. Tribunal appointed to inquire into certain issues arising out of the operations of the Crown Agents as financiers on their own account in the years 1967–74 (Chairman, Sir David Croom-Johnson), *Report*, HC 364 (1981–2) p. 157.
28. For an example, Fay Committee, *Report*, pp. 106–7.
29. The originator of the tradition is probably Thomas Balogh: see his comments in Radcliffe Committee, *Memoranda*, vol. 3, pp. 31–47. For 'incompetence' explanations of the banking crisis see Tom Lester, 'The Secondary Scandal', *Management Today*, October 1974; Robert Heller and Norris Willatt, *Can You Trust Your Bank?* (London: Weidenfeld & Nicolson, 1977) pp. 96–105. The Croom-Johnson reasoning is in, for instance, its *Report*, pp. 521–4.
30. Wilson Committee, *Second Stage Evidence*, vol. 4, p. 98.
31. For a brief review of the background, 'The secondary banking crisis', *BEQB*, 18 (1978) pp. 230–1.
32. Kindleberger, *Manias, Panics and Crashes*, pp. 207–9.
33. 'The secondary banking crisis', *BEQB*, 18 (1978) pp. 230–1.
34. Inspectors' Report, *London and County Securities*, p. 235.
35. The full list is in Wilson Committee, *Second Stage Evidence*, vol. 4, pp. 101–2.
36. The best brief account is in Crowther Committee, *Report*, pp. 31–49.

Notes and References 175

37. The case is summarised in Crowther Committee, *Report*, pp. 62–3.
38. Ibid.
39. Channon, *British Banking Strategy*, pp. 94–5.
40. Wilson Committee, *Second Stage Evidence*, vol. 4, pp. 96–7; 'The secondary banking crisis', *BEQB*, 18 (1978) pp. 230–1.
41. Crowther Committee, *Report*, p. 63. The phrase is the Committee's.
42. Fay Committee, *Report*, pp. 44ff.
43. Croom-Johnson, *Report*, pp. 226–7.
44. Ibid., pp. 213–230.
45. Ibid., p. 229.
46. Department of Trade Inspectors' Report, *London and County Securities*, pp. 1–2.
47. See Governor in HC 166–i (1977–8), pp. 11–12.
48. Department of Trade Inspectors' Reports into *London and County Securities*; into *Ferguson and General Investments*; into *Lonrho Limited* (London: HMSO, 1976) pp. 255–6; and Fay Committee, *Report*.
49. The procedure is well described in Department of Trade Inspectors' Report, *London Capital Group, formerly British Bangladesh Trust* (London: HMSO, 1977) pp. 203–4; and in Crowther Committee, *Report*, p. 63.
50. Bank memo quoted in Department of Trade Inspectors' Report, *London Capital Group*, p. 53.
51. Ibid., p. 206.
52. Ibid.
53. Ibid., pp. 206–7.
54. Harold L. Wilensky, *Organisational Intelligence* (New York: Basic Books, 1967) pp. 88–93.
55. Department of Trade Inspectors' Report, *Ferguson and General Investments*, p. 253. The words are those of Mr Jack Dellal, joint Managing Director of Keyser Ullmann.
56. Wilensky, *Organisational Intelligence*, p. 92.
57. Tom Hadden, *Company Law and Capitalism* (London: Weidenfeld & Nicolson, 1972) pp. 64–72.
58. Quoted in Department of Trade Inspectors' Report, *Peachey Property Corporation Limited* (London: HMSO, 1979) pp. 24–5.
59. Roberta Wohlstetter, *Pearl Harbor: Warning and Decision* (Stanford University Press, 1962).
60. 'Foreword' to Wohlstetter, *Pearl Harbor*.
61. Cited in Charles Raw, *Slater Walker: an investigation of a financial phenomenon* (London: Andre Deutsch, 1977) p. 347.
62. In HC 166–i (1977–8) p. 11.
63. Croom-Johnson, *Report*, pp. 346–7.
64. Recent issues in industrial policy are discussed in Grant, *The Political Economy of Industrial Policy*.
65. 'The secondary banking crisis', *BEQB*, 18 (1978) p. 231. See also HC 166–i (1977–8) p. 2.
66. Wilensky, *Organisational Intelligence*, pp. 76–7.
67. See Governor in HC 166–i (1977–8) p. 2.
68. Kindleberger, *Manias, Panics and Crashes*, pp. 161–81.

176 The Politics of Banking

69. For neglect of shareholders see, for instance, Anne Segall, 'Anatomy of a rescue', *Investors Chronicle*, 13 December 1974, pp. 1021-3.
70. Anne Segall, 'Euromarket questions affect Bank's thinking at home', *Investors Chronicle*, 16 August 1974.
71. HC 258 (1969-70) p. 284.
72. For examples: HC *Debates*, vol. 861, col. 1249 (24 October 1973).
73. For instance, Mr Ian Wrigglesworth, HC *Debates*, vol. 958, col. 1528 (23 November 1978).
74. HC 166-i (1977-8) p. 6.
75. For the contemporary air of equanimity see Michael Brett, 'London and County is rescued but will the lessons be learnt?', *Investors Chronicle*, 7 December 1974, pp. 1032-4.
76. Vividly described in Reid, *The Secondary Banking Crisis*, pp. 1-10.
77. HC 166-i (1977-8) p. 7.
78. For Discount Houses' problems, *Financial Times*, 'U.K. Banking Survey', 16 September 1974.
79. Reid, *The Secondary Banking Crisis*, p. 8.
80. Ibid., p. 14.
81. Wilson Committee, *Evidence*, First Stage, vol. 6, p. 134.
82. These details are from HC 166-i (1977-8) pp. 7-9.
83. Reid, *The Secondary Banking Crisis*, pp. 15, 17.
84. For instance: comments in *Annual Reports* by Chairmen of Barclays and of the Midland, quoted in *The Banker*, March 1975, pp. 366-7.
85. Details from HC 166-i (1977-8) p. 9; and 'The secondary banking crisis', *BEQB*, 18 (1978) p. 233.
86. 'The secondary banking crisis', p. 235.
87. Ibid., p. 234.
88. HC 166-i (1977-8) p. 9.
89. 'The story of the City crisis', *The Banker*, February 1974, pp. 87-9.
90. 'The secondary banking crisis', *BEQB*, 18 (1978) p. 233.
91. The Governor has described the idea in HC 166-i (1977-8) p. 8.
92. Ibid.
93. For this see Reid, *The Secondary Banking Crisis*, p. 123.
94. In HC 166-i (1977-8) p. 8.
95. 'The secondary banking crisis', *BEQB*, 18 (1978) p. 233.
96. Fay Committee, *Report*, p. 148, put the figure at £26 million; but Croom-Johnson, *Report*, p. 355, more authoritatively quotes £60 million.
97. Bank of England evidence in Select Committee on Nationalised Industries, *Seventh Report*, HC 672 (1975-6) pp. 2-3, 20-1; and in HC 166-i (1977-8) p. 13.
98. Blunden, 'The supervision of the UK banking system', p. 192.
99. The Stern affair is in Croom-Johnson, *Report*, pp. 165-7.
100. Croom-Johnson, *Report*, p. 354.
101. The Governor, in Wilson Committee, *Evidence,* First Stage, vol. 5, p. 242,
102. *Investors Chronicle*, 28 February 1975, p. 609.
103. 'The secondary banking crisis', Appendix 1, *BEQB*, 18 (1978) p. 237.
104. For how this was done, see HC 166-i (1977-8) pp. 10-11.

105. Fay Committee, *Report*, p. 156; Bank of England *Annual Report* 1981, p. 14, says merely that lending by the Support Group was 'less than one quarter of its peak' of £1,285 million; hence my estimate.

CHAPTER 6: RULES, RISKS AND THE LAW

1. 'Banking supervision', *BEQB*, 14 (1974) p. 262; Blunden, 'The supervision of the UK banking system', pp. 190–2.
2. Blunden, ibid., p. 190; Wilson Committee, *Second Stage Evidence*, vol. 4, p. 98.
3. 'Banking supervision', *BEQB*, 14 (1974) p. 262; later developments were announced in 'New banking statistics', *BEQB*, 15 (1975) pp. 162–5.
4. Blunden, 'The supervision of the UK banking system', p. 191.
5. 'Banking supervision', p. 262.
6. Wilson Committee, *Second Stage Evidence*, vol. 4, p. 98; Blunden, 'The supervision of the UK banking system', p. 191.
7. Blunden, *ibid*; the Governor, 'Banking Tomorrow', *BEQB*, 15 (1975) pp. 367–9 (369).
8. 'The capital and liquidity adequacy of banks', *BEQB*, 15 (1975) pp. 240–3.
9. Ibid., p. 243.
10. Banking Act, 1979, Elizabeth II, Chapter 37.
11. *The Licensing and Supervision of Deposit-Taking Institutions*, Cmnd 6584 (1976); note also the Minister's account in HC *Debates*, vol. 958, col. 1500 (23 November 1978).
12. HC *Debates*, ibid.
13. Two good studies of the European side of banking regulation are Jane A. Sargent, 'Pressure Group Development: A Case-Study of the British Bankers' Association', and Alan Butt Philip 'A Tale of Nine Cities: Pressure Groups and Policy in the European Communities'; both papers given to the Annual Conference of the Political Studies Association, University of Hull, April 1981.
14. John Cooper, 'Dirigisme or empiricism?', *The Bankers' Magazine*, October 1980, pp. 20–3. Mr Cooper was then chairman of the executive committee of the BBA.
15. For a review: J. Revell, 'Improving the Solvency and Liquidity of various Financial Institutions', in J. E. Wadsworth, J. S. G. Wilson and H. Fournier (eds), *The Development of Financial Institutions in Europe, 1956–1976* (Leyden: Sijthoff, 1977) pp. 203–13.
16. Banking Act, 1979, Part II, Sections 25 and 27.
17. HC *Debates*, vol. 958, col. 1511 (23 November 1978).
18. For details, Wilson Committee, *Report*, p. 293.
19. HC *Debates*, Standing Committee A, col. 186 (16 January 1979).
20. For example, HL *Debates*, vol. 399, col. 67 (6 March 1979: Lord Selsdon).
21. Speech to the Institute of Bankers, *BEQB*, 14 (1974) p. 54.
22. 'Banking Tomorrow', *BEQB*, 15 (1975) pp. 367–8.
23. This information is drawn from private conversations, but also fits closely the tone of the Governor's comments in note 22 above.

24. Lowi, 'Four Systems of Policy', pp. 298–310.
25. Banking Act, 1979, Schedule 2, Part I.
26. HL *Debates*, vol. 399, col. 1060 (20 March 1979).
27. Christopher Fildes, 'City Notebook', *Investors Chronicle*, 6 August 1976. The point is confirmed in private conversations.
28. Keegan and Pennant-Rea, *Who Runs the Economy?*, pp. 102–4.
29. Christopher Fildes, 'City Notebook', *Investors Chronicle*, 11 November 1977.
30. Moran, 'Finance Capital and Pressure-Group Politics'.
31. On the CLCB, see London Clearing Banks, *Evidence to the Wilson Committee*, p. 176; on the BBA, Jane Sargent, 'Pressure Group Development: A Case-Study of the British Bankers' Association'.
32. For details: Cooper, 'Dirigisme or empiricism?'; 'The banks and the Banking Bill' (by 'a leading banker'), *The Banker*, October 1978, pp. 19–24.
33. Moran, 'Finance Capital and Pressure-Group Politics'.
34. See, for instance, *Committee Stage* contributions on the Deposit Protection Fund, Sixth Sitting, 18 January 1979.
35. The Minister of State in HC *Debates*, vol. 958, col. 1509 (23 November 1978).
36. For example, HC *Debates*, vol. 958, col. 1535 (23 November 1978).
37. 'The banks and the Banking Bill', *The Banker*, October 1978, p. 20.
38. HL *Debates,* vol. 399, cols 1039–42 (20 March 1979).
39. On the third tier see the Bill's *Committee Stage*, Third Sitting (12 December 1978).
40. La Porte, *Organised Social Complexity*, p. 3.
41. See, for instance, Banking Bill, *Committee Stage*, Eighth Sitting (30 January 1979); ibid., First Sitting (5 December 1978); HL *Debates*, vol. 399, cols 1730–45 (2 April 1979).
42. HL *Debates*, vol. 399, cols 57 and 60 (6 March 1979).
43. HL *Debates*, vol. 399, col. 1085 (20 March 1979). For Lord Selsdon, ibid., cols 66–9 (6 March 1979).
44. Bank of England, *Annual Report*, 1979, p. 35.
45. 'Banking supervision and the Banking Act', *BEQB*, 20 (1980) pp. 205–8.
46. Martin Karmel, 'First and Second Division Banking', *The Bankers' Magazine*, October 1979, pp. 8–10; and Karmel 'First and Second Division Banking revisited', ibid., June 1980, pp. 20–1. Mr Karmel is Deputy Secretary, Committee of London Clearing Bankers.
47. On the importance placed on these values see Blunden, 'The supervision of the UK banking system'.
48. *The Banker*, August 1981.
49. 'The assessment of capital', *BEQB*, 20 (1980) pp. 324–30; 'Liquidity Ratios: US banks voice their fears', *The Banker*, August 1980, pp. 13–14; 'Liquidity: a new era is ushered in', interview with Peter Cooke, *The Bankers' Magazine*, August 1980.
50. For details see *The Bankers' Magazine*, June 1981, p. 22 and August 1981, p. 14.
51. Wilson Committee, *Report*, p. 69.
52. Richard S. Dale, 'Prudential Regulation of Multinational Banking', *Na-*

tional Westminster Bank Quarterly Review, February 1981, pp. 14–24 (15).
53. Wilson Committee, *Report*, p. 68.
54. Tony Killick, 'Euromarket recycling of OPEC surpluses', *The Banker*, January 1981, pp. 15–23.
55. For the Polish debt problem, *The Banker*, March 1982, pp. 81–2.
56. For instance, J. N. Robinson, 'Is it possible to assess country risk?', *The Banker*, January 1981, pp. 71–9, and references therein.
57. HC 166–i (1977–8) p. 13.
58. Select Committee on Nationalised Industries, *Seventh Report*, HC 672 (1975–6) p. xxxii.
59. My discussion of the Basle Committee relies heavily on a series of papers by its chairmen, notably, George Blunden, 'International co-operation in banking supervision', *BEQB*, 17 (1977) pp. 325–9; Blunden, 'Control and Supervision of the Foreign Operations of Banks', in Wadsworth, Wilson and Fournier (eds), *Development of Financial Institutions in Europe*, pp. 193–202; Peter Cooke, 'Banking regulation, profits and capital generation', *The Banker*, August 1981, pp. 21–3; Cooke, 'Developments in co-operation among banking supervisory authorities', *BEQB*, 21 (1981) pp. 238–44.
60. The quotation is from Blunden, 'Control and Supervision of the Foreign Operations of Banks', p. 194; on the EEC, see Bank of England, *Annual Report*, 1979, p. 17.
61. Blunden, 'International co-operation in banking supervision', p. 327.
62. Ibid.
63. Cooke, 'Developments in co-operation', p. 241.
64. On the IASC see 'International Accounting Firms: A study of a Multinational Service Industry', *Multinational Business*, 3 (1980) pp. 1–13.
65. Blunden, 'Control and Supervision of the Foreign Operations of Banks', p. 195.
66. Ibid., p. 196.
67. Cooke, 'Developments in co-operation', p. 240.
68. Dale, 'Prudential Regulation of Multinational Banking', pp. 20–1.
69. On this point, Cooke, 'Developments in co-operation...', p. 240.
70. The key document is *Inflation Accounting: Report of the Inflation Accounting Committee* (Chairman: Sir F. Sandilands), HMSO, Cmnd 6225 (1975). For examples of the disputes and the complexities, Edward Stamp, 'Half-baked ideas in the Sandilands Report', *Accountancy Age*, 12 November 1975; Richard Briston, 'Support for the Sandilands Way', *Accountancy Age*, 30 January 1976.
71. For an account which stresses the ability of multinationals to manipulate governments see Richard J. Barnet and Ronald E. Muller, *Global Reach: The Power of the Multinational Corporations* (London: Jonathan Cape, 1975). By contrast, Steven I. Davis, *The Management Function in International Banking* (London: Macmillan, 1979) describes the enterprises themselves struggling to cope with complexity.
72. Cooke, 'Developments in co-operation...', p. 239.
73. 'Interbank communication', *The Bankers' Magazine*, March 1981, pp. 7–12.

74. Charles Raw, Godfrey Hodgson and Bruce Page, *Do you sincerely want to be rich?* (London: Andre Deutsch, 1971).
75. The huge scale of lending to Eastern Europe and the attendant problems are well illustrated in Table C of 'The International banking markets in 1980–81', *BEQB*, 22 (1982) pp. 42–55.

CHAPTER 7: COMPLEXITY, TRUST AND POLICY MAKING

1. Michael Oakeshott, *On Political Education* (Cambridge: Bowes & Bowes, 1951) p. 22.
2. Oliver Williamson, *Markets and Hierarchies* (New York: Free Press, 1975) p. 9.
3. Ibid., pp. 26–8.
4. James B. Rule, *Private Lives and Public Surveillance* (London: Allen Lane, 1973) pp. 18–43.
5. La Porte, *Organised Social Complexity*, p. 3.
6. This paragraph is drawn from *Financial Weekly*, 1 June 1979 and 31 August 1979; *Financial Times*, 19 July 1978.
7. Seidman, *Politics, Position and Power*, p. 190.
8. Peter Hall, *Great Planning Disasters* (Harmondsworth: Penguin, 1981) pp. 208 ff.
9. Christopher C. Hood, *The Limits of Administration* (London: John Wiley, 1976) pp. 17–29.
10. Richard Titmuss, *The Gift Relationship: from human blood to social policy* (London: Allen & Unwin, 1970); John H. Goldthorpe, 'Social inequality and social integration in modern Britain', in Dorothy Wedderburn (ed.), *Poverty, inequality and class structure* (London: Cambridge University Press, 1974); Alan Fox, *Beyond Contract: work, power and trust relations* (London: Faber, 1974).
11. Fred Hirsch, *Social Limits to Growth* (London: Routledge & Kegan Paul, 1977) pp. 139, 131 and 143.
12. Ibid., pp. 178–90.
13. Clarke, *Fallen Idols*, pp. 26–83, 172–222.
14. On rules over discretion see especially F. A. Hayek, *Law, Legislation and Liberty*, vol. III (London: Routledge, 1979) pp. 98–104. On rules in general and the monetary rule in particular, Friedman, *Capitalism and Freedom*, pp. 37–55.
15. Hood, *Limits of Administration*, Part 2.
16. Hirsch, *Social Limits to Growth*, pp. 157–8.
17. For the background to this I draw on Hood, *Limits of Administration*, pp. 169–89.
18. For the background to abortion law I have drawn on R. F. Gardner, *Abortion* (Exeter: Paternoster Press, 1972) Part I.
19. For the background to the obscenity laws I rely on Patricia Hewitt, *The Abuse of Power: Civil Liberties in the United Kingdom* (Oxford: Martin Robertson, 1982) pp. 95–101; Martin Tomkinson, *The Pornbrokers* (London: Virgin Books, 1982).
20. Rule, *Private Lives and Public Surveillance*, pp. 308–20.

21. Ibid., pp. 320ff.
22. Goodhart, *Money, Information and Uncertainty* pursues the economic policy implications in a highly theoretical way.
23. Michael Carley, *Rational Techniques in Policy Analysis* (London: Heinemann, 1980).
24. Ibid., pp. 161-3.
25. Peter Self, *Econocrats and the Policy Process* (London: Macmillan, 1975).
26. See, for instance, Donald Madgwick and Tony Smythe, *The Invasion of Privacy* (London: Pitman, 1974) pp. 20-40.
27. Aaron Wildavsky, *Budgeting: A Comparative Theory of Budgetary Processes* (Boston: Little, Brown, 1975) part IV.
28. Hall, *Great Planning Disasters*, pp. 149, 214-22; Harvey M. Sapolsky, *The Polaris System Development: bureaucratic and programmatic success in government* (Cambridge, Mass: Harvard University Press, 1972).
29. Wildavsky, *Budgeting*, pp. 330-4.
30. The classic study is Karl W. Deutsch, *The Nerves of Government* (New York: Free Press, 1966); an excellent account with practical applications is Robin Hambleton, *Policy Planning and Local Government* (London: Hutchinson, 1978) pp. 281-314.
31. Donald A. Schon, *Beyond the stable state: public and private learning in a changing society* (London: Temple Smith, 1971) pp. 116-79.
32. T. Burns and G. M. Stalker, *The Management of Innovation* (London: Tavistock, 1961).
33. Schon, *Beyond the stable state*, pp. 123-7.
34. Gordon Tullock, *The Politics of Bureaucracy* (Washington: Public Affairs Press, 1965); Anthony Downs, *Inside Bureaucracy* (Boston: Little, Brown, 1967); William A. Niskanen, *Bureaucracy and Representative Government* (Chicago: Aldine-Atherton, 1971).
35. Keith Hartley, 'Defence: A Case-Study of Spending Cuts', in Christopher Hood and Maurice Wright (eds), *Big Government in Hard Times* (Oxford: Martin Robertson, 1981) pp. 125-51 (146); P. D. Henderson 'Two British errors: their probable size and some possible lessons', in Christopher Pollit *et al.* (eds), *Public Policy in Theory and Practice* (London: Hodder & Stoughton, 1979) pp. 222-49.
36. Hirsch, *Social Limits to Growth*, p. 129, and references therein.
37. See, for instance, Williamson, *Markets and Hierarchies*, p. 253.
38. Terence J. Johnson, *Professions and Power* (London: Macmillan, 1972).
39. Seidman, *Politics, Position and Power*, pp. 149-50 is illuminating on this point.
40. Hadden, *Company Law and Capitalism*, pp. 64-72.
41. Phillipe C. Schmitter and Gerhard Lehmbruch (eds), *Trends Toward Corporatist Intermediation* (Beverly Hills: Sage, 1979).
42. Charles Perrow, *Complex Organisations: a critical essay* (Glenview: Scott, Foresman, 1972) pp. 1-60.

Index

Names of official committees and reports are indexed under name of chairman.

abortion, 149
Accepting Houses Committee, 19
accounting, 136, 160
   see also Chartered Accountants, Institute of; auditors
Accounting Standards, Committee on, 136
adversary politics, 29, 39–41, 126, 156–7
Agricultural Credits Act (1928), 87
Agriculture, Ministry of, 87
Allen, Sir D., 51, 52
Allison, G., 29, 47, 167n, 170n
arbitrage, 70, 71–2
Armstrong, R., 38
Armstrong, Sir W., 36, 68
Artis, M., 166n
Auditors, 93, 95–6
   see also accountants; Chartered Accountants, Institute of

Bagehot, W., 1, 17, 77, 173n
Balacs, P., 172n
Balogh, T., 26, 165n, 174n
Bank Charter Act (1844), 17
Bank of England
   aversion to bureaucracy, 24, 25, 91–2, 94
   Court of, 23
   Deputy Governor of, 77–8, 97, 103, 108, 110
   devises Competitions and Credit Control, 2, 39, 40, 47–51, 52
   Governor of, 4, 15, 16, 23, 24, 25, 26, 30, 31, 38, 40, 48, 49, 59, 61, 82, 83, 102, 103, 110, 117, 121, 122, 130, 135
   lobbyist, 13, 19–21, 23, 24, 46
   manager of financial markets, 24, 26
   Official functions, 12, 18, 22–7
   in regulating banks, 1, 11, 14–15, 17–19, 20, 21, 22, 23, 24, 84–96, 114ff., 135–9
   relations with government, 22–7
   Supervision Division, 114–15, 116, 117
   see also Cobbold, Lord, Cromer, Lord, Cunliffe, Lord, Hollom, J., Norman, M., O'Brien, L. K., Richardson, G.
Bank for International Settlements, 109, 135
Bank Rate, 23, 26, 32, 47, 56, 68
   see also interest rates; Minimum Lending Rate
Bankhaus Herstatt, 99, 109, 134–5
banking
   cartels, 12, 15–16, 31, 41, 51
   community, 9, 11, 14–15, 27, 49, 94, 131
   industrial structure, 12–16, 42–3
   international, 42, 86, 109–10, 113–14, 133–9
   lobby, 13, 19–21, 125–30
   and manufacturing industry, 12–13, 14, 15
   merchant, 13, 14, 102, 116
   municipal, 128
   penny, 128

Index

primary, 11, 42, 48, 92
prudential regulation of, 1, 3, 5,
   17–19, 81–2, 84–96, 114–39
recognised, 119, 123, 127, 130–1
rescues, 17, 19, 76, 97–111
retail, 11, 41–2
Scottish, 11, 103, 128
secondary, 11, 42, 70, 70–112
   passim, 115
wholesale, 11, 42–3, 48–9, 132–3
see also crises; licensed deposit
   takers; markets
Banking Act (1979), 11, 17, 87, 114
consultations over, 125–6
implementation, 130–2
origins of, 118–21
in Parliament, 126–30
Barber, A., 4, 55, 57, 66, 67, 69, 71, 172n
Barber boom, why misnamed, 67–8
Barclays Bank, 11, 42, 43, 44, 45
Bardsley, D., 76, 77
Baring crisis, 17, 98
Barnett, R., 179n
Bay Area Rapid Transit System, 143
Beer, S., 169n
Benson, Sir H., 136
Benthamites, 35
Biffen, J., 75
Blackaby, F., 163n, 171n
Blunden, G., 114, 117, 135, 166n, 176n, 177n, 178n, 179n
Bolton, Sir G., 167n, 170n
Boyle, A., 166n
Brett, M., 176n
Bridges, Lord, 24, 26
Brittan, S., 166n, 167n, 168n, 171n, 173n
Broackes, N., 173n
Briston, R., 179n
British Bangladesh Trust, 93
British Bankers' Association, 12, 119, 125–8, 130, 131
British Overseas Banks, 117, 132
Building societies, 41, 68, 69, 72
Bureaucratic politics, 29, 49–53
Burke's Peerage, 14
Burns, T., 155, 181n

Cabinet, 68, 69, 72, 122, 124
Callaghan, J., 124
capitalism, 144–6
Carley, M., 152, 154, 181n
case-studies, 3, 4, 140
cash and liquidity ratios, 31, 70, 81
Cedar Holdings, 77, 102
central bankers, 35, 57, 109, 135–9
Certificates of Deposit, 43
Chancellor of the Exchequer, 39, 40, 64, 74, 110, 127
   see also Barber, A.; Jenkins, R.; Maudling, R.
Channon, D., 174n, 175n
Chapman, R., 167n
Chartered Accountants, Institute of, 96
   see also accounting; auditors
Checkland, G., 164n
Chester, Sir N., 166n
Clapham, Sir J., 165n
Clarendon Schools, 15
Clark, R., 166n
Clark, R. W., 168n
Clarke, M., 146, 173n, 180n
Clay, Sir H., 166n, 167n
Clearing Banks
change in, 43–5
influence on Competition and Credit Control, 44–6, 49–50, 70
market shares, 41, 127
regulation of, 117–18, 126–30
in secondary banking crisis, 77–8, 101–11
structure of, 11, 13–14, 15, 31–2, 34, 132
Clegg, Sir C., 45, 170n
Coates, D., 169n, 173n
Cobbold, Lord, 167n
Colwyn Committee, 23
Committee on Banking Regulations, 135–7
Committee of London Clearing Bankers, 12, 19, 44, 125–9
Companies Act (1948), 87
Companies Act (1967), 88
Competition and Credit Control
consequences for banking

184 Index

Competition and Credit Control *cont.*
    industry, 44, 55, 97–112
    consequences for monetary control, 4, 5, 58–73
    consequences for property market, 4, 80–1
    costs of, 1, 4, 111–12
    implementation of, 28, 58–73
    origins, 2, 24, 27, 28, 29–54
    summarised, 30–3
competition, in government, 155–8
complexity
    administrative, 6, 7, 8, 53, 65, 90, 92, 95, 142–3
    intellectual, 6, 7, 8, 49, 53, 59–60, 70, 133, 138, 140–1, 143
    social, 6, 7, 8, 49, 53, 59–60, 69, 70, 71, 87, 95, 128, 133, 141–3
Concorde, 143, 156
Confederation of British Industry, 67
Conservative Party, 5, 39, 40, 64
consumer credit, 21, 31, 34, 40, 73, 88, 128–9
    see also Crowther Committee
Consumer Credit Act (1974), 128–9
consumer sovereignty, 157
Control Committee
    costs, 78, 104–8, 111–12
    disagreements in, 106–9
    origins, 78, 101–3
    workings, 97, 101–11
Cooke, P., 135, 179n
Cooper, J., 177n, 178n
coordination, problems of, 7, 65, 90–2, 155
Coppock, D., 171n
corporatism, 160–1
country risk, 134
Courakis, A., 171n
Cox, A., 174n
Craig, M., 169n
crises
    in banking history, 17, 98, 145
    causes of, general, 76–7
    in international banking, 86, 109–10, 133–7
    management of, 114–16, 136–7
    in secondary banking, 17, 77–8, 83–4, 85–96, 120
    social functions of, 113, 114, 136–7, 154, 162
Crockett, A., 168n, 172n
Cromer, Lord, 26
Croome, D., 166n, 168n, 169n
Croom-Johnson inquiry, 85, 91, 174n, 175n, 176n
    see also Crown Agents; Fay Committee
Crouch, C., 166n
Crown Agents, 98, 100
    dealings, 80, 84, 90–1, 108–9
    losses, 90, 111, 112, 163n
    failure to regulate, 90–2
    see also Croom-Johnson inquiry; Fay Committee
Crowther Committee, 31, 34, 40, 49, 167n, 168n, 170n, 174n, 175n
    see also consumer credit
Crowther, Lord, 31
Cunliffe, Lord, 26
Cunningham, G., 100
Currency Commission, 74
custom, place of, 9, 22, 24, 41, 47, 49, 64–5, 91, 93–4, 98, 162
cybernetics, 154

Dale, R., 137, 178n, 179n
Dalton, H., 23
Davidson, P., 168n
Davies, D., 119, 121
Davis, E., 165n, 172n
Davis, S., 179n
defence policy, 53
Dellal, J., 175n
Dennis, G., 163n
Deposit Protection Fund, 118–19, 120, 122, 124, 126–8
de-regulation, 148–50
Deutsch, K., 181n
Dicks-Mineaux, L., 38
Discount Houses, 11, 14, 15, 16, 18, 31, 33, 42, 70, 82, 102, 116, 123
Discount Market, 11, 14, 31, 42, 43, 138–9
Discount Office, 18, 86, 92, 93, 94, 114–15
discretion, in economic management,

57, 58, 69, 74, 146
Dondelinger Committee, 135
Dow, C., 65
Downs, A., 155, 181n
Dunleavy, P., 34, 35, 168n
Dunsire, A., 164n
Durkheim, E., 144
dustbin men, 159

economists
  and Bank of England, 26, 37, 66
  in policy making, 36–9, 45
  and theories of banking, 36–9
Eliot, T. S., 10
energy policy, 53
esoteric politics, 5, 27–8, 35, 40, 47–9, 52, 53–4, 59, 87, 91, 94, 100, 104, 113, 116, 118, 129, 156
  see also exoteric politics
Etonians, 15
eurocurrencies, 11, 42–3, 92, 109, 133–4
European Economic Community, 119, 135
Exchange Control Act (1947), 87
Exchequer and Audit Department, 91
exoteric politics, 5, 27–8, 39, 156
  see also esoteric politics
Expenditure Committee, 172n

fashion, and policy change, 29, 33–5
Fay Committee, 108, 112, 174n, 175n, 176n, 177n
  see also Croom-Johnson inquiry; Crown Agents
Fildes, C., 178n
finance houses, 21, 40, 88, 128, 130
Finance Houses Association, 21, 66
Finer, S., 168n, 169n
First National Finance Corporation, 76, 92
Fisher, Sir W., 24
Fletcher, G., 165n, 166n
Foot, M., 168n
foreign banks, 22, 43, 109–10, 132
Foreign Office, 91, 132
Fournier, J., 177n, 178n

Fox, A., 143, 180n
Friedman, M., 36, 37, 58, 146, 171n, 180n
fringe banks, *see* banking, secondary; crises

gambling, 141, 148–9
Gardner, R., 180n
Germany, 12, 13, 99
gilt-edged, *see* markets
Goffman, E., 168n
Gold Standard, 22, 23
Goldthorpe, J., 143, 180n
Goodhart, C., 171n, 172n, 180n
Goodhart's Law, 60
Goodin, R., 164n
Gowland, D., 70, 163n, 168n, 171n, 173n, 174n
Grant, W., 166n, 175n
Greenaway, J., 167n
Greider, W., 164n
Griffiths, B., 37, 165n, 168n, 169n, 173n

Hadden, T., 175n, 181n
Hall, P., 143, 154, 156, 180n, 181n
Halperin, M., 29, 167n
Hambleton, R., 181n
Harrington, R., 172n
Harris, R., 169n
Hartley, K., 156, 157, 181n
Hawksmoor, N., 10
Hayek, F., 180n
Heath, E., 2, 4, 57, 67, 68, 77
Heclo, H., 53, 167n, 170n
Heller, R., 174n
Henderson, P., 156, 181n
Hewitt, P., 180n
Hill Samuel, 76
Hirsch, F., 143–6, 148, 153, 157, 158, 165n, 168n, 180n, 181n
Hockley, G., 163n
Holliman, S., 169n
Hollom, Sir J., 111
  see also Bank of England, Deputy Governor of Hong Kong and Shanghai Banking Corporation, 132
Hood, C., 147, 180n, 181n

housing market, 51, 57, 79
  see also building societies
Humble, J., 169n
Hunsworth, J., 168n

incrementalism, 6, 153–4
industrial disengagement, 2
industrial relations, 21, 148, 159, 161
Industrial Relations Act (1971), 2
industrial rescues, 19, 97–8
Institute of Economic Affairs, 36, 37
institutional investors, 102, 108
insurance industry, 10, 14
interest rates, 31, 32, 52, 69, 72, 82
  see also Bank Rate; Minimum Lending rate
International Monetary Fund, 36, 51, 74

Jay, P., 171n
Jenkins, R., 40
Jenkins, W., 163n
Johnson, H., 37, 45, 166n, 168n, 169n, 170n
Johnson, T., 181n
Jordan, A. G., 169n
Joseph, Sir K., 64, 172n

Karmel, M., 178n
Keegan, W., 172n, 178n
Keogh, J., 114, 115
Keynes, J. M., 34, 38
Keynesianism, 4, 36, 65–8, 69
Killick, T., 179n
Kindelberger, C., 19, 99, 165n, 174n, 175n
King, A., 164n
King, R., 170n

Labour Party, 24, 79
Laidler, D., 171n
Lambert, R., 174n
La Porte, T., 6, 141, 164n, 178n, 180n
law in banking, 18, 49, 86–9, 118–32
Law Society, 128
leasing, 142

Lehmbruch, G., 181n
Leijonhufvud, A., 172n
lender of last resort, 17, 18, 19, 43, 81, 99
Lester, T., 174n
liability management, 81–2
licensed deposit takers, 119, 123, 127, 128, 130–1
lifeboat, *see* Control Committee
Lilley, P., 173n
Lindblom, C., 164n
Lipset, S., 165n
Lisle-Williams, M., 14, 165n
Lloyds Bank, 11, 43
Lloyds, Corporation of, 10, 49
  see also insurance industry
Lomax, D., 172n, 173n
Lombard Street, 9, 11, 19, 125, 127
London and County Securities, 76, 77, 83, 87, 101, 102
London, City of, 10, 12–13, 14, 15, 18, 21, 24, 26, 27, 49, 53, 87, 93, 101, 116, 126
London Discount Market Association, 19
Lords, House of, 128, 129
Lowe, A., 169n
Lowi, T., 3, 122, 163n, 178n
lunatic asylums, 34

MacDougall, Sir D., 172n
McKay, D., 174n
MacKenzie, W. J. M., 27, 167n
Macmillan Committee, 12–13, 26, 164n, 167n
Macmillan, M., 163n
Madgwick, D., 181n
markets
  adaptation in, 8, 31, 53, 70–1, 96, 113, 145
  financial, 10, 94
  gilt-edged, 10, 31
  inter-bank, 11, 43
  local authority, 11, 42
  power of, 75
  secondary, 11, 42, 81–2
Marriott, O., 173n
maturity transformation, 81
Maudling, R., 51

Index   187

Maunder, W., 163n, 172n
Medium Term Financial Strategy, 74
Midland Bank, 103
Minimum Lending Rate, 32, 56, 68–9, 73
  see also Bank Rate; interest rates
monetarism, 38, 57, 58, 66, 75, 146–7
monetary base control, 74
monetary targets, 35, 57, 74
Moneylending Laws, 88, 90
money supply
  control of, 4, 5, 32, 38, 73–5, 147
  and complexity, 58, 147
  and democracy, 57
  measurement of, 31, 60–3
  see also monetarism
Monopolies Commission, 34, 35, 37, 43, 48, 50, 51, 132, 166n
moral suasion, 20, 21
Moran, M., 165n, 170n, 178n
Morgan, E. V., 166n, 172n
Mosley, Sir O., 13
Muller, R., 179n

National Board for Prices and Incomes, 33, 34, 35, 37, 38, 41, 48, 49, 168n
National Economic Development Council, 67
National Institute of Economic and Social Research, 36
Nationalised Industries, Select Committee on, 25, 164n, 166n, 167n, 169n, 170n, 173n, 174n, 175n, 176n, 179n
National Westminster Bank, 11, 43, 45, 107
Nevin, E., 165n, 173n
Niskanen, W., 155, 181n
Norman, M., 24, 25, 26
North, Lord, 16–17
nuclear power, 53
Nuffield School, 35

Oakeshott, M., 180n
O'Brien, Sir L., 25, 35, 50, 66–7, 77, 100, 123
  see also Bank of England, Governor of
Opie, R., 37, 169n
opportunism, 140–3, 154, 157, 158–9
Orwell, G., 141
Overend Gurney crisis, 98

Parkin, M., 171n
Parliament
  and Banking Act, 126–30
  and banking politics, 18, 20, 27, 100, 112
  and Competition and Credit Control, 2
Pay policies, 66–7, 142, 148
Pearl Harbor, 96
Pennant-Rea, R., 172n
pension funds, 103
Perrow, C., 161, 181n
Peston, M., 172n
Peters, G., 164n
Poland, 134, 139
Policy
  change, theories of, 29–30
  implementation, 6–7, 141
Policyholders' Protection Act (1975), 120
Pollard, S., 165n
Pollitt, C., 181n
pornography, 149–50
Post Office Superannuation Fund, 80
Presnell, L., 165n
Pressman, J., 164n
Prest, A., 171n
Price, D., 47
Prime Minister, 110–11
professionalism, 158–60
property market
  bank lending to, 57, 79–84
  boom in, 80–1
  crisis in, 81–4, 105
  invention in, 79–80, 84
  rescue of, 97, 104, 110–11
property speculation, 4, 57, 80–1, 86, 103
public borrowing, 5, 23, 64, 71
public learning, 7, 154–5

Raab, E., 165n

Index

Radcliffe Committee, 21, 23, 25, 26, 59, 129, 165n, 166n, 167n, 174n
rationality, 151–5
Raw, C., 175n, 179n
Reid, M., 163n, 173n, 176n
reintermediation, 59–61
reserve asset ratios, 31, 32, 50, 70–1
restrictive practices, 15–16, 21, 30–1, 45
Revell, J., 169n, 170n, 174n, 177n
Richardson, G., 77, 109, 110, 170n
  see also Bank of England, Deputy Governor of
Richardson, J., 169n
Robinson, J., 179n
Rose, R., 164n, 167n
Rothschild, 13
Rule, J., 152, 153, 180n
Ryan, A., 172n

Sandilands Report, 179n
Sapolsky, H., 154, 181n
Sargent, J., 177n, 178n
Sayers, R. S., 36, 164n, 165n, 166n, 167n, 168n
Schelling, T., 96
Schmitter, P., 181n
Schon, D., 154, 155, 181n
secrecy, 53–4
  see also esoteric politics
Seebohm, Lord, 129–30
Segall, A., 176n
Seidman, H., 7, 142, 164n, 180n, 181n
Self, P., 153, 181n
self regulation, 121
Selsdon, Lord, 129
Selsdon Man, 39, 44
Sewill, B., 125, 169n
Sheppard, D., 165n
Simon, H., 164n
Skinner, D., 100
Slater, J., 97
Slater Walker Securities, 92, 97, 108, 111, 112
Smythe, T., 181n
Special Deposits, 32, 40, 56, 71
Stalker, G., 155, 181n
Stamp, E., 179n

Standard Chartered Bank, 132
statistics, economic, 58–9
Stern, F., 165n
Stern, W., 84
Stern properties, 110
Stewart, M., 169n
Stock Exchange, 10, 49, 77, 102
Stonehouse, J., 93, 94
The Sunday Times, 'Business News', 93
Sutherland, G., 168n
Sydney Opera House, 143

Tapsell, P., 120
Tax laws, 141–2
Tew, J., 171n, 173n
Thatcher, M., 5, 57, 75
Thomas, W., 166n
Thompson, J., 168n, 170n
Thorpe, J., 77
Titmuss, R., 143, 180n
Tomkinson, M., 180n
Trade, Board of, 88, 90
Trade, Department of, 87, 93, 173n, 174n, 175n
Trades Union Congress, 67, 172n
travel agents, 128
Treasury Bills, 11, 14, 16, 31, 32, 68
Treasury, H.M.,
  and Bank of England, 1, 22, 23–7, 32
  and Banking Act, 118–25
  and commercial banks, 23, 44, 46
  and implementation of Competition and Credit Control, 61, 62
  and origins of Competition and Credit Control, 37, 39, 49, 51–2
Treasury and Civil Service, Committee on, 171n
Trescott, P., 164n
trust
  in banking, 16, 18, 76, 94
  creation of, 158–61
  exploitation of, 95, 158–9
Tufte, E., 171n
Tullock, G., 155, 181n

Unemployment, 63–4, 66–7
United Dominions Trust, 88, 92
United States, 12, 13, 22, 60, 137
universities, *see* lunatic asylums

Van Gelder, S., 174n

Wadsworth, J., 165n, 177n, 179n
Walters, A., 37, 169n
Weber, M., 154
Wedderburn, D., 180n
Westaway, T., 172n
Weyer, D., 169n, 170n, 173n
Whale, P., 164n
Whitehall village, 53
Whittesley, C., 165n
Wildavsky, A., 53, 153, 154, 164n, 167n, 170n, 181n
Wilensky, H., 94, 95, 98, 175n
Willatt, N., 174n
Williams and Glyn's Bank, 11

Williams, M., 167n
Williams, R., 170n
Williamson, O., 140, 141, 180n, 181n
Wilson Committee, 50, 98, 103, 129, 165–6n, 169n, 170n, 171n, 174n, 175n, 176n, 177n, 178n, 179n
Wilson, Sir H., 167n
Wilson, J., 165n, 170n, 177n, 179n
Winch, P., 172n
Wohlstetter, R., 175n
Wood, G., 168n, 173n
Wrigglesworth, I., 176n
Wright, M., 170n, 181n

Yeomans, K., 172n
Yom Kippur War, 77, 83
Young, S., 169n

Zaire, 134
Zawadzki, K., 163n, 168n, 173n